ODYSSEY OF THE PSYCHE

JEAN KIMBALL

Odyssey of the Psyche

JUNGIAN PATTERNS IN JOYCE'S *ULYSSES*

Southern Illinois University Press
CARBONDALE AND EDWARDSVILLE

Printed in the United States of America
00 99 98 97 4 3 2 1

Library of Congress Cataloging-in-Publication Data
Kimball, Jean.
Odyssey of the psyche : Jungian patterns in Joyce's Ulysses / Jean Kimball.
p. cm.
Includes bibliographical references and index.
1. Joyce, James, 1882–1941. Ulysses. 2. Joyce, James, 1882–1941—Knowledge—Psychology. 3. Jung, C. G. (Carl Gustav), 1875–1961—Views on literature. 4. Psychoanalysis and literature—Ireland. 5. Archetype (Psychology) in literature. I. Title.
PR6019.O9U6726 1997
823′.912—dc20 96-27129
ISBN 0-8093-2110-6 (alk. paper) CIP

The paper used in this publication meets the minimum requirements of American National Standard for Information Sciences—Permanence of Paper for Printed Library Materials, ANSI Z39.48-1984. ♾

THIS BOOK IS LOVINGLY DEDICATED
TO MY HUSBAND, JACK F. KIMBALL,
AND TO THE MEMORY OF MY PARENTS,
LESTER G. SEACAT AND MAE M. SEACAT

CONTENTS

PREFACE

Like most people who write about Joyce, I was introduced to *Ulysses* in a college course: an undergraduate course in the early fifties called "The Modern Novel," which was taught by a medieval scholar steeped in the notion of the scriptural tradition as a frame for medieval literature—and for Joyce. Our reading started with Dostoevsky's *Crime and Punishment* and *The Brothers Karamazov* and ended with Faulkner's *Sanctuary*, *The Sound and the Fury*, and *As I Lay Dying*. Joyce's *Dubliners*, *Portrait of the Artist as a Young Man*, and *Ulysses*, treated as a trilogy, formed the center of the course. The rationale for selecting these novelists was that all three recognized and dramatized the doubleness of the human personality that was the mark of the modern novel—indeed, the "split subject" that Julia Kristeva links to Freud's revolutionary insistence on the determining influence of unconscious forces on conscious behavior. That doubleness is also the basic premise for the New Testament view of human nature, a view that was bred in the bone for the Irish Catholic Joyce. Such an introduction, to borrow from Frost, "has made all the difference" in my approach to this great novel, and I wish here to express my gratitude to the late Bernard F. Huppe, who demonstrated to me the fascination of exegesis and convinced me of the beauties of a contextual frame for the novel.

Ulysses is a book without a hero but with two protagonists who are together its subject. It is a critical truism that Stephen and Bloom are opposites, but together, I became convinced, they represent Joyce's vision of The Artist as a divided self working toward integration. It is perhaps to be expected that I initially saw their relationship—and still do, for that matter—as analogous to the hypostatic union of two natures in the Christ of Christian dogma—truly God and truly man—in one person. The church asserts that two contradictory natures are joined in the person of Jesus Christ but remain at the same time eternally separate. It is a significant part of my thesis in this study that the paradoxical pattern of the coincidence of contraries without integration that distinguishes the Christian hypostasis is repeated in Joyce's presentation of Stephen and Bloom in *Ulysses*.

My exploration of this view of the divided self in *Ulysses* led me (by a path I cannot now recall) to C. G. Jung's *Integration of the Personality*, which introduced me to Jung's claims for the psychological validity of Christian symbols in the relations between the conscious personality and the unconscious. I thus came to Jung through Joyce, and it was only when I was invited to participate in a panel on Jungian approaches to Joyce at the Seventh International James Joyce Symposium (1979) in Zurich that I began to focus more deliberately on the patterns I was seeing in *Ulysses* in a frame of Jung's theories. I wish to thank Sheldon Brivic, a scholar who is unusually receptive to the ideas of others, for identifying my approach as Jungian and inviting me to my first Joyce symposium as well as for his steady encouragement since.

Over the years after that first symposium presentation of a Jungian scenario for *Ulysses*, I became, little by little, convinced of a more comprehensive congruence between the patterns in Joyce's autobiographical fiction and the interior drama of Jung's individuation process, and it is this congruence I have addressed in *Odyssey of the Psyche*. Anyone who deals with a psychoanalytic context for fiction is aware of the lurking presumption that he or she is forcing the fiction to fit psychoanalytic categories and assumptions, but it is my claim that the parallels between Joyce's fiction and Jung's theory forced themselves upon me rather than the other way around. I have developed great respect and affection for Jung, but my book is about Joyce and his *Ulysses*.

This book has thus developed over many years, during which I have accumulated more debts to others than I can enumerate or even remember. These debts are institutional as well as personal, and I should like to recognize, first of all, a debt, which all Joyceans share, to the James Joyce Foundation and to the spirit of its founders: Fritz Senn, Thomas Staley, and the late Bernard Benstock. The openness, good humor, and flair, which all these men have combined with their unquestioned literary taste and knowledge, have come to characterize the operations of the James Joyce Foundation. I am grateful for the opportunities provided by this institution to test out insights of my own as well as to become familiar with the insights of others at meetings the foundation arranges and through publications it sponsors.

Because this study has developed over a period of many years, I have been very aware of the way one generation of critics builds on the work of previous generations. My own indebtedness to this long line of critical works is acknowledged in the notes, but I wish to single out four, not available when I first read *Ulysses*, which were particularly helpful to me. The first and still foremost, despite questions raised in the past few years, was Richard Ellmann's 1959 *James Joyce*, which, along with his edition of Joyce's *Letters*, changed the way we saw the connection between the portraits of Stephen and more especially Bloom to the facts of Joyce's life. Although Stanislaus Joyce's *My Brother's Keeper* (1958) reinforced the effect of Ellmann's biography, it was his *Dublin Diary* in 1962 (later *The Complete Dublin Diary of Stanislaus Joyce*) that provided an even more immediate sense of the roots of *Ulysses* in Joyce's life in Dublin, which was extremely valuable to me. Weldon Thornton's immensely useful *Allusions in* Ulysses, which appeared in 1961, is just what its subtitle promises—*A Line-by-Line Reference to Joyce's Complex Symbolism*—and this volume has proved an indispensable reference. Stanley Sultan's *Argument of* Ulysses, published in 1964, provided a coherent story line for the novel, which had not been established before. All four have been of inestimable value to me in my work with *Ulysses*.

Writing has always been a solitary pursuit for me, so that little in my published work has been importantly influenced by informal discussion or, I must admit, by friendly critiques of my writing in progress. In the case of this book, however, I was truly blessed when I accepted Elliott Gose's offer to read and critique the chapters of the book as I wrote them. Gose is a scholar who understands and appreciates both Joyce and Jung and who combines kindness and tact with an intellectual and rhetorical rigor that are very nearly irresistible—and helpful beyond any expectation I could have had. He is, as another Joycean told me, "a good reader," and this book has benefited greatly from his reading. My gratitude for this gift cannot be adequately expressed.

I have depended greatly on the services of librarians. Whether I was examining material in the Joyce collection at Cornell University, the Richard Ellmann collection at the McFarlin Library of the University of Tulsa, the Otto Rank papers at Columbia University, the library of the Jung Institute in Küsnacht, or the Zentralbibliothek in Zurich, or borrowing material from other libraries through the interlibrary loan service here at the University of Northern Iowa, library staff members have been uniformly courteous, interested, and helpful. I am grateful to them all, though few have names in my memory, and many may not still be where I remember them. My thanks go to Lucy Burgess and Elaine Smyth of the Department of Rare Books at the Cornell University Library; Bernard Crystal at the Butler Library of Columbia University; Lori Curtis at the McFarlin Library in Tulsa; L. Köhler at the Zentralbibliothek in Zurich; and Rosemary Meany and Edward F. Wagner (now retired) of the Rod Library at the University of Northern Iowa. All these representatives of their profession served me cheerfully and served me well.

I wish also to express my gratitude to the National Endowment for the Humanities for a Summer Stipend in 1985, which enabled me to translate several early psychoanalytic works, translations that have contributed to this study.

A certain amount of the material that makes up this study has appeared, though in different contexts, in articles I have published over many years in various outlets. For permission to use this material in my book, I am indebted to the following:

To International Universities Press for material from "James and Stanislaus Joyce: A Jungian Speculation," in *Blood Brothers: Siblings as Writers*, ed. Norman Kiell (1983), 73–113.

To the *James Joyce Quarterly* for material from "The Hypostasis in *Ulysses*" 10 (summer 1973): 422–38; "Freud, Leonardo, and Joyce: The Dimensions of a Childhood Memory" 17 (winter 1980): 165–82; "Family Romance and Hero Myth: A Psychoanalytic Context for the Paternity Theme in *Ulysses*" 20 (winter 1983): 161–73; "Love and Death in *Ulysses*: 'Word known to all men' " 24 (winter 1987): 143–60; " 'Lui c'est Moi': The Brother Relationship in *Ulysses*" 25 (winter 1988): 227–35; "Love in the Kidd Era: An Afterword" 29 (winter 1992): 669–77; and "An Ambiguous Faithlessness: Molly Bloom and the Widow of Ephesus" 31.4 (summer 1994): 455–72.

To the *Journal of Modern Literature* for material from "Jung's 'Dual Mother' in *Ulysses*: An Illustrated Psychoanalytic Intertext" 17.4 (spring 1991): 477–90.

To *Mosaic, a journal for the interdisciplinary study of literature*, for material from

"From Eve to Helen: Stages of the Anima-Figure in Joyce's *Ulysses*" 20.2 (spring 1987): 29–40.

To Penn State Press for material from "A Jungian Scenario for *Ulysses*," *Comparative Literature Studies* 19.2 (summer 1982): 195–207. Copyright 1982 by The Pennsylvania State University. Reproduced by permission of The Pennsylvania State University Press.

And to the University of Texas Press for material from "Autobiography as Epic: Freud's Three-Time Scheme in *Ulysses*," in *Texas Studies in Literature and Language*, vol. 31, pp. 475–96; by permission of the University of Texas Press.

I thank Norman Kiell for tirelessly prodding me to complete this study and for providing me a clipping service from New York City; and I acknowledge a debt of gratitude also to Ruth Bauerle and Barbara Lounsberry for their advice and encouragement. Finally, for their practical help to me in completing this book, I owe thanks to Jack Miller and his staff at the Computer Consulting Center at the University of Northern Iowa and to two successive English Department heads, Mary Rohrberger and Jeffrey Copeland.

My debt to my husband is acknowledged in the dedication. His unswerving support of me in whatever I wanted to do has been with me through my entire adult life, and my gratitude for this is more than I can express.

ABBREVIATIONS

BK	Joyce, Stanislaus. *My Brother's Keeper: James Joyce's Early Years*. Ed. Richard Ellmann. New York: Viking, 1958.
CDD	Joyce, Stanislaus. *The Complete Dublin Diary of Stanislaus Joyce*. Ed. George Healy. Ithaca: Cornell University Press, 1971.
CW	Jung, C. G. *The Collected Works of C. G. Jung*. 18 vols. Ed. H. Read, Michael Fordham, and Gerhard Adler, trans. R. F. C. Hull. New York: Bollingen Foundation and Princeton University Press, 1953–78.
D	Joyce, James. *Dubliners*. New York: Viking, Compass, 1968.
E	Joyce, James. *Exiles: A Play in Three Acts*. New York: Viking, Compass, 1961.
F-J	McGuire, William, ed. *The Freud-Jung Letters: The Correspondence Between Sigmund Freud and C. G. Jung*. Trans. Ralph Manheim and R. F. C. Hull. Bollingen Series, no. 94. Princeton: Princeton University Press, 1974.
FP	Joyce, James. "A Portrait of the Artist" (1904). In *The Workshop of Daedalus: James Joyce and the Raw Materials for "A Portrait of the Artist as a Young Man."* Ed. Robert E. Scholes and Richard M. Kain, 56–74. Evanston, Ill.: Northwestern University Press, 1965.
FW	Joyce, James. *Finnegans Wake*. New York: Viking, 1958.
JJ	Ellmann, Richard. *James Joyce*. Rev. ed. New York: Oxford University Press, 1982.
Letters	Joyce, James. *The Letters of James Joyce*. 3 vols. Vol. 1, ed. Stuart Gilbert. Vols. 2 and 3, ed. Richard Ellmann. New York: Viking, 1966.
MDR	Jung, C. G. *Memories, Dreams, Reflections*. Rev. ed. Recorded and ed. Aniela Jaffe, trans. Richard and Clara Winston. New York: Vintage Books, 1965.
P	Joyce, James. *A Portrait of the Artist as a Young Man*. New York: Viking, Compass, 1964.
PU	Jung, C. G. *Psychology of the Unconscious: A Study of the Transformations and Symbolism of the Libido*. Trans. Beatrice M. Hinkle. New York: Moffat, Yard, 1916.
SE	Freud, Sigmund. *The Standard Edition of the Complete Psychological Works of Sigmund Freud*. Ed. and trans. James Strachey, in collaboration with Anna Freud. London: Hogarth and the Institute of Psycho-Analysis, 1953–74.
SH	Joyce, James. *Stephen Hero*. Ed. John J. Slocum and Herbert Cahoon. New York: New Directions, 1944.

SL Joyce, James. *Selected Letters of James Joyce*. Ed. Richard Ellmann. New York: Viking, 1975.

TC Rahner, Karl, ed. *The Teachings of the Catholic Church as Contained in Her Documents*. Comp. Josef Neuner and Heinrich Roos, trans. Geoffrey Stevens. Staten Island: Alba House, 1967.

U Joyce, James. *Ulysses: The Corrected Text*. Ed. Hans Walter Gabler, with Wolfhard Steppe and Claus Melchior. New York: Random, 1986.

PART ONE

Prologue

ONE

Introduction

The Split Subject of *Ulysses*

This study addresses the most obvious, and possibly the most fundamental, question that most readers have asked about *Ulysses*: just what *is* the relationship between Stephen Dedalus and Leopold Bloom, and what does it mean? This is a two-part question, of course, and the answer to the question of meaning depends on what a reader decides about how the two protagonists are related to each other. The obvious difference in age, for example, has led interpreters to the father-son paradigm as determining the nature of the relationship, as well as suggesting the simple relation of youth to maturity as a guide to meaning. The action of the novel appears to insist on the importance of the meeting of the older and younger man, and even if we bow to a contemporary suspicion of the search for meaning and ask instead, "How does it work?,"[1] the nature of the relationship between the protagonists remains central.

The earliest identification, somewhat more unequivocal than later interpretations tended to be, was offered by Valéry Larbaud in a lecture at the 7 December 1921 "séance" sponsored by Sylvia Beach to promote Joyce's novel before its publication (*JJ* 519). Larbaud assured the soon-to-be-confused reader of *Ulysses* that the "key" to the relationship was the title and advised him or her that "Stephen Dedalus is Telemachus, and Bloom is Ulysses."[2] This tidy equation has served as an underpinning for the enduring father-son identification, enhanced by the casting of Bloom as Stephen's "spiritual father," a role suggested by Larbaud and endorsed by Stuart Gilbert,[3] though vehemently rejected by Joyce's friend John Francis Byrne, who claimed that "St. Thomas takes his besom and sweeps into the discard the notion of the human 'spiritual father.' "[4]

Early in the 1970s, Edmund Epstein, interpreting Bloom's "fatherly" moves as a threat to Stephen's "becoming an independent creator," denied that Stephen was searching for a father and pointed to the evidence in the novel that the young artist, "no longer a son," was instead "striving to *become* a father."[5] By 1980, Sheldon Brivic, though mentioning Bloom's "spiritual father[ing]" of Stephen and his "paternal position in the novel's structure," concluded that both protagonists are sons with "essentially identical complexes."[6]

Over the years, multiple identifications have been proposed for the relationship between the two protagonists, many of them complementary rather than mutually exclusive, and most approaches to meaning, even now, can be fitted in under one or more of eight broad categories suggested by Richard Kain in his 1972 survey of fifty years of interpretations of the meeting of the two protagonists: "isolation," "creativity," "ambiguity," "trinitarian," "classical temper," "existential," "biographical fact," and "psychological projection."[7] But Kain found no consensus in the interpretations at the fifty-year mark, and there is no consensus now, though the fact of the significance of the meeting has not been seriously challenged.

ASSUMPTIONS OF THE STUDY

Several broad assumptions are essential to my consideration of the relationship between the two protagonists of *Ulysses*. First, I accept as a basic premise the autobiographical nature of Joyce's fictional undertaking, agreeing with William Empson's judgment some years back that "we must not take simply [Joyce's] claim to be writing autobiography," but "we must take it deeply."[8] I assume that Joyce is presenting a vision of the artist that is not only a complex self-portrait, with existential roots that go deep into his personal experience, but also a myth of The Artist, particular to his own time but at the same time universal. I assume, too, a measure of self-discovery in the crafting of this personal myth, as well as the author's felt obligation toward self-revelation, however devious or disguised. I believe, in fact, with Richard Ellmann that "nothing has been admitted into [*Ulysses*] which is not in some way personal and attached" (*JJ* 364), though obviously Ellmann's "in some way" allows a wide latitude for interpretation.

I also have assumed the contextual interplay in this novel of two great systems: the centuries-old system of Christian doctrine and the twentieth-century system of psychoanalysis, "the most influential and elaborate system of recent times," according to Jameson, who claims that psychoanalysis is "the only really new and original hermeneutic developed since the great patristic and medieval system of the four senses of scripture."[9] These systems share assumptions, however differently expressed, about the dual nature of the human personality, assumptions that are significantly relevant to problematic aspects of the relationship between Stephen Dedalus and Leopold Bloom. Joyce's thinking has been informed by both these systems, which reinforce each other in a number of ways. Both Christian doctrine and psychoanalysis have a biographical-cum-autobiographical base, which underscores their common assumption of the extraordinary importance of self-knowledge as well as its potential for universal validity. The basic texts of Christianity, after all, give great prominence and significance to biographical and autobiographical material. The biographical narratives of the Gospels and the

Acts of the Apostles combine with autobiographical material in Paul's Epistles to provide the underpinnings of Christian doctrine, the foundation for later elaboration by the church fathers. Nor should we forget that Saint Augustine's *Confessions* have their own place in the writings of the fathers.

The intricate structure of exegesis and definition that belongs to the Roman Catholic Church belongs also to Joyce by birth and training, and the place of Catholicism in his work has always been recognized. Mary Colum, raised in the same tradition that produced Joyce,[10] titled her early review of *Ulysses* "The Confessions of James Joyce" and judged it "one of the most Catholic books ever written."[11] This judgment is reinforced by Father William Noon's expressed conviction that "no modern artist is more preeminently the artist of a Catholic site and place" than Joyce. Indeed, in his review of Richard Ellmann's 1959 *James Joyce*, Father Noon warned that Ellmann's failure to take seriously the power of the Catholic tradition in Joyce's life had led to "major distortions in perspective" in the biography.[12] The importance of the Catholic tradition for *Ulysses* has been equally clear to those outside the fold. C. G. Jung, a Swiss Protestant, recognized in the "anti-world" of *Ulysses* the "quintessentially Catholic atmosphere of . . . Erin" (*CW* 15:120); and Frank Budgen, Joyce's friend and confidant in Zurich, though he acknowledged Joyce's intermittent hostility toward the church, pointed to the importance of "the rich mine of material" in the tradition "for the construction of his own myth."[13]

Also contributing to Joyce's personal myth were the speculations of the new "science" of psychoanalysis, which, as T. S. Eliot commented in his influential critique of *Ulysses*, helped "to make possible what was impossible even a few years ago."[14] However debatable the scientific nature of psychoanalysis might be,[15] its validation of the unconscious as a fact of conscious life provides an inevitable overall context for *Ulysses*. In addition, the explicit textual allusions in the novel to psychoanalytic texts go far beyond the one allusion that Weldon Thornton has identified.[16] Psychoanalysis, of course, was contemporary with Joyce: its beginnings as a movement coincided with Joyce's early development as an artist, and its "second capitol," Zurich, home of Jung and the "Zurich school,"[17] was also Joyce's home from mid 1915 to late 1919. During his residence in Zurich, he had access to a wealth of early psychoanalytic writings, both books and journals, in the public library of that city, the Zentralbibliothek Zurich,[18] and it was in Zurich that he wrote much of *Ulysses*.

Furthermore, Joyce's acquaintance with psychoanalysis predated his move from Trieste to Zurich, and hence he was aware of psychoanalytic speculations about the nature and power of the unconscious well before *Ulysses* was under way. Although Joyce's grasp of psychoanalytic literature became obvious in *Finnegans Wake*, the question of whether psychoanalytic assumptions had informed the earlier novel was the subject of considerable debate in the years following the publication of *Ulysses*. Wyndham Lewis, for example, assumed that "it was in the company of that old magician, Sigmund Freud, that Joyce learnt the way into the Aladdin's cave where he manufactured his *Ulysses*,"[19] but Joyce's Triestine friend Italo Svevo asserted positively that as late as 1915 Joyce "knew nothing of psycho-analysis . . . [which] thus cannot boast of having fathered Joyce's work."[20]

As the years passed, and as Joyce himself had opportunities to poison the wells, the hesitancy about inquiring into the nature of the connection grew, until it became almost taboo to suggest a direct influence. Mark Shechner might with justice assert in his 1974 *Joyce in Nighttown* that the view of *Ulysses* as a "Freudian" novel had "settled into commonplace,"[21] but there appeared to be an equally common agreement to assume that Joyce got there entirely on his own, without anyone else's insights to light the way. Thus, when Maria Jolas was asked at the 1973 Joyce symposium about Joyce's attitude toward Freud and Jung, she could respond that "it was a remarkable sign of his intelligence that he didn't fall for psychoanalysis when it was so current. He started beyond it."[22]

But in 1977, as an appendix to *The Consciousness of Joyce*, Ellmann published a listing of Joyce's Trieste library, which included four early psychoanalytic works, three of them purchased by Joyce during the Trieste years, probably around their publication dates: Jung's 1909 "Significance of the Father in the Destiny of the Individual," Freud's 1910 psychobiography of Leonardo da Vinci, and the 1911 German translation of Ernest Jones's 1910 essay, "The Oedipus Complex as an Explanation of Hamlet's Mystery." In this essay, which expanded on Freud's footnote in the first edition of *The Interpretation of Dreams* about Shakespeare's *Hamlet* having "its roots in the same soil as *Oedipus Rex*" (*SE* 4:264), Jones quoted extensively from Otto Rank's *Myth of the Birth of the Hero*, the work in which Freud's "Family Romance" was first published.[23] Joyce had thus been sufficiently interested in what Rosa M. B. Bollettieri calls "this new adventure in thought"[24] to spend money, which was always scarce in his catch-as-catch-can household, on his investigation of what psychoanalysis had to offer.

For a number of reasons, but not least because of their focus on sexuality, Joyce had a natural affinity for the materials of psychoanalytic literature. Stanislaus Joyce's judgment that his brother's temperament, "like Catholic morality," was "predominantly sexual" (*Letters* 3:104) is strikingly verified by the sexual emphasis in Joyce's writings. In addition, Joyce's often-quoted claim, in a letter to Stanislaus, that if he "put down a bucket" into his "own soul's well, sexual department," he would draw up everyone else's water with his own (*Letters* 2:191) is based on an assumption of the universal validity of self-knowledge that is linked to his Christian tradition and at the same time is very close to Freud's working hypothesis in his *Interpretation of Dreams*.

The significance of personal experience is an assumption that the Christian tradition shares with psychoanalysis. For the Christian, the necessity for self-examination and the validity of the understandings derived from such examination is ultimately based on the Genesis account of God's creation of man in His own image as the culminating act of His creation of the universe, also presumably stamped with His image. Thus, what Étienne Gilson calls "Christian Socratism" expands the meaning of the Delphic Oracle's "know thyself" into the promise of universal knowledge—of neighbor, of the world, and of God—through knowledge of the self. Gilson quotes an anonymous medieval meditation that promises: "He then who seeks God's image in himself, seeks there his neighbour no less than himself; and whoso seeking finds it, finds it as it is in all mankind."[25] Surely it is some kind of extension of this inherited faith in the universality of the *imago Dei* that underlies Stephen's declaration in *Ulysses* that "his own image to a man with that queer thing genius is the standard of all experience, material and moral" (*U* 9:432–33). However we may quibble about the degree to which Stephen is to be equated with Joyce, this pronouncement certainly harmonizes with Joyce's practice.

Moreover, from the perspective of Genesis, the whole creation takes on a sacramental character; not only is man made in the image of God, but, as Gilson points out, the physical world itself is seen as an "analogue of God,"[26] so that the history of human experience, whatever form it takes, may be considered to reflect this divinity. Joyce claimed such a reflection in his fictional history, comparing it, as Stanislaus reports, to "the mystery of the Mass," in that he was "converting the bread of everyday life into something that has a permanent artistic life of its own" (*BK* 103–4); and Edmund Wilson, in the first decade after the publication of *Ulysses*, pointed out that in this novel Joyce had "exploited together, as no writer had thought to do before, the resources both of Symbolism and of Naturalism."[27]

This dual vision of the equivalence of being and meaning finds a rationale in the Christian tradition. Saint Augustine, for example, in a chapter of *The City of God*, headed "*Of Paradise, that it can be understood in a spiritual sense without sacrificing the historic truth of the narrative regarding the real place*," lists a full page of representative allegorical interpretations of the Garden of Eden. He concludes, however, that "these and similar allegorical interpretations may be suitably put upon Paradise . . . while yet we believe the strict truth of the history, confirmed by its circumstantial narrative of facts,"[28] an admonition that could be transferred to *Ulysses* with little or no editing. It is also Saint Augustine who points out that "those things which are past and cannot be revoked belong to the order of time, whose creator and administrator is God,"[29] a belief that provides an essential context for the declaration by the Stephen of *Stephen Hero* that "so long as this place in nature is given us it is right that art should do no violence to the gift" (*SH* 79). Joyce in effect reflected this point of view in his response to Grant Richards's demands for deletions from *Dubliners*: "he is a very bold man who dares to alter in the presentment, still more to deform, whatever he has seen and heard" (*Letters* 2:134).

Autobiography also plays a prominent role in the literature of psychoanalysis. Otto Rank could have been speaking for the great originators of the psychoanalytic movement and for Joyce too when he wrote in his 1905 daybook as a very young man: "It comes only to this, that one has the courage to universalize his experience; whoever has this courage, his generalizations are correct."[30] To begin with, psychoanalytic speculations are supported by the mediated autobiography of the case study. In addition, the movement originates at the beginning of our century in Freud's extraordinarily confessional *Interpretation of Dreams*, which, to be sure, conceals even as it reveals,[31] but which has by now been reviewed, rearranged, and cross-referenced,[32] so that its autobiographical nature has become clear. Henri Ellenberger points to the "unprecedented degree" to which *The Interpretation of Dreams* is "bound to the life and personality of its author," making it "an autobiography in disguise."[33] Ronald R. Thomas goes farther, identifying Freud's dream book as an autobiographical novel of sorts, "vitally affiliated with the novel as a literary form."[34]

Jung's psychology is similarly determined by his own experience. Indeed, George Hogenson, in his study of the relationship between Freud and Jung, claims that "the works and actions of someone like Jung, and . . . Freud as well, are so mythic and self-reflexive that they can only be seen as expressions of what I am terming *metabiography*," a word coined "to clarify the significance of the use of biographical information in the development and validation of psychoanalysis."[35] And Jung himself pointed out that "every psychology—my own included—has the character of a subjective confession" (*CW* 4:336).

At the same time, however, Jung affirmed the potential for universality in these highly personal analyses, insisting that Freud, through *his* "subjective confession," had "assisted at the birth of a great truth about man" (*CW* 4:334). In turn, Jung's extraordinarily personal and directed "confrontation of the unconscious," described in his autobiographical *Memories, Dreams, Reflections* (*MDR* 170–98),[36] also yielded, he assumed, universal insights that formed the basis for his analytical psychology.[37] And Peter Homans, whose *Jung in Context* represents a significant contemporary reassessment of Jung's life and work, asserts that "[i]n the very act of naming his own personal experiences, Jung created a unique system of psychological ideas."[38] Thus, the two great names in the origins of depth psychology as theory and therapy exemplify Friedrich Nietzsche's claim that "every philosophical system is nothing but a disguised confession."[39]

THE TEXTUAL DIALOGUE

Balancing and enriching the biographical bases of Joyce's work, however, is an immensely productive dialogue with a range of other texts, a dialogue that is a defining characteristic of his style. And this kind of textual dialogue is also a significant characteristic of the literature of the Christian Church and psychoanalysis, the latter drawing on the Old and New Testaments of the Christian Bible[40] as well as other mythologies that have informed both systems. Joyce himself reminded Frank Budgen that, "to get the correct contour on me, you ought to allude to me as a Jesuit" (*JJ* 27), while he identified for August Suter the principal gain from his Jesuit training as "how to gather, how to order and how to present a given material."[41]

The Jesuit discipline has traditionally involved what one Christian commentator has called "acquisitive adaptation" of any truth that can contribute to the church's truth.[42] Thus Cardinal John Henry Newman was reaffirming an assumption deeply embedded in the tradition of the Catholic Church when he claimed for the church, for the purpose of "enlarging the range and refining the sense of her own teaching,"[43] whatever the heathen had said rightly. To the enormous wealth of the Jewish Scriptures, reinterpreted to harmonize with the Christian revelation, the fathers of the early church had added, with hardly a tremor, the treasures of classical Greek and Roman literature, also suitably modified, including, it should be noted, the figure of Homer's Odysseus.[44]

When Joyce was introduced to Ulysses by the Jesuits at Belvedere, it was in the context of this tradition,[45] which surely had some influence on his vision of Ulysses tied to the mast as "the artist, who will lay down his life rather than renounce his interest" (*JJ* 417). The Christ-derived "lay down his life" combines oddly with the Ulyssean (and Joycean) concern for "his interest," but it illustrates Joyce's assumption of his freedom to treat inherited contexts as his own.[46] For there is no aspect of Joyce's artistic stance in which he is more truly a child of the fathers than in the freedom with which he appropriates insights from any source and adapts them to his own artistic purposes. With his stunning sense for analogy, he has tapped into some of the main arteries of Western thought, including psychoanalysis, arteries that have themselves become intricately interconnected through their shared history.

The psychoanalytic texts that were available to Joyce were often products of a dialogue with a range of other texts; and like the medieval Christian writers, the early psychoanalysts appropriated from tradition whatever fit into their own constructions, adapting it for their own purposes. Their writings thus combined, in an odd way, the congeniality of a method familiar to Joyce with the appeal of a new message, with which he himself, in some aspects at least, was in sympathy. And Joyce, a past master at creative appropriation, added this contemporary intertext to the inventory of possibilities for his fiction.

Joyce's wholesale appropriation cannot accurately be called "borrowing," nor can we properly speak of simple "influence," a caution that is significant in this study of Jungian patterns in Joyce's *Ulysses*. Indeed, until M. M. Bakhtin's notion of "dialogue" entered our critical vocabulary, first introduced by Julia Kristeva as "intertextuality,"[47] we really did not have a satisfactory word for Joyce's use of other texts. But Bakhtin might well be describing Joyce when he writes in "Discourse in the Novel" of the novelist who constructs his own style by "welcom[ing] heteroglossia and language diversity of the literary and extraliterary language" into his novel. This generic novelist, who "makes use of words that are already populated with the social intentions of others and compels them to serve his own new intentions"[48] is surely kin to Joyce, whose great and unique gift is his uncanny ability to recognize and appropriate insights and ambiences from a staggering variety of sources and to transform them into an integral part of his own symbolic statement.

Bakhtin's almost muscular picture of the novelist who "compels" other texts to serve the requirements of his own artistic will is unusually apt for Joyce's habitual use of allusion. He worked into his fiction whatever he might find in other texts that resonated with his own thinking or his own experience and could add a dimension to the fiction. What did not relate, he ignored. Like his fictional surrogate, Stephen Dedalus, he "retained nothing of all he read save that which seemed to him an echo or a prophecy of his own state" (*P* 155),[49] and it is a ruling assumption of this study that the truth that is served by any allusive material is Joyce's truth—first. Otherwise he does not respond to the material at all. The mature Joyce, I think, was all but impervious to "influence," as it is commonly understood, but at the same time his sensitivity to confirmation from other thinkers was phenomenal. Like the Coleridge of John Livingston Lowes's classic study of influence, *The Road to Xanadu*, Joyce's mind, equipped, like Coleridge's, with "an almost uncanny power of association," moved "like the passing of a magnet" over his reading and "drew and held fixed whatever was susceptible of imaginative transmutation"[50]—even more, whatever related to his own life and consequently to his autobiographical fiction.[51]

Joyce has thus synthesized into the complex integrity of *Ulysses* bits and pieces of insights from other thinkers and writers that are congruent with his own vision, and I should emphasize that the parallels I am examining in this study between Joyce's fiction and Jung's theory follow this general rule. The similarity between the patterns of psychic development in Jung's individuation process and the patterning of *Ulysses* is organic, primarily a matter of congruence rather than influence. These parallels are thus a particularly significant example of the mutual confirmation that literature and psychoanalysis have offered each other since the beginnings of psychoanalysis.[52]

Freud's acknowledgment of the poet as precursor of the psychoanalyst is, of course, a commonplace, and he himself has established this connection more or less permanently by naming the core complex of his theory after Sophocles's Oedipus, while Freud's Oedipus complex has in turn provided a ready model for psychoanalytic readings of literature ever since. Jung's dependence on the literature of the past, however, reaches beyond the individual poet or myth to archetypal themes and symbols, so that, as J. P. Hodin has pointed out in his study of modern art, Jung's "complex psychology" presents a "parallelism of thought and vision" to the vision of the artist rather than any well-defined model.[53] Such a parallelism is basic to the Jungian patterns I see in *Ulysses*.

The multiple intertexts with which *Ulysses* is in dialogue are often also congruent with one another, so that the layering of one pattern upon another adds extraordinary density and resonance to Joyce's own structure. Theoharis Constantine Theoharis has recently pointed out, however, that Joyce's "prodigal allusiveness," as it "surrounds a topic with numerous, variously interdependent contexts," results in a certain competition among these contexts for "primary control" over a given subject,[54] producing a problem for interpretation. For, as Robert Martin Adams recognized some thirty years ago, the "major complications" of *Ulysses* force the critic to choose one perspective, even though, by doing so, he is "in a sense, 'composing' a picture in the simple act of selecting a perspective from which to view it."[55]

More recently John Paul Riquelme and Brook Thomas have expanded on Adams's caution, and both have printed the same picture of Ernst Hans Gombrich's classic rabbit-duck optical illusion to illustrate identical analogies between reading Joyce and looking at an optical illusion: a viewer of either text or picture can always see more than one thing, but not *both at the same time.*[56] This is a caution whose consequences must be taken seriously, especially in a consideration of the relationship between Stephen and Bloom, for the textual picture we see depends on the vantage point from which we view it. The Artist, who is the intensely singular subject of *A Portrait* in the person of Stephen Dedalus, has become in *Ulysses*, by a kind of cell division, a split subject: *both* Stephen *and* Bloom. At the same time, each of the protagonists has a story that is realized in the novel; and although Stephen can be fitted into Bloom's story, and Bloom can be fitted into Stephen's story, the two separate stories of Stephen's day and Bloom's are conspicuously not integrated in the narrative of *Ulysses*.

I have come to believe that a coherent account of what the relationship is and what it means—or how it works—requires a choice of perspective between Stephen and Bloom. And, as will become clear, the focus of this study is Stephen's story, in which Bloom has a crucial function. Looking at the whole novel from Stephen's perspective, that is, I see the relationship between the two protagonists of *Ulysses* as the embodiment of Joyce's symbolic statement about the divided Self of the autobiographical artist-hero of *Ulysses* and the terms of its integration into a unified personality, an essential prerequisite for the productive artist.[57]

OPPOSITION AND IDENTITY: THE HYPOSTASIS

Perhaps not since *Don Quixote* has an author presented two such fully developed characters, so specifically identified with opposing views of the nature of reality, who are at the same time so identified with each other. Like their great progenitors, Don Quixote and Sancho Panza, Stephen and Bloom are characters with quite separate personalities, growing out of separate, well-documented personal circumstances. And one fact of the text of *Ulysses* on which there has always been a measure of consensus is that, also like Don Quixote and Sancho Panza, the two main characters represent opposing ways of being in the world. Gilbert Seldes, in his 1922 review of *Ulysses*, saw this opposition in autobiographical terms: "If it is true, as Mr. Yeats has said, that the poet creates the mask of his opposite, we have in *Ulysses* the dual mask—Bloom and Stephen—of James Joyce."[58] R. P. Blackmur also insisted, a generation later, that the "true polarity in 'Ulysses' is in Joyce himself. Bloom is exactly as autobiographical as Stephen."[59] Similarly, for H. E. Rogers, also writing at the end of the forties, Bloom and Stephen are "opposing forces of a single personality in search of integration" in the "schizoid plot of *Ulysses*."[60]

At the fifty-year mark in *Ulysses* criticism, Robert Scholes put a new spin on the autobiographical contrast with his distinction between the two *kinds* of autobiography embodied in Stephen and Bloom, which he labels "bioenergetic" (Stephen) and "cybernetic" (Bloom). "Stephen," Scholes points out, "is Joyce in his skin, with all the significant features that would make him recognizable. And with no features that Joyce himself did not possess," whereas "Bloom contains large elements of Joyce's neural circuitry without being recognizable as Joyce."[61] Also in the seventies, James H. Maddox, Jr., presented the contrast between the protagonists as finally pointing to "the need the two men have of one another." Each incomplete in himself, Maddox says, "the two men are fragmentary and complementary."[62] Brivic, on the other hand, explores the opposition in a frame of Jungian typology, identifying Stephen's attitude as introverted in contrast to Bloom's extraverted attitude.[63]

Whatever the critical agreement about the opposing natures of Stephen and Bloom, we have also discovered that the text insistently exhibits evidences of some kind of paradoxical shared identity between the two, the most incontestable of which are the recurring appearances of the thinking of one in the mind of the other.[64] Often the idiom shifts as the idea moves from one mind to the other, as, for example, in Stephen's observation that "we walk through ourselves . . . always meeting ourselves" (*U* 9:1044–46), which appears in Bloom's drowsy musing as "Think you're escaping and run into yourself" (*U* 13:1110). These are general, though not quite commonplace, observations, but when another piece of Stephen's Shakespeare lecture—"In a rosery of Fetter Lane of Gerard, herbalist, he walks, greyedauburn" (*U* 9:651–52)—appears almost word for word in Bloom's mind (*U* 11:907), the limits of reasonable coincidence have been passed, at least for Adams, who objects at some length to "Bloom's thinking Stephen's thoughts."[65]

This shared identity, however, is indicated structurally as well in the fact that time starts over at 8:00 A.M. in "Calypso," the episode that introduces Leopold Bloom, while the duplicated experience of the cloud that covers the sun, "slowly, wholly," in both Stephen's world and in Bloom's (*U* 1:248, 4:218) further insists on some kind of interfusion of personality. Thus, by the time Bloom reflects, in the appalling idiom of "Eumaeus," that "a certain analogy there somehow was, as if both their minds were travelling, so to speak, in the one train of thought" (*U* 16:1579–81), the cumulative evidence for this analogy has become an impressive fact of the text of *Ulysses*. But whatever the strength of the analogy, however clear the movement of the novel toward the protagonists' meeting, when they do meet, they simply separate instead of consolidating in any way, and this textual fact has been a source of hermeneutic frustration.

The textual paradox of opposition and identity suggests a model for the relationship between Stephen and Bloom in the central Christian dogma of the hypostasis, the union of the two contradictory natures—"truly God" and "truly Man," the divine Word and the humble flesh—in the one person of Christ. This is a model obviously close to Joyce, whose easy familiarity with the figure of Jesus, both as a human being and as the Christ of Christian dogma, is prominently displayed in *Stephen Hero*, where the author's intentions and assumptions are much more explicitly stated than in any of the works he published. Stephen's "preparative abstinences" before the time he is to deliver his paper, for example, are compared to Christ's forty days in the wilderness (*SH* 69); his demand that Cranly "explain the hypostatic union" is connected with Christ's "interest in loose women" (*SH* 141); and he compares the speeches of Yeats's Owen Ahern and Michael Robartes to "the enigmas of a disdainful Jesus" (*SH* 178; see also 114, 116–17, 133, 139–41, 189–90, 191, 222).

Some years ago I presented the case for an analogy between the union of the two natures in Christ and in the artist,[66] and I do not mean to repeat the argument here, except to note the broad outlines for the analogy. The church teaches that, in the incarnation, "the divine Word united himself to the flesh while each (*nature*) remained what it is" (*TC* 159, item 26), and in Joyce's *Ulysses*, the opposing natures of the artist represented by Stephen and Bloom move toward some kind of union, even though each remains unchanged. At the end of Bloomsday, Stephen is still Stephen, and Bloom is still Bloom, but they are united textually in a "new man" who contains them both. "Ithaca" concludes with the vision of "Darkinbad the Brightdayler" (*U* 17:2329–30), the opposites united in "the manchild in the womb" (*U* 17:2317–18). It is not unreasonable to identify "Darkinbad the Brightdayler" with the flesh and spirit of the incarnated artist, for, as Augustine has said, "Not unfitly do we liken the spirit to the day and the body to the night."[67] And, also not unfitly, critics have since the publication of *Ulysses* identified the spirit with Stephen and the flesh with Bloom.

Rebecca West, for one, identifies the opposition between the two in Manichaean terms that reflect the dark-and-light opposition of Joyce's "Darkinbad the Brightdayler" as "Ormuz and Ahriman, the dark force of matter . . . and the spirit of light."[68] Jung, personalizing this opposition, sees in Bloom and Stephen the "disintegration" of Joyce's personality into "Bloom, *l'homme moyen sensuel*, and the almost gaseous Stephen Dedalus, who is mere speculation and mere mind" (*CW* 15:114). And Jung's conclusion—that the Ulysses of the title is "the creator-god in Joyce" and the whole book "a microcosm of James Joyce" (*CW* 15:127)—is reinforced by Adams, who sees "the mind of Joyce-over-the-novel," not only as "that toward which Stephen's mind is developing" but also as the "*terminus-ad-quem*" of the novel,[69] the end toward which everything in *Ulysses* moves. We may be reminded of Ellmann's speculation that Joyce "conceived of his entire book as a silent, unspoken portrayal of an archetypal man who would never appear and yet whose body would slowly materialize as the book progressed, linguafied as it were into life."[70]

Joyce himself, of course, identified Ulysses with the artist, as well as with Christ (*JJ* 416); and in this autobiographical novel, it is hardly a stretch to equate this "new man," the "manchild in the womb" at the end of "Ithaca," with Joyce in his larger identity as the productive artist of the future, who contains in himself both Stephen and Bloom, or, as they are renamed in "Ithaca," "Blephen" and "Stoom" (*U* 17:549–54). Thus the pronouncement of Lynch's Cap in "Circe" is fulfilled in this artist of the future: "Jewgreek is greekjew. Extremes meet" (*U*

15:2097–2298). Like the Shakespeare of Stephen's theory, the productive artist is "the boy of act one [and] the mature man of act five. All in all" (*U* 9:1020–21), echoing Saint Paul's vision of the "new man, which is created after the image of him that created him: Where there is neither Greek nor Jew . . . but Christ is all and in all" (Col. 3:10–11).

In this view, as in the Christian hypostatic union, the protagonists are not simply opposites, who may in some way instruct or redeem each other, but complementarities, who are absolutely necessary to each other and who together form one person with two conflicting natures which *never* lose their separate identities. For Joyce's artist, as for Christ, "each of the two natures does what is proper to it in communion with the other, the Word doing what pertains to the Word, and the flesh doing what pertains to the flesh. One of them shines out with miracles, the other is subjected to insults" (*TC* 153, item 251). The union of the two natures in the artist, as in the dogmatic Christ, is "according to the hypostasis, for . . . union by composition not only preserves from confusion what has come together, but also tolerates no separation" (*TC* 157, item 257).

The union of opposites in one person that is insisted upon in Christian doctrine is also central to Jung's vision of human personality. This union is in fact the aim of the core process of his psychology, which he names *individuation* and which he has defined as "the process by which a person becomes a . . . separate, indivisible unity or 'whole' " (*CW* 9.1:275). The goal of the process, which Jung equates with self-realization, is some apprehension by the conscious personality of the existence in himself of a greater personality, both conscious and unconscious, the Jungian Self, which, "as a totality," Jung says, "is indescribable and indistinguishable from a God-image." He therefore concludes that "self-realization—to put it in religious or metaphysical terms—amounts to God's incarnation" (*CW* 11:157) and, in fact, elsewhere identifies Christ as a symbol of the Self (*CW* 9.2:36–71).

Thus the amalgam of Christian and psychoanalytic contexts that informs Joyce's *Ulysses* is also characteristic of Jung's theory. Indeed, Homans points to the role of "prophet or reinterpreter of traditional Christianity" as one essential aspect of Jung's "threefold" personal identity, around which this contemporary reinterpreter of Jung organizes his assessment of Jung's work. Besides the prophetic post-Christian role, Homans includes "psychotherapist and critic of Freud," as well as "moralist and social critic of modernity," noting that Jung's system is "a genuine alternative to both Christianity and psychoanalysis but draws aspects of these orientations into a fresh synthesis."[71]

At the same time, Homans stresses "the double movement in Jung's psychology, in which both rejection and affirmation [of traditional Christianity] were present," a double movement that also characterizes Joyce's approach to Catholicism in his work. Homans emphasizes that Jung's approach to Christianity was "a *re*-interpretation" and a significant aspect of Jung's "attempt to integrate traditional and modern orientations to life." Even though his rejection of traditional Christianity was sincere, Jung wanted to save for modern man the truth that had been attached to the figure of Christ, and, Homans says, he saw in psychoanalysis a means of "revivify[ing] among intellectuals a feeling for symbol and myth," which could salvage valid insights originally Christian in a modern setting. Thus, as Homans points out, not only was individuation "the lens through which Jung viewed the Christian faith" but, in turn, "the classical Christian experience provided an absolutely essential matrix . . . out of which the individuation process took its peculiar shape."[72]

Jung's theory of the nature and development of the psyche may thus be viewed as a twentieth-century psychoanalytic reformulation of the coincidence of contraries that Christian doctrine posits in Christ and, by extension, in the human personality as well.[73] In Jung's modern formulation, to be sure, the opposites, labeled *Word* and *flesh* or *God* and *man* in the doctrinal Christ figure, are relabeled *conscious* and *unconscious* or *Ego* and *Shadow*, though in both Christian and psychoanalytic constructs the relationship between these opposites is complementary: contradictory as they are, both elements are necessary for the whole person.

Jung's view of the relationship between these opposites, however, adds to the Christian view of the union of Word and flesh the notion, which has no place in Christian doctrine—or, for that matter, in Freud's theory—of the *compensatory* role of the unconscious in relation to the conscious personality, an important dimension in the consideration of Bloom's function in *Ulysses*, where, as has been noted by uncounted readers and critics over the years, Bloom clearly has qualities that Stephen needs. Jung's "theory of compensation" goes beyond Freud's "repression theory" (*CW* 10:15) to assert that the psyche is "a self-regulating system that maintains its equilibrium just as the body does" (*CW* 16:153) through a "natural, automatic function" of compensation (*CW* 10:18), so that unconscious forces, created in part by repression, constantly work to correct imbalance in the conscious personality. At the same time, in Jung's modern construct, the hierarchical Christian relationship between Word and flesh as superior and inferior extends to the psychoanalytic opposites of conscious and unconscious, for, however "valuable and congenial [an] asset" the unconscious may be (*CW* 10:14), Jung asserts that "it is man's capacity for consciousness alone [that] makes him man" (*CW* 8:210).

The truth of Jung's theory is not at issue here, and I make no claim that this perspective is the only approach to meaning or that it accounts for everything in the novel or that it nullifies any of the many other helpful approaches in the critical tradition. Any such claim would be foolish in the face of the multidimensional artifact that is *Ulysses*. In addition, I make no simple equation between the psychic events I identify in Joyce's *Ulysses* and psychic developments in the author's life, even though it is clear that I see a strong connection. We cannot finally know these developments, however autobiographical the basis for the fiction and however much we may be tempted to extrapolate them from his fiction. With no claim, then, to direct influence, to exclusive truth, or to an analysis of Joyce's mind, what I do claim is that this examination of parallels between psychic events in *Ulysses* and Jung's theoretical descriptions of psychic happenings in the course of the individuation process focuses on a strand of meaning that *holds* all the way through the novel, supported by the text and contexts of *Ulysses*.

FICTION AND THEORY: A PARALLEL DEVELOPMENT

I am persuaded that the meaning of the coming together of Stephen Dedalus and Leopold Bloom, which, structurally at least, has always seemed to be the point of *Ulysses*, is clarified by considering their encounter and its ramifications in the context of Jung's theory of the integration of the personality. This study accordingly examines patterns in *Ulysses* as they harmonize with patterns in Jung's theoretical individuation process, a theory of the composition and development of the psyche that was significantly influenced by the Christian tradition that played so dominant a role in the early development of both Jung and Joyce but at the same time was grounded in a culture that was contemporary with Joyce in his productive years.

Jung's psychology, which departs from Freud's emphasis on childhood as the key to adult development and refocuses on the middle years of the adult as they complete the development of the personality, reinforces Joyce's own conviction of the significance of these middle years. For Joyce has registered his agreement with Jung's identification of the period between the ages of thirty-five and thirty-eight as the "turning of life."[74] In *Ulysses*, for example, Stephen points out that Shakespeare was thirty-five when he wrote *Hamlet* and quotes the beginning of the *Inferno* in this connection: "*nel mezzo del cammin di nostra vita*" (in the middle of the journey of our life) (*U* 9:831). For Dante also began his *Divine Comedy* at about thirty-five.

What is more and what probably determines the inclusion of this observation in Stephen's lecture is that Joyce was writing *Ulysses* when he was about thirty-five, in the middle of his life's journey, a coincidence he liked to point to both in correspondence and in conversation (*JJ* 393, 449). When he talked with Georges Borach about the beginnings of *Ulysses*, for example, he confided that "Now in *mezzo del cammin* I find the subject of Ulysses the most human in world literature" (*JJ* 416), placing himself, as was his habit, in the company of the truly great.

Jung's psychic descriptions tend to be more dramatic, even melodramatic, than systematic, a "dramatic, mythological way of speaking," which he justifies as "more exact" in describing the "living processes of the psyche" (*CW* 9.2:13). He thus defines his theoretical individuation process in terms of an interior drama, whose characters are the personified psychic forces that interact in the process of individuation. These characters, whose names are familiar to most of us, serve in this study as clarifying parallels, or glosses, for the main characters in *Ulysses*, and I capitalize the names of these personifications throughout: the *Ego* for Stephen, the *Persona* for Mulligan, the *Shadow* for Bloom, the *Anima* for Molly, and the *Self* for the nonappearing but ever-present productive artist of the future, Ulysses.

The essential first confrontation in Jung's psychic drama, the confrontation that opens the way for any other development of a larger personality, is the encounter between the Ego and the Shadow,[75] even as the central relationship in *Ulysses* is that between Stephen and Bloom. The "realization of the Shadow," as Jung names this beginning stage of mature individuation (*CW* 8:208), means the recognition, as a part of oneself, of a hitherto unknown subpersonality that includes "all those qualities we find painful or regrettable" (*CW* 12:177, note 118) and, beyond that recognition, an accommodation to this alien personality. In theory and in reality as well, the discovery of the Shadow is often extremely threatening to an individual's self-concept, and the accommodation to this discovery may well be an extraordinarily painful psychic task.

In the first decade of the twentieth century, Jung and Joyce, in widely different circumstances, faced this psychic task as each underwent a uniquely painful life experience that revealed to him the existence and strength of a hitherto unrealized aspect of his personality, a psychic reality that Jung would later universalize as the Shadow in his theory of individuation and one that Joyce would fictionalize in his portrait of Leopold Bloom in *Ulysses*. Each of these men was forced to integrate this "alien 'other' " (*CW* 13:348) into his understanding of himself, and the acceptance of the validity of the "other" as a part of himself changed the course of each man's lifework.

For Jung the discovery was a significant impetus for his move beyond Freud's psychoanalytic ideas to an exploration of the archetypes of the collective unconscious and eventually to the formulation of a new psychology. For Joyce the parallel experience in 1909 opened up a new dimension in his understanding of the subject of his autobiographical fiction, a personal introduction to "the subterranean forces, those hidden tides which govern everything," which he later identified as the "modern theme,"[76] a theme that dominates *Ulysses* and *Finnegans Wake*. Thus these parallel experiences provide the autobiographical base for Jung's descriptions of the realization of the Shadow and also for Joyce's creation of Leopold Bloom.

Because Jung and Joyce can without exaggeration be called giants of the twentieth century, each in his own area of endeavor, I am assuming that parallels in their lives and in their work are meaningful, even though, as I have earlier indicated, I do not see these parallels as importantly connected to influence. We may recognize "influence" as literary criticism's equivalent for the causal principle so important to science, but it is another principle that underlies the life parallels that I examine in the following chapter and also underlies the parallels in the work of Jung and Joyce that are the subject of this study: the "acausal connecting principle" that Jung named *synchronicity*.[77] Jung recognized when he coined the word that such a principle was "in complete contradiction" to Western "scientific and causal thinking" and therefore "outside the scope of our scientific judgment, indeed incomprehensible to it" (*CW* 15:55). But he was convinced that an accurate understanding of reality required that this principle of acausal meaningful coincidence supplement the principle of cause and effect. At no time did Jung dismiss the causal principle as invalid,[78] although his insistence that an acausal principle was also valid was doubtless a part of what Edward Glover, in his notably hostile discussion of "what is wrong" with Jung's psychology, termed the "unscientific mystical feelings" that Jung had injected into Freud's ideas.[79]

But Glover's dismissal of the "unscientific" and "mystical" in Jung's psychology, so influential at mid century, is not so convincing in the scientific world of the nineties. Indeed, Jung's recognition of the need for a principle beyond causality is in harmony with the new worldview forced on Western scientists by developments in atomic and subatomic physics in our century, a view, as Fritjof Capra has pointed out in his *Tao of Physics*, that recognizes a meaningful "interconnectedness" in the universe that is not dependent on cause and effect.[80] The new scientific respectability accorded Jung's notion of synchronicity has in turn trickled down to popular culture in an album, *Synchronicity*, recorded in 1983 by The Police. Indeed, one song in this album, with words and music by Sting, expands, in quite another idiom to be sure, on the acausal connectedness that is essential to Jung's concept, as well as its validation by subatomic physics. And the song is titled "Synchronicity I."

TWO

The Autobiographical Base

Some Synchronicities

Almost thirty years ago, a Jungian analyst pointed out that in *Ulysses* Joyce's use of "acausal rather than causal connecting links" to show the relationship of Stephen and Bloom was "anticipating Jung's later formulations of synchronicity."[1] Jung in fact coined the term to categorize "psychic parallelisms" which "simply cannot be related to each other causally, but must be connected by another kind of principle altogether" (*CW* 15:56), a description that fits the recurring signals of relationship between the two protagonists of *Ulysses*. It has become ever clearer that these verbal and situational "correspondences" or "coincidences" are used, as William York Tindall early asserted, to "gather, carry, and deposit meanings,"[2] and meaning, of course, is an "inherent quality" in Jung's concept of synchronicity (*CW* 8:513). Thus one event may be meaningfully connected to another without any question of causality at all.

Sheldon Brivic has in recent years introduced—or reintroduced—*synchronicity* into the Joycean critical vocabulary, listing a sampling of more than one hundred "synchronicities" in *Ulysses* as an appendix to his 1985 *Joyce the Creator*.[3] Brivic, however, interprets the acausality that is essential to Jung's use of the term as referring simply to the absence of physical causality, equating synchronicity with "psychic causality."[4] But synchronicity, as Jung proposed the term, does not designate a special *kind* of causality but the *absence* of causality. Neither is the principle a substitute for cause and effect; it is rather "an intellectually necessary principle" added to "the recognized triad of space, time, and causality" (*CW* 8:511).

To be sure, Jung's definitions of synchronicity never progressed completely beyond the tentative.[5] With the air of trying to arrive at a definition, he offers a series of related synonyms: "causeless order," for example, which he amends to "meaningful orderedness"; "psychophysical parallelism" (*CW* 8:506); or "acausal orderedness" (*CW* 8:516). Indeed, he acknowledges that synchronicity "explains nothing, it simply formulates the occurrence of meaningful coincidences" in which "no reciprocal causal connection can be shown to obtain between parallel events," and "the only recognizable and demonstrable link between them is a common meaning, or equivalence" (*CW* 8:531). It is this kind of equivalence I am primarily concerned with in this study.

Jung further identifies synchronicity as a "modern differentiation" of the alchemical theory of correspondence, "based not on philosophical assumptions [as was the alchemical theory] but on empirical experience and experimentation" (*CW* 8:531). And here we may see one of a fairly impressive number of synchronicities that are discoverable in the experience and thinking of Jung and Joyce. For, paralleling Jung's interest in alchemical assumptions as foreshadowing aspects of his theoretical individuation process is Joyce's view of the artist as alchemist, a view that is made explicit in *Finnegans Wake*, in which, according to Barbara DiBernard, "Joyce consciously and deliberately chose alchemy as a central metaphor."[6] Any Joycean is familiar with the description of Shem the Penman in Joyce's final work—"the first till last alshemist" (*FW* 185.35)—but is perhaps not so predictably familiar with the same identification in Joyce's first "Portrait of the Artist," written in one day at the beginning of 1904, though rejected for publication.[7]

In this strange "essay narrative," which Ellmann calls "the extraordinary beginning of Joyce's mature work" (*JJ* 144), Joyce describes the young artist who is the subject of this first portrait as being "like an alchemist, bent upon his handiwork, bringing together the mysterious elements, separating the subtle from the gross." The young author goes on to identify priorities that would characterize Joyce's fiction for the rest of his life: "For the artist the rhythms of phrase and period, the symbols of word and allusion were paramount things" (*FP* 63–64), an emphasis that may remind us in turn of Jung's assertion that the "moral concepts" of the alchemists "moved entirely on the planes of synonym and analogy, in a word, of 'correspondence' " (*CW* 14:249).

In *Ulysses* the meaningful coincidences or correspondences that link Stephen and Bloom, which, with Brivic, I would call synchronicities, are invented by Joyce; they are in the text because he plans it that way, and they are meaningful because he sees such correspondences as meaningful. There is also evidence that Joyce took living coincidences at least as seriously as does Jung. One of the more bizarre examples of this faith in coincidence was his proposal that James Stephens might finish *Finnegans Wake*, a proposal based entirely on a series of coincidences in their lives, the clinching one being that both these Irishmen were born on the same day, or, as Stephens himself reported the perceived coincidence, "in the same country, in the same city, in the same year, in the same month, on the same day, at the same hour, six o'clock in the morning of the second of February" (*JJ* 593).[8]

THE ZURICH CONNECTION

Jung and Joyce, of course, were born in different countries—Switzerland and Ireland—though both died and were buried in Switzerland, Jung in Küsnacht, on the shores of Lake Zurich, and Joyce in Fluntern Cemetery in the City of Zurich. The names of both live on in the Zurich area, in the Jung Institute at Küsnacht and in the Zurich James Joyce Foundation, as well as the James Joyce Pub. To be sure, Jung's image as the "old wise man of Küsnacht" contrasts sharply with Joyce's often-noted appearance of never-aging youth, which led Wyndham Lewis, for example, to characterize him as "a 'young man' in some way embalmed"[9] and Nino Frank to see him as "immutable, never growing old, frozen once and for all in the appearance he had given himself," indeed "fixed in Stephen Dedalus' adolescence at the Martello Tower."[10]

But it is a fact that Jung and Joyce were contemporaries: Jung was born on 26 July 1875 and Joyce on 2 February 1882, six and one-half years apart. Moreover, both lived in Zurich during the First World War at a time when each man was engaged in a central endeavor of his career: Jung was developing the framework of his psychology and Joyce was writing *Ulysses*. There is no record of any direct contact between Jung and Joyce during these wartime years, although Ellmann's biography includes the story of Edith Rockefeller McCormick's offer to pay for Joyce to be analyzed by Jung, whom she was "heavily endowing" (*JJ* 422), even as she was subsidizing Joyce, who, the story goes, "vehemently refused" the offer. He memorialized it, however, in *Finnegans Wake* (*JJ* 466) with the command, "Get yourself psychoanolised!" and the boastful response, "I can psoakoonaloose myself any time I want" (*FW* 522.35–6).

Beyond this near miss in their lives, moreover, Jung and Joyce knew something about each other's work; in fact, Jung was the only one among the early psychoanalysts to make reference to Joyce, whose name appears in Jung's *Collected Works*, along with the names of his books, in a number of significant contexts.[11] In addition, Jung's essay "*Ulysses*: A Monologue," paired with an essay on Picasso, appears in his *Spirit in Man, Art, and Literature* (*CW* 15:109–32).[12] Jung in fact sent a copy of the essay to Joyce with a conciliatory letter, which includes his often-quoted description of "Penelope" as "a string of veritable psychological peaches" (*CW* 15:133–34; *JJ* 629).

Joyce never publicly acknowledged his ownership of Jung's aggressively Freudian essay, "The Significance of the Father in the Destiny of the Individual" (1909), but Jung's 1912 *Wandlungen und Symbole der Libido* (Transformations and Symbols of the Libido)[13] is the only psychoanalytic title, so far as I can discover, that Joyce ever mentioned in his correspondence or in reported conversation. Writing to Frank Budgen in December 1919, two months after his return to Trieste from Zurich, he complained that Ottocaro Weiss, whom he by now held responsible for Mrs. McCormick's withdrawal of financial support (*JJ* 467–69),[14] had failed to fulfill a promise to send Joyce "as a gift Doktor JUNG's (prolonged general universal applause) Wandlungen der LIBIDO (shouts *Hear*! *Hear*! from a raughty tinker and an Irishman in the gallery)" (*SL* 244). Although the mockery in Joyce's complaint is evident, its vehemence prompted Budgen to record his puzzlement at his friend's "big grouse about not getting that book he was promised—*Wandlungen der Libido*."[15]

Transformations of the Libido was an extraordinarily significant work for Jung, marking his escape from what he later called "the constricting atmosphere of Freudian psychology" (*CW* 5:xxiii). Homans identifies it as "a key text in the study of the formation of Jung's ideas" and points out that Jung repeatedly said that its contents were "the source of his break with Freud."[16] Suggesting that the 1912 work might more accurately be considered the *result* of the accumulation of disagreements that led to the final break, John Kerr has pointed to the "lack of clarity" in the "hodgepodge of different ideas" in *Transformations* as evidence of Jung's emotional upset as he wrote it.[17] And this supposition is supported by Jung's admission to a 1925 seminar called "Analytical Psychology" that, though it took him years to realize it, in *Transformations* he was "analyzing my own fantasy function," so that the work "can be taken as myself," saturated as it is with "my own unconscious processes."[18] The break with Freud, of course, was agonizingly drawn out and far from simple. But whatever the other factors in this historic split, the *Transformations* volume has been a convenient focus for explanation.

Transformations of the Libido was also remarkably pertinent to Joyce's fictional agenda in *Ulysses*, since Jung shifted in this work from the typically Freudian emphasis on the father that characterized his 1909 essay and focused on "the mother-complex,"[19] a focus that fits in with Stephen's story in *Ulysses*. For Stephen's mother enters the novel with him in the first episode and literally haunts him through the day until he dispatches her in "Circe." And at a time when Joyce was putting together the "Circe" episode of *Ulysses* in Trieste, it is not surprising that he remembered his impression of Jung's *Transformations* and complained that it was not available to him as it had been in Zurich.[20]

Joyce had returned to Trieste in October 1919 and wound up in Paris by mid 1920, but his connection to Zurich remained. His ophthalmologist, Dr. Alfred Vogt, was there, as were supportive friends like the Giedion-Welckers and the Jolases, and during the Paris years Joyce made intermittent trips to the city for consultation about his eyes. By the 1930s Lucia Joyce's worsening schizophrenia made it relevant that the world-famous Burghölzli Psychiatric Hospital was also in Zurich, as was Jung, whose special interest in schizophrenia dated back to his 1907 work, translated into English in 1909 as *The Psychology of Dementia Praecox* (*CW* 3:1–316).[21]

It was thus only natural that Maria Jolas should suggest that Joyce consult Jung about Lucia (*JJ* 659), a suggestion that Joyce did not act on until two years later,[22] when in late September 1934 he had Lucia transferred from the Burghölzli to a private sanatorium where Jung was on the staff, "the twentieth doctor to be consulted for Lucia" (*JJ* 676). It is thus another shared fact of Joyce's biography and Jung's that Lucia was briefly treated by Jung, marking the only time that Jung and Joyce actually talked with each other. It was at this time that Joyce wrote the following inscription in Jung's copy of *Ulysses*: "To Dr. C. G. Jung, with grateful appreciation of his aid and counsel. James Joyce. Xmas 1934, Zurich" (*CW* 15:134).

THE FAMILY BACKGROUND

Nor are the parallels between their lives confined to the Zurich connection. A number of "psychophysical parallels" may be discerned in the years before Joyce left Ireland for the Continent.

Both men were brought up in what Ellenberger calls "an impoverished middle-class family."[23] Jung remembers his first awareness of "how poor we were" when he entered the gymnasium in Basel, where his classmates came from wealthy families, whereas he, the son of a "poor country parson," had "holes in his shoes and had to sit for six hours in school with wet feet" (*MDR* 24). As for the Joyce family, their progressive descent into poverty is a given of Joyce's biography and is reflected in the autobiographical fiction. The father, John Joyce, heir at twenty-one to property that brought him a living, supplemented by a political job that enabled him to marry (*JJ* 15, 18), mortgaged his inherited property, piece by piece, as his family grew, until nothing was left (*JJ* 21). Removed from his political job at the age of forty-two, with only a small pension, he never held a steady job again and of necessity moved his family—sometimes under cover of night to avoid paying the rent—to less and less desirable houses in less and less desirable locations (*JJ* 34).

In each family the father was in some sense—quite different for each man—a failure, though for both sons there was an ambiguity in this judgment. Jung's dissatisfaction with his "dear and generous" father, who "never tyrannized over me" (*MDR* 55),[24] centered on his deep disillusion with his father's unwillingness or inability to come to grips with essential questions about the Christian religion of which he was a minister. Jung records his feeling of "vehement pity" for his father when he realized "the tragedy of his profession and his life" (*MDR* 55), for Jung came to believe that the cause for the "impatience and defensive anxiety" with which his father met attempts to discuss religious questions with him was that "my poor father did not dare to think, because he was consumed by inward doubts" (*MDR* 73). This intellectual "immaturity," Ellenberger suggests, was the source of the "strong resentment" that Jung felt for his father "during his whole life."[25]

Joyce's father, on the other hand, was an unambiguous and spectacular failure, not only as a provider but in his whole relationship to his family. Stanislaus Joyce has recorded the specifics of his father's failure in convincing detail in his diary.[26] "Domineering and quarrelsome" (*CDD* 5), this "crazy drunkard" calls "all his children bastards as a habit" (*CDD* 6), personalizing his abuse as he taunts them with "their deformities. 'Ye dirty pissabed, ye bloody-looking crooked-eyed son of a bitch. Ye ugly bloody cornerboy, you've a mouth like a bloody nigger.' 'Ye black-looking mulatto. You were black the day you were born, ye bitch' " (*CDD* 28).

James Joyce appears to have maintained a good-humored detachment from this phenomenon, in contrast to his brother's anger and in contrast also to Jung's resentment of Paul Jung's intellectual failure. The reality of Stanislaus's portrait, however, is reflected in Joyce's fiction, even though nonjudgmentally. In *A Portrait*, for example, when a disembodied voice floats down to the Dedalus kitchen with the angry query, "Is your lazy bitch of a brother gone out yet?" Stephen's response is to laugh at his father's assumption that "a bitch is masculine" (*P* 175). In *Ulysses* the substance of Stanislaus's indictment of "Pappy" is acted out in Simon Dedalus's encounter with Dilly in "Wandering Rocks," the only scene in which Simon appears as a father. He taunts his daughter for her poor posture as she asks him for money and publicly mimics her, delivering an abbreviated tirade against all his daughters, "insolent pack of little bitches," and absolutely refusing to provide for his family (*U* 10:654–704). Again in this scene the nonjudgmental perspective of the son-author is reflected by the fictional daughter, who grins at Simon as he mocks her need and says, "You're very funny" (*U* 10:705).

And so he is in this scene, very funny, a fictional example of Joyce's skill in turning painful reality into comic irony, a skill that Constantine Curran saw as "an impregnable defence against intrusion on the inner sanctuary,"[27] and Carola Giedion-Welcker identified as a means for "liberation from the burden of reality into the more sublime regions of the intellect and imagination."[28] Ironic detachment was apparently Joyce's predominant defense against pain, reliably available to him in the face of the reality of his father's failure and the squalor of his home. Jung's "vehement pity" for his father, on the other hand, reflects his habitual assumption of a certain superiority in his own understandings—moral, intuitive, and intellectual—a superiority that he counted on.

Parallels such as these in the facts of the lives of Jung and Joyce, mingled as they are with contrasts and varying as they do in significance, add weight to the meaning of the parallels I am exploring in their work, without being in any necessary way a cause for this parallelism. We may thus consider them synchronicities—meaningful acausal coincidences.

We come now to the most dramatic of these synchronicities and the most significant for the lifework of each man. During the same period of time in 1909, each of these men discovered an aspect of himself that was shocking to him at the time, a psychic reality that Jung would personify in his individuation theory as the Shadow and Joyce would fictionalize in *Ulysses* as Leopold Bloom. The seeds for this discovery in each case were planted in 1904, when Sabina Spielrein came into Jung's life in Zurich and Joyce met Nora Barnacle in Dublin. For each man this love relation was at the center of the revelation of the Shadow, though the circumstances surrounding the experience were strikingly different, as was the nature of the subpersonality that was revealed. The Shadow erupted in each case in the context of a triangle, though again the nature of the triangles differed sharply. The year of the crisis was 1909, but the individual—and quite different—stories begin for each man in 1904.

DISCOVERY OF THE SHADOW: JUNG AND SABINA

In 1904, Jung, not yet thirty years old, had been a resident at the Burghölzli Psychiatric Clinic since 1900 and had been married to Emma Rauschenbach, the daughter of a wealthy industrialist, since February 1903. He had not yet met Freud or written to him, although he had read Freud's *Interpretation of Dreams* twice and "discovered how it all linked up with my own ideas" (*MDR* 147). In August 1904 Sabina Spielrein was admitted to the Burghölzli and became Jung's patient, suffering from what he later labeled "psychotic hysteria."[29] Until the 1974 publication of the Freud-Jung correspondence, including a number of letters about Spielrein, her name hardly appeared in the history of psychoanalysis.[30]

In 1977, however, Sabina Spielrein's name was definitively rescued from obscurity through the discovery of a carton of her personal papers in the basement of the Palais Wilson in Geneva, where Spielrein had practiced as a Freudian analyst in the twenties. This discovery was communicated to Aldo Carotenuto, a Jungian analyst in Italy, who was investigating the relationship between Jung and Spielrein, having been intrigued by the identification of Spielrein in the Freud-Jung correspondence as an early patient of Jung's and even as a factor in "a potentially disastrous scandal, barely covered up, implicating the two of them in an illicit romance."[31] Among her papers Carotenuto found confirmation of his speculative assumption of her importance to Jung, for these papers, as he lists them in the introduction to his 1982 *A Secret Symmetry*,[32] included "the correspondence between Sabina Spielrein and Jung (forty-six letters from Jung and twelve from Sabina), the correspondence between Spielrein and Freud (twenty letters from Freud and two from Sabina), and Spielrein's diary from 1909 to 1912."[33]

Carotenuto expressed the hope that his "partial publication" of the papers would "stimulate further research on Sabina Spielrein,"[34] and indeed it has. Since the publication of *A Secret Symmetry* two other caches of relevant documents have been unearthed,[35] and the research on Spielrein has resulted over the past several years in a spate of publications about this woman and her odd, triangular relationship with Jung and Freud. Among these the most substantial is Kerr's *Most Dangerous Method*, but full chapters in recent books, as well as a number of articles, have also been devoted to her story.[36] Although these writings differ in emphasis and context, they all depend on Carotenuto's book for the basic narrative of Spielrein's life and her relationships with Jung and Freud. For, with the publication of *A Secret Symmetry*, her significance in Jung's life and work, as well as her position at the heart of the relationship between Freud and Jung, was dramatically clarified.

Carotenuto's book made it apparent that her virtual omission from the history of psychoanalysis demanded redress, for Spielrein's significance to psychoanalysis is multiple. She was the first patient Jung treated with Freud's methods; she became herself an analyst, counting among her analysands Jean Piaget;[37] and she was the first woman analyst to contribute importantly to psychoanalytic theory, directly through her own publications and indirectly through her influence on Jung's theoretical development.[38] Moreover, her case formed, from beginning to end, a bridge between Jung and Freud. As Kerr puts it, "she had been closest to [Jung] during that personal transformation that first made Jung into a Freudian. Likewise, she had been at the center of the sudden squall of distrust that led to the break with Freud."[39]

Much of what has been written about Sabina Spielrein is not directly relevant to my purpose, which is to indicate how Jung's complicated interactions with this young woman, especially during the crisis of 1909, which also involved Freud, revealed to him his own Shadow. For this we need to know something of who she was, the development of her relationship with Jung before 1909, and the circumstances of Jung's betrayal of that relationship in 1909. I have tried to stay within these limits in the following abbreviated account, although, like the story of the relationship between Freud and Jung, to which this one is an addendum, the details are highly emotional and more finely nuanced than a strict summary can indicate.

Sabina Spielrein, the daughter of a prosperous Russian Jewish businessman and his university-educated wife, was nineteen years old when she was admitted to the Burghölzli. Being wealthy, Russian, and Jewish, Spielrein was a rare patient for the Burghölzli, which was roughly comparable to a state hospital in the United States, and patients with means ordinarily chose a private sanatorium instead.[40] Although she was severely disturbed, she was also highly intelligent and well educated, with a gymnasium degree. She was indeed, Kerr points out, "the perfect sort of person on whom to try out Freud's newest ideas,"[41] which were of great interest to the staff of this teaching hospital.

That Spielrein was a Jewess was almost certainly a part of her appeal for Jung. Sabina herself wrote, "He told me that he loved Jewish women, that he wanted to love a dark Jewish girl".[42] Another significant factor in the development of the young Jewess's relationship with Jung was her very nearly incredible naïveté about sexual matters. Although the oldest of five children, she had, by design, been raised in complete ignorance of the sexual facts of life. Her mother, in fact, even managed to have the gymnasium curriculum changed so that her daughter would not learn about reproduction in biology class. Sabina was thus "consciously ignorant of what the procreative act was all about" and did not bring this knowledge to consciousness until after she entered medical school in 1905.[43] This enforced ignorance, followed by sudden enlightenment when she was an adult, must surely have had a bearing on the nature of her relationship with Jung.

Jung later described Sabina's condition at the time of her admission to the Burghölzli in a paper presented to the First International Congress of Psychiatry and Neurology in Amsterdam in September 1907 (included in Jung's *Collected Works* as "The Freudian Theory of Hysteria" [*CW* 4:10–24]). Alternating between "deep depressions and fits of laughing, crying, and screaming," Sabina "could no longer look anyone in the face, kept her head bowed, and when anybody touched her stuck her tongue out with every sign of loathing" (*CW* 4:21). In this paper, Jung used Spielrein's case to exemplify Freud's theory that hysteria is rooted in "a bit of sexual repression from childhood"—in Sabina's case "anal eroticism." Kerr justifiably labels it "bad manners" for Jung to have abstracted "the erotic history of a young woman who already meant a good deal to him personally" and used it in this public, even though anonymous, way.[44] For by 1907 when Jung delivered his paper, Spielrein, about to enter her third year of medical school, had become a valued associate and a friend of Jung's. At the same time, the apparent fact that this young woman could move from the condition Jung described before the congress to a successful career as a medical student in such a relatively short time dramatizes the truth of Bruno Bettelheim's observation: "However questionable Jung's behavior was from a moral point of view—however unorthodox, even disreputable, it may have been—somehow it met the prime obligation of the therapist toward his patient: to cure her."[45]

What was Jung's behavior? To begin with Bettelheim's positive point about the cure, Jung's "analysis" of the case, as Kerr has reconstructed the treatment,[46] was completed by December 1904, after which Spielrein, who planned to enter medical school, was assigned "work therapy" with Jung and Franz Riklin in the psychology laboratory while she continued her sessions with Jung. Still living at the Burghölzli, she enrolled at the University of Zurich in April 1905, although she was not allowed to begin classes until her formal discharge from the clinic in June. In September 1905, as Spielrein was beginning the fall semester in medical school and nine months before the Freud-Jung correspondence actually began, Jung wrote Freud what appears to be a letter of introduction for Spielrein, which was never sent but was retained by Spielrein. This letter, in which Jung described Sabina as a "highly intelligent and gifted person of great sensitivity," places Spielrein, Kerr maintains, "in her dual capacity as former patient and as fledgling medical student, at the center of the relationship between Jung and Freud—even before it had properly begun."[47]

And when the correspondence did begin in 1906, Spielrein's case surfaced in Jung's second letter to Freud, dated 23 October 1906, as a "difficult case, a 20-year-old Russian girl student, ill for 6 years" (*F-J* 4J). Jung then gave an abbreviated summary of the history of the patient's case, asking for comments from Freud, to which Freud responded with gusto on 27 October, pointing, for one thing, to the advantage "that your Russian girl is a student [since] uneducated persons are at present too inaccessible for our purposes" (*F-J* 5F). Nine months later, the relationship between Jung and Spielrein had progressed to a more dangerous stage, as is suggested in Jung's report to Freud on 6 July 1909 of the dream of a "hysterical patient," whose "greatest wish is to have a child by me" (*F-J* 35J), giving no indication, however, that this is the same patient, whose name, it should be noted, has never been mentioned to Freud. By 1908, Carotenuto supposes, Jung "probably realized he was in love with the patient,"[48] and by the end of that year he had begun to sense the dangers to his more public ambitions of this now intense relationship.

Two days after the birth of his first son, an event of great significance for Jung, he wrote to Sabina, apparently, Kerr speculates, after an attempt to break off with her. He acknowledges in the letter that he has behaved unprofessionally and begs her not to revenge herself on him, to understand that "it is my misfortune that my life means nothing to me without the joy of love, of tempestuous, eternally changing love." The letter ends with an extraordinary appeal: "Return to me, in this moment of my need, some of the love and guilt and altruism which I was able to give you at the time of your illness. Now it is I who am ill."[49] This is a desperate man.

The question of whether their affair was sexually consummated remains a matter of debate. Kerr, for example, finds it "at least possible that the two stopped short of intercourse," although Fisher concludes that "almost certainly" the affair "was consummated sexually," and Haynal says flatly that Jung "became *her lover* when the treatment was finished" (Haynal's emphasis).[50] Thomas, however, has no doubt that the two "confined themselves to kisses and speechless gazing," and the authors of *Freud's Women* conclude that "however the question of the sexual consummation of their relationship is answered, Jung and Spielrein had been acting for some years as if they were engaged in an illicit affair."[51]

As Sabina reviews the relationship in her diary, she records her own assessment, that "our love grew out of a deep spiritual affinity and common intellectual interests," and summarizes for herself the progress of the affair: "We came to know each other, we became fond of each other without noticing it was happening; it was too late for flight; several times we sat 'in tender embrace.' Yes, it was a great deal!"[52] "It was my first love," she recognizes, admitting that because of "the force of my passion and of our spiritual kinship," she has played with the idea of trying to "snatch him away from his wife," but she follows this with the claim, "I am far from being his wife's enemy," which she supports convincingly with her rueful commentary about the pain she has already brought to Emma Jung and the impossibility of happiness for her and Jung if he were to abandon his wife and children.[53]

As she considers the possibility of having a child—"a little boy"—by Jung and then sending him back to his wife, she recognizes the emotional pain as well as the practical problems of raising the child by herself and then asks herself, "What if I did not even get pregnant? Then our pure friendship would be destroyed by the intimate relationship, and our friendship is what is so terribly dear to me."[54] Here in her diary, Spielrein, it seems to me, is writing about intercourse as a first-time sexual experience that is the only way to have a child but is also a sure way, in her particular circumstances, to destroy a "pure friendship." She writes of Jung as "my friend" throughout the diary entries and in her letters to Freud; and however passionate the friendship, I must agree with those who conclude that the relationship was never technically adultery. But certainly it was a love affair, and even though Carotenuto labels Jung's relationship with Sabina a "psychotic countertransference," he acknowledges that, like "transference love," "countertransference love" cannot reliably be distinguished from the real thing.[55] In 1909 there were no built-in safeguards in psychoanalytic practice against this powerful involvement,[56] and whatever the hazards, Jung was still meeting secretly with Spielrein as the new year began.

In mid-January, however, Jung received a letter from Spielrein's mother, who was herself acting on an anonymous letter, presumably from Emma Jung, warning her that her Sabina, having been saved by Jung, was in grave danger of being ruined by her savior. Mrs. Spielrein begged Jung, as Sabina later reported to Freud in a long, confused letter, "not to exceed the bounds of friendship."[57] At this point, Jung went into a panic. His reply to Mrs. Spielrein, copied out for Freud by Sabina, is a model of callous defensiveness, in which he outlines a sophistical distinction between the relationship of doctor to patient and that of friendship, a distinction based entirely on the matter of payment of fees. He points out to this anxious mother that a patient "may expect her doctor to give her all the love and concern she requires" and still be confident that he will never go beyond certain limits because "he is *paid* for his troubles."

Jung then suggests to Mrs. Spielrein that "if you wish me to adhere strictly to my role as doctor, you should pay me a fee as suitable recompense for my trouble" and quotes his fee as "10 francs per consultation." Although Jung assures Sabina's mother that his remarks "conceal no baseness," it is hard to imagine, especially in the context of his five-year relationship with Sabina, a response that could be *more* base. This letter was followed by a second, in which Jung assured Mrs. Spielrein that he had "always told [Sabina] that a sexual relationship was out of the question," and a third letter that Sabina considered too insulting to herself even to paraphrase for Freud.[58]

At this point in the affair, having said nothing to Sabina of the correspondence with her mother, Jung cut off his visits to Sabina and suggested a weekly one-hour appointment instead. Understandably bewildered, Sabina stayed away altogether for three weeks; then she appeared at the appointed time on 26 February 1909 only to be treated to a "long sermon about all he had done for me," with no acknowledgment at all that "only a short time ago we could sit in speechless ecstasy for hours."[59] This was indeed a *long* sermon, and in response Sabina attacked Jung, in fact, drew blood. Then she fled.[60] If Jung had been desperate before, he was now beside himself with anxiety about how she might avenge herself.

Meanwhile, there was no mention of any of these developments in Jung's correspondence with Freud, who remained happily firm in his determination to make Jung his scientific heir; indeed the first issue of the *Yearbook for Psychoanalytic and Psychopathological Research*, with Jung's name on the masthead as editor, had just been published when Jung had his disastrous encounter with Sabina at the end of February. Two weeks went by before Jung, in response to Freud's telegram of inquiry, wrote on 7 March 1909 with a flurry of excuses, the "last and worst straw" being the developments with Spielrein. Identifying her as "a woman patient, whom years ago I pulled out of a very sticky neurosis with unstinting effort," Jung accuses this still-unnamed patient of having "kicked up a vile scandal solely because I denied myself the pleasure of giving her a child" and claims that he has "always acted the gentleman towards her," though because of his "rather too sensitive conscience," he does not feel "clean." He concludes his account by admitting that "until now I had a totally inadequate idea of my polygamous components" (*F-J* 133J). Freud at this point had not yet heard from Spielrein, and his response to Jung's account was soothing: "To be slandered and scorched by the love with which we operate—such are the perils of our trade" (*F-J* 134F).

By the time Sabina wrote to Freud at the end of May, requesting "a brief audience," Jung's ambitions for the future were even more closely tied to his relationship with Freud, for he had been invited to accompany Freud on the historic trip to America for the twentieth anniversary celebration at Clark University in September. This introduction to the American scientific community as part of a gathering in Worcester, Massachusetts, of internationally prominent scientific figures was, as Saul Rosenzweig points out, "momentous for Freud and psychoanalysis" and for Jung the realization of his long-standing dream of journeying to America. In addition it was an undreamed of opportunity for international prominence, including the awarding of an honorary degree, which was extraordinary for a man of thirty-four.[61] His relationship with Freud was even more than before central to the realization of his ambitions, and Sabina, with her entirely unpredictable revelations, represented an enormous threat, so that when Freud wired him a request for further information about Spielrein's case, his reply of 4 June 1909 was defensive and still not quite honest.

Naming Spielrein for the first time, Jung identifies her as the patient described in his Amsterdam lecture, his "test case" and hence the object of his "special gratitude and affection," and he justifies his "prolonged" relationship with her as a measure to prevent her relapse. Claiming to have broken with her when he realized that she was "systematically planning my seduction," he reports that she has been "seeking revenge" by spreading rumors. After more explanation and excuse, none of it edifying, Jung concludes: "To none of my patients have I extended so much friendship and from none have I reaped so much sorrow" (*F-J* 144J).[62] And again, Freud's reply was reassuring—in intent, if not in effect. Recognizing that "such experiences, though painful, are necessary and hard to avoid," he reports that he has written to Spielrein, "affect[ing] ignorance" and asking her to state the nature of her business (*F-J* 145F).

Jung was well aware that he had been far from candid with Freud, and when Freud wrote that Sabina had named Jung as the object of her concern and also reported his own suggestion to the young woman that she try to work out the change in her relationship with Jung for herself without the intervention of others (*F-J* 147F),[63] this did nothing to alleviate Jung's agonizing suspense. Nor was he relieved by Freud's advice that he not "go too far in the direction of contrition and reaction," since "in view of the kind of matter we work with, it will never be possible to avoid little laboratory explosions" (*F-J* 147F), for Jung still had no idea how fully and how clearly Sabina would state her case.

In all this correspondence, neither of these great men, engrossed as they were in assuring and reassuring each other, indicated any real awareness of the overwhelming distress of this troubled and troublesome patient and certainly no sympathy. But Sabina had given considerable thought to her case "for over three months," she tells Freud, as she begins to draft her response to his letter of 8 June, in which he has indicated to her that he believes Jung to be "incapable of frivolous or ignoble behavior."[64] Although she recognizes that Freud's letter is "unfavorable" to her, it has convinced her that Freud "deeply loves and respects" Jung and is therefore the one who can understand her. For she too deeply loves and respects Jung and is looking for someone to "demonstrate to me that he is worthy of love, that he is no scoundrel."[65]

Beginning on 10 June, Spielrein drafted a marathon letter to Freud over a period of ten days, reviewing the history of her relationship with Jung. The document is, as Kerr says, "vivid, impassioned, and chaotic,"[66] and when Freud received the letter itself, he characterized it as either "amazingly awkward" or "very inhibited," but certainly "hard to read and hard to understand. All I can gather from it is that the matter means a great deal to her and that she is very much in earnest" (*F-J* 149F). But by the time Spielrein's letter reached Freud on 30 June 1909, he had received a letter from Jung, dated 21 June 1909, in which Jung admitted fully his own culpability in the Spielrein affair and by implication his betrayal of Sabina.

Sabina herself had required that he write Freud, and her strength in insisting on this is perhaps again a measure of the success of Jung's treatment of her case. Having spent ten days reviewing the course of their relationship in her draft letter, she confronted Jung at his home for what Jung called "a *very decent* talk," during which she assured him that she had not been the source of rumors about him (*F-J* 148J) and that she was not seeking revenge. But she also extracted a promise that he write Freud "an honest account of everything,"[67] for Sabina was concerned with Jung's moral salvation. In the draft letter to Freud, she relates her conviction that "he could not be saved by being publicly disgraced, that is, he would be incapable of realizing what he had done." And she exclaims, "If he were capable of being honest with himself, how happy I should be!"[68] Jung's confession to Freud appears to be at least very close to Spielrein's hope for him:

> Although not succumbing to helpless remorse, I nevertheless deplore the sins I have committed, for I am largely to blame for the high-flying hopes of my former patient. . . . Thus I imputed . . . wishes and hopes entirely to my patient without seeing the same thing in myself. When the situation had become so tense that the continued perseveration of the relationship could be rounded out only by sexual acts, I defended myself in a manner that cannot be justified morally. Caught in my delusion that I was the victim of the sexual wiles of my patient, I wrote to her mother that I was not the gratifier of her daughter's sexual desires but merely her doctor, and that she should free me from her. In view of the fact that the patient had shortly before been my friend and enjoyed my full confidence, my action was a piece of knavery which I very reluctantly confess to you as my father. (*F-J* 148J)

He then asks Freud to inform Spielrein of his confession and apologizes for "my stupidity that drew you into this imbroglio," though he does not apologize for his evasions and misstatements to Freud. Jung could not have written this letter without realizing what he had done, which, of course, was Sabina's intention; but such a confession, though probably good for the soul, which was Sabina's hope, makes a galling memory.[69] It documents the existence and activities of a person who is

Jung and yet not Jung, indeed, Jung beside himself, a person who has been cowardly and cruel and dishonorable, qualities that are radically foreign to his concept of himself. Through the whole experience with Spielrein, and especially through his cruel denial of his relationship with her, which he alludes to in his letter to Freud, Jung has been forced to recognize an alien other in himself, a psychic reality that he would later personify as the Shadow.[70]

This recognition was not, of course, the end of the story, but it became a different kind of story as Jung began the process of accommodation to this shocking realization. One can only speculate what influence the recognition of his cowardice in the Spielrein affair had on his increasingly open expression of disagreements with Freud over the next few years, especially in his 1912 *Transformations of the Libido* and his Fordham lectures in the fall of that year, which clarified his disagreements with Freud.[71] Freud and Jung each had a great professional stake in the continuation of their personal relationship and struggled to maintain it in the face of a variety of conflicts,[72] but what they had seen in each other in the course of the resolution of the affair with Sabina Spielrein was surely an important factor in a change of attitude on both sides, and the split between Freud and Jung gradually widened. By the beginning of 1913, they had ended their personal correspondence; in mid 1913, Jung resigned as editor of the *Yearbook*; and in April 1914, he resigned as president of the International Psychoanalytic Association.

Jung's later determination to be absolutely open in his long-term relationship with Toni Wolff was a striking contrast to his fearfulness about his affectional tie with Sabina Spielrein. Spielrein records in a diary entry of 23 September 1909 her realization after a meeting with Jung that "we both loved each other fervently again" but records also Jung's reminder that "we would always have to be careful not to fall in love again; we would always be dangerous to each other."[73] And what record we have indicates that this line was not crossed. Spielrein left Jung's world when she received her medical degree in 1911 and moved to Vienna, where she was a member of the Vienna Psychoanalytic Society and became identified with Freudian psychoanalysis, then to Berlin, to Geneva, and finally back to Russia, where she apparently was exterminated by the invading Germans during World War II.[74] Married to a doctor in 1913, she had two daughters and maintained an intermittent correspondence with both Jung and Freud until after World War I.

Although Jung makes no explicit reference in his autobiography to his experience with Sabina Spielrein, he has elsewhere acknowledged the crucial importance of that experience in two letters, widely separated in time. In one of his last letters to Sabina, dated 1 September 1919, after Jung had emerged from his long period of solitude and even near madness and had formulated his metapsychology, he wrote,

> *The love of S. for J.* made the latter aware of something he had previously only vaguely suspected, that is, of a power in the unconscious that shapes one's destiny, a power which later led him to things of the greatest importance. The relationship had

to be "sublimated" because otherwise it would have led to delusion and madness. . . . Occasionally one must be unworthy, simply in order to be able to continue living.[75]

Many years later, as a wise old man of eighty, he wrote to Theodor Bovet, a Swiss psychiatrist, pointing out that "I would hardly have been able to form the concept of the shadow had not its existence become one of my greatest experiences." Asserting that "my shadow is indeed so huge that I could not possibly overlook it in the plan of my life," he spells out what he means when he speaks theoretically about the "accommodation" to the Shadow in the course of the individuation process: "I had to see it as an essential part of my personality, accept the consequences of this realization, and take responsibility for them."[76]

Kerr surmises that Jung's "misadventure with Spielrein had left him feeling both threatened and exhilarated" and that "his whole intellectual saga since that time was predicated on the attempt to recapture the sense of exhilaration while escaping the sensed dangers of the . . . fantasy that had first brought it into being."[77] This kind of paradoxical response may also be said to characterize the effect on Joyce of his confrontation with his Shadow in 1909 during his devastating experience of jealousy in Dublin, the experience that provides the autobiographical base for Bloom's story in *Ulysses*.

JEALOUSY AND THE SHADOW: JOYCE AND NORA

Again, the story begins in 1904. As every Joycean knows, 16 June 1904 is the day of *Ulysses*, which is celebrated every year in Dublin and elsewhere as Bloomsday. This is the day, according to the generally accepted explanation offered by Richard Ellmann, when Joyce "began to fall in love" with Nora Barnacle, for it was on 16 June that they first went walking together, though their first meeting appears to have been on 10 June (*JJ* 155–56). Of course, not everyone agrees with Ellmann's conjecture. Rodney Wilson Owen, for example, in his study of the origins of *Ulysses*, suggests that the date was chosen because it offered the closest correspondence to the first day back in Ithaca for Homer's Odysseus.[78] I myself feel that 16 June could well have been chosen because it was a Thursday, as was 2 February 1882, the date of Joyce's birth. For Joyce has testified to his rebirth through Nora, "the girl I loved, who had red-brown hair and took me so easily into her arms and made me a man" (*Letters* 2:233), and certainly it would be fitting that both birth and rebirth be on the same day for "Thursday's child" (*U* 15:3687). But whatever we may decide about the rationale for Joyce's selection of 16 June 1904 as the historical day of *Ulysses*, and it may well have been multiple, most of us could agree that the fictional day of the novel celebrates in some way a crucial event in the true story of Joyce's life of feeling: his commitment to Nora.

But this event took place over time. On 8 October 1904, when Joyce and Nora left Dublin, without a marriage certificate and with just enough money to get them to Paris, "neither," Ellmann says, "wholly trusted the other" (*JJ* 179). But what they left behind held no promise at all. Nora was already an exile twice over, having been sent to live with her Grandmother Healy in Galway before she was five simply because there were too many children in the home, and having run away from Galway at nineteen to escape her Uncle Tommy's beatings. Not yet twenty, she was totally alone in Dublin, though she did have a job as a chambermaid, which provided room and board at Finn's Hotel.[79] Joyce at twenty-two, almost two years after receiving his degree from University College, Dublin, was jobless, though he had been moved to start an autobiographical novel after the rejection of his first "Portrait of an Artist" in January. His home and family, never a reliable source of comfort or security, had fallen into chaos after his mother's death in August 1903. "The house," Stanislaus wrote in his diary, "is and always has been intolerable with bickering, quarrelling and scurrility" (*CDD* 17), and so unreliable were John Joyce's moods and sobriety that the three brothers took turns staying home to protect their sisters from his drunken attacks (*CDD* 24).

The loss of his mother was a psychic disaster for Joyce. With her death, he entered upon the "interval of loose living" that is pictured in *Ulysses*, a time that Constantine Curran remembers as short but "startling, being lived openly and in defiance of convention, and . . . in plain contradiction with his life before and after."[80] Although May Joyce had been continually in conflict with her eldest son about religion, she believed in his genius and wholeheartedly supported him. Joyce's sister Eileen remembered that "all the relatives were saying that Jim should get a job and help with the big family—he being the eldest, but Mother never took that point of view. She always did everything in her power to help him follow his bent."[81] Certainly May Joyce's letters to her eldest son during his feckless adventure in Paris (*Letters* 2:20–41) fully support Eileen's judgment that "he completely depended on her," and they testify also to her complete dependability.

When she was gone, as Eileen said, "he had to have someone."[82] And in Nora, ten months after his mother's death, Joyce found a woman who loved him almost as unreservedly as his mother had and let him know it, a woman who had the courage to throw in her lot with him. The initial commitment to Nora in 1904 thus represented, at least in part, the solution for Joyce to the loss of his mother. Words being a kind of ultimate reality for Joyce, he could not quite bring himself to say that he loved her, although he acknowledged "my great respect for that love of yours which it is my desire to deserve and to answer" and conceded that "perhaps my affection for you is a kind of love" (*JJ* 176–77).

Puzzling out his feelings for Nora in a letter to Stanislaus after the couple had been some months in Pola and Nora was pregnant with Giorgio, Joyce wrote that Nora's "disposition, as I see it, is much nobler than my own, her love also is greater than mine for her. I admire her and I love her and I trust her—I cannot tell how much. I trust her. So enough" (*JJ* 191). And it was enough—just barely. Their commitment to each other was strained during their first five years by the practical inadequacy of both these young people for a stable married life. Nora did not speak Italian, and neither of them knew how to manage money, which was never adequate. The addition of Stanislaus to their disorderly household in 1905 was a mixed blessing, as, for that matter, were the births of their children: Giorgio in 1905 and Lucia, born in 1907 in the pauper's ward of the Trieste city hospital at the same time her father was hospitalized there with rheumatic fever. All of this has been described and documented in convincing detail in Ellmann's account of these first years of their life together (*JJ* 195–275).[83]

At the end of July 1909, not quite five years after he and Nora had left Dublin, Joyce made his first trip back to Dublin, taking Giorgio with him and leaving Stanislaus to deal with his chronically unstable household, his wife and daughter, and his creditors in Trieste.[84] Although he had "practical objectives" to justify the trip—a contact with Maunsel & Co. about *Dubliners* and the possibility of a professorship at his old university (*JJ* 276)—his main purpose was to see and be seen by those he had left behind, his family and his friends. One of the first of these friends to be contacted was Vincent Cosgrave, a schoolmate and longtime fellow idler, memorialized in both *A Portrait* and *Ulysses* as Lynch. Cosgrave in turn told Oliver St. John Gogarty that Joyce was in town, and Gogarty, the model for Buck Mulligan in *Ulysses*, immediately got in touch with Joyce and invited him to his house. Joyce, according to his letter to Stanislaus, told Gogarty that he intended to include in his novel his brief stay with Gogarty at the Martello Tower, and although Joyce assured Gogarty that he bore him no ill will, he reminded him that "I must write as I have felt." Joyce "relished" this meeting, Ellmann says, "as the fulfillment of a daydream, in which he, the lofty, cool, untouchable hero had discomfited his suppliant enemy" (*JJ* 278).

Joyce also visited John Francis Byrne, the original of Cranly in *A Portrait*, taking with him "in beaming pride" his four-year-old son for a pleasant afternoon.[85] In 1909 Byrne was living at Number 7 Eccles Street, which, of course, is the Blooms' address in *Ulysses*, and Byrne writes in his memoirs: "Joyce had good reason to remember No.7 Eccles Street, for it was to that house one subsequent afternoon that he came, in a state of utter perturbation, to see me."[86] Byrne does not reveal the source of Joyce's distress, but Ellmann does as he pieces together the story (*JJ* 278–82) from Byrne's account, from Joyce's letters of 6 and 7 August 1909 to Nora, and from an interview with Stanislaus Joyce almost half a century later.

Two days before he appeared at Byrne's door on 8 August, Joyce had been told by Vincent Cosgrave that during the time surrounding 16 June 1904, the day of *Ulysses*, Nora was, in Joyce's own words "dividing [her] body" between Cosgrave and Joyce; and apparently Joyce believed him without question, despite the "inherent improbability" of Cosgrave's boast (*JJ* 279) and despite his own experience of Nora's steadfastness. His assurance to his Aunt Josephine three months into their adventure that "I have not been able to discover any falsehood in this nature which had the courage to trust me" (*JJ* 189) was temporarily annulled. For the young man who had debated with himself about whether or in what way he loved the young woman who had joined her fate to his was overwhelmed by a debilitating jealousy he had never experienced before. The ironic detachment that had been his dependable protection against painful situations for years deserted him; he was in undiluted agony. He was beside himself.

Byrne describes the figure that confronted him on 8 August: "I had never before this afternoon seen anything to approach the frightening condition that convulsed him. He wept and groaned and gesticulated in futile impotence as he sobbed out to me the thing that had occurred. Never in my life have I seen a human being more shattered."[87] This is a far cry from the "lofty, cool, untouchable hero" of the meeting with Gogarty, and we might think Byrne was exaggerating, since the picture of a sobbing, groaning James Joyce does not fit any other picture we have of him, either as a young man—the model, after all, for the cool, detached Stephen Dedalus—or in his middle years, when by all accounts, the detachment was even more pronounced.[88] But Ellmann also includes in his account the letters that Joyce wrote to Nora from the irrational depths of his jealous despair (*JJ* 279–81), and the primitive quality of these letters, which present a startling contrast to any other writing we have from Joyce, entirely confirms the picture presented by Byrne, a picture that is, I think, a candid shot of the Bloom in Joyce, in at least one of his attitudes.

An hour after his conversation with Cosgrave, Joyce put his feelings on paper in a letter to Nora, which does not admit to any doubt about the "disclosures" he had heard. He "can never believe again" now that he knows that "*every second night*" during their courtship she was meeting Cosgrave and exchanging kisses with him. "What else did you do together?" Picturing for Nora his agony, with his eyes full of "tears of sorrow and mortification" and his heart "full of bitterness and despair," he assures her that he will "cry for days" because "[m]y faith in that face I loved is broken," and he has "learnt that the only being I believed in was not loyal to me." His love for her in this letter is all in the past tense, indeed "dead," though he does ask her to write, presumably to answer his question, "is all to be over between us?" (*JJ* 279–80).

During a nearly sleepless night, he apparently pictured "what else" may have occurred in these supposed assignations, and by the following morning his jealous imaginings had expanded beyond Cosgrave. He wrote another letter flinging questions at Nora about specifics of her sexual past that are reminiscent of Molly's report in *Ulysses* of Bloom's "question and answer would you do this that and the other with the coalman yes with a bishop yes . . . who is in your mind now tell me who are you thinking of who is it tell me his name . . . " (*U* 18:89–90). "Is Georgie my son?" Joyce asks Nora, reminding her that "[t]he first night I slept with you in Zurich was October 11th and he was born July 27th. That is nine months and 16 days. I remember that there was very little blood that night. Were you fucked by anyone before you came to me?" He has been a fool, he laments, and supposes that "the rumour here is circulated that I have taken the leavings of others. Perhaps they laugh when they see me parading '*my*' son in the streets." He vows to return to Trieste "as soon as Stannie sends me the money" and again asks her for reassurance: "Is there any hope yet of my happiness?" (*JJ* 280–81).

The following morning he wrote to Stanislaus, asking for his fare home, but without further explanation of the reason for his change in plans, and in the afternoon he poured out his anguish to Byrne. Byrne pronounced Cosgrave's boast "a blasted lie" (*JJ* 281) and "succeeded in quieting" Joyce, who spent the night with Byrne and got up the following morning, Byrne reports, "fully out of the gloom," leaving after breakfast, "humming as he went." He bought "a trinket" for Nora, which he showed to Byrne, and returned energetically to his business in Dublin and his plans for taking his sister Eva back with him as soon as Stanislaus raised the money.[89] His belief in Cosgrave's story had apparently been dissipated, but it was ten days before he reported this to Nora, asking her "to forgive me for my contemptible conduct" but asking her also to "say . . . a word of denial and O I shall be so transported with happiness!" (*Letters* 2:235).

His behavior *had* been contemptible. The twenty-seven-year-old Joyce had almost eagerly accepted his wife's unfaithfulness as a fact; he had poured out his unjustified jealousy in wounding letters to her at a great distance; he had humiliated himself in a blubbering confession to his friend Byrne. None of this could be gratifying to contemplate in retrospect. He had discovered another personality in himself that he had not known about before, and the ironic detachment that was his trusted weapon against inner pain vanished as he gave himself over to maudlin self-pity and wailing reproach. But this newly discovered personality was at the same time one that he could not really deny or reject or even entirely disapprove. For he had also discovered that this internal uproar, painful though it might be, was just about the most exciting thing that had happened to him.

As was the case with Jung after his recognition of another and, by his conscious standards, an inferior, personality in himself, Joyce's similarly disquieting discovery was followed by a period of accommodation to the new recognition. Having experienced the excitement of his jealous imaginings, Joyce apparently sought to repeat and prolong this excitement, most immediately and perhaps most importantly through the notorious pornographic letters that he and Nora exchanged during the remainder of his stay in Dublin on this first trip and during a second separation from October 1909 till January 1910, when Joyce again traveled to Dublin.[90] Joyce's part of the correspondence is, of course, available in Ellmann's edition of the *Selected Letters* (*SL* 180–93), and even though Nora's letters do not survive, they can be reconstructed, as Maddox points out, from Joyce's responses.[91]

Much has been written about this correspondence, but I focus here on the value of these letters to Joyce's understanding of the true dimensions of his autobiographical fiction, which had to encompass what he had discovered about himself in the totally uncharacteristic eruption of emotion that accompanied his experience of jealousy. Nora's letters, by intention and by Joyce's own direction, presented to him—at a distance and through words on paper—a picture of himself as her lover, a separate person engaged in a remarkable range of perverse sexual activities. For Joyce these letters were tantamount to a voyeuristic experience, and he responded, not only through the masturbation that the letters were intended to stimulate but also through words on paper, thus bringing this polymorphous perverse aspect of his love life to full consciousness. But at the same time, in a kind of antiphonal chorus, he put into words his love for Nora in the language of worship, committing himself to her unconditionally and irretrievably. As Joyce prepared to return to Trieste in December 1909, he wrote, "I will *never* leave you again" (*Letters* 2:273), and Nora knew that he meant it.

The separation from his ongoing life—represented by his two trips to Dublin, along with the objectification and legitimation, through the letters, of this other person he had recently discovered as himself—parallels, though on a much smaller scale, Jung's self-styled "confrontation with the unconscious," that period of comparative isolation from 1913 to 1918, during which he struggled to understand and accept submerged levels of himself. Jung also approached this confrontation, in part at least, through writing out his fantasies, and if "something emotionally vulgar or banal" came up in his writing, even though he might recognize that he had "thought and felt this way at some time or other," he came to see that he "need not accept this banality . . . in perpetuity." He discovered that he could strip these unconscious forces of their power over him by "personifying them and at the same time bringing them into relationship with consciousness" (*MDR* 186–87). This defensive maneuver is, of course, analogous to the writing of autobiographical fiction, and it is one that Joyce followed in the creation of Bloom, through whom he wove into his autobiographical fiction the emotional vulgarity and the banality revealed to him through his experience of jealousy in 1909.

Through this technique, Jung eventually fitted the personified unconscious forces into a universal developmental pattern, the individuation process, a technique that is paralleled, though with admitted differences, by the process that Joyce initiated in the 1909 exercise in pornography, which, Maddox says, was over even before the end of Joyce's second stay in Dublin and was never resumed.[92] Words, especially written words, certify reality for Joyce. His brother's diary, written during the period following their mother's death, gave Joyce an objective view of himself, unparalleled in its authenticity, as the young artist struggling to reorient himself after this crushing loss. And surely the figure of Stephen in *Ulysses* owes much to Stanislaus's written portrait, which complemented Joyce's own intimate experience of the upheaval in himself during this period. Similarly the letters to and from Nora presented Joyce with an extraordinary opportunity to see himself as the cuckold *imaginaire* who eventually took shape as Leopold Bloom.

Once Joyce had chosen Nora as his companion in exile in 1904, the uxorious Bloom, who in the "Ithaca" episode of *Ulysses* complacently contemplates an unbelievably long and wildly assorted list of his wife's "lovers" (*U* 17:2133–42), became a possibility, the "manchild in the womb" of the end of "Ithaca" (*U* 17:2317–18). But this Bloom was born not in 1904, when Joyce left Dublin with Nora, but during Joyce's devastating 1909 experience of jealousy in Dublin, the experience that provides the autobiographical base for Bloom's story in *Ulysses*. He was, in effect, born at Number 7 Eccles Street in August 1909 and only gradually matured into the other self of the fictional artist whose earlier development Joyce pictured in *A Portrait.*

Joyce's translation of this aspect of his experience into his fictional self-portrait took some years, during which he was working out the fictional childhood and youth of the artist-hero of his fiction in *A Portrait of the Artist as a Young Man.* His first attempt to work through the 1909 experience was in his only play, *Exiles*, which Joyce had begun to write by November 1913 (*Letters* 2:65) and had completed by April 1915 (*Letters* 2:338). Ellmann connects the composition of *Exiles* with another episode of jealousy, this time Joyce's discovery that the Venetian journalist Roberto Prezioso had propositioned Nora "some time in 1911 or 1912" (*JJ* 316), reviving, we might suppose, the contradictory emotions attendant upon the earlier experience of 1909.[93]

In *Exiles* Joyce attempted a literal translation of his experience, attributing to Richard Rowan—who is, like Stephen, a bioenergetic self-portrait, recognizable as Joyce—the self-willed jealous doubts that he had come to see in himself in the wake of his ordeal of jealousy. Richard reveals the perverse nature of his motivation in dialogue that is rhetorically akin to the clean parts of the "dirty letters." Speaking, for example, to Robert Hand, a trial version of a second self, Richard admits that "in the very core of my ignoble heart I longed to be betrayed . . . by you, my best friend, and by her . . . passionately and ignobly, to be dishonoured for ever in love and in lust" (*E* 70). Although the overt sexual perversity that was attached to the 1909 experience in Joyce's life is not explicitly revealed in *Exiles*, a peculiar miasma of sexual obsession pervades the play, and we may suppose that the writing of *Exiles* was a therapeutic success for Joyce, judging from his 1916 comment on Nora's dream about a weeping Prezioso: "the motive from which I liberated myself in art he is unable to liberate himself in life" (*JJ* 437). As art, however, *Exiles* is a widely acknowledged failure.[94]

In *Ulysses* Joyce split his autobiographical subject into two opposite persons, each of whom could reveal a part of the contradictory truth about himself. *A Portrait* had traced the development of Stephen, the self-conscious artist of Joyce's original conception of his autobiographical fiction. The 1909 experience, however, including both the unfounded jealousy and its aftermath in the pornographic letters, which wallow in excremental language and mawkish sentimentality at the same time, had revealed to Joyce, as an essential part of his true personality, "those poisonous subtleties which envelop the soul, the ascending fumes of sex," which he associated with the "modern theme."[95] Stephen simply could not encompass the whole, for this realm of Joyce's psyche does not belong to the artist-self that has been developed through Stephen in *A Portrait*, a basic incompatibility that Joyce must have realized when he attempted to attach this particular "poisonous subtlety" to Richard Rowan.

In fact, to personify all the forces in this extended, extraordinarily powerful epiphany, Joyce needed more even than Bloom, and he "pulled out of his own long pocket," à la the Shakespeare of Stephen's theory (*U* 9:741–42), that wonderfully named fantasy creature Blazes Boylan. Boylan does not appear to have had a local habitation or a clear model in the Dublin of 1904, any more than Bloom does,[96] but he is, I suspect, as real as Bloom and just as close to Joyce's heart. Although Ellmann labels Boylan Joyce's "villain" (*JJ* 378), he may instead be considered heroic in a special sense, that is, as the projection of a kind of ideal phallic self, a fantasy of the unadulterated, indiscriminate, physical sexuality that dominates the pornographic letters. Blazes Boylan is, I think, a specialized and short-lived aspect of Joyce's self-portrait, and the picture Molly paints of him in her soliloquy may stand as a memorial to Joyce's youthful libido, of which the middle-aged author of *Ulysses* is perhaps more than a little proud, more than a little ashamed, and also more than a little jealous. But Bloom, as Mary Colum recognized in her review of *Ulysses*, "is the one character whom Joyce really loves,"[97] for, as St. Paul wrote to the Ephesians, "no man ever yet hated his own flesh" (Eph. 5:29).

And with Bloom, Joyce moved from the nineteenth-century pattern of the *Bildungsroman*, which largely governed his *Portrait*, into a twentieth-century pattern for his autobiographical fiction, consciously personifying, even glorifying, a facet of his personality retrieved from the unconscious, though never acknowledged in his lifetime. Distancing himself from both artist and cuckold, whom he separated into Stephen and Bloom, he assigned to each a separate aspect of the determining experience of jealousy, which is mastered for each in a different and appropriate way. To Stephen, the acknowledged artist-surrogate, he assigned the whole question of the "incertitude" of biological paternity that he himself faced in 1909—"Is Georgie my son?" And Stephen, with access to the fully matured intellectual virtuosity of his creator, rings changes on the "paternity theme" throughout *Ulysses*, meshing it with Christian dogma and with his artistic ambitions to become the creator of "the word that shall not pass away" (*U* 14:293–94), the "son consubstantial with the father" (*U* 9:480–81), the artwork that, with its paternity certain, guarantees the personal immortality of the artist.

And through Bloom, the unacknowledged, infinitely adaptable surrogate, Joyce could reveal freely the polymorphous perverse sexual tendencies that are demonstrably an aspect of his mind, though not the only aspect revealed in Bloom. He attached this revelation to the experience of jealousy, which became a significant event in his life and is at the center of Bloom's story in *Ulysses*. By assigning all this to Bloom, he could bring the factually unacceptable picture of his jealousy and its obsessive fascination for him under the control of his comic genius, which enabled him not only to entertain generations of readers but also to reveal, as an essential part of his autobiographical fiction, his own hidden world and at the same time—at least for his lifetime—*keep* it hidden.

THREE

From Bildungsroman *to Individuation*

A Portrait as Prelude

A notation in the British Museum notesheets for "Circe" contains the equation "SD + LB = idem."[1] Since *idem* may be translated "same" or "self" and, further, forms the stem for "identity," this equation suggests the "equivalence" which Blackmur saw between Stephen and Bloom[2] and also supports my assumption that it takes both Stephen and Bloom to reveal the dimensions of the autobiographical artist-hero of *Ulysses*. To be sure, as Joseph Prescott pointed out a generation ago, if Stephen had not been "so fully realized in advance of *Ulysses*,"[3] there would be no way for a reader to assign him enough weight to provide a balance for the weight given Bloom in the novel, and we should recognize that one of the demands that Joyce makes of his reader, among many that are much more strenuous and even bizarre, is that in order to understand *Ulysses*, he or she must have read the novel to which it is a sequel, in which Stephen is not only the undisputed hero, but almost the sole actor.

Prescott feels that this expectation is "tantamount to an admission that, as regards Stephen, *Ulysses* does not constitute an artistic whole,"[4] but surely Joyce was implying just that when he told Georges Borach in Zurich, "When I had finished about half the *Portrait*, I realized that the Odyssey had to be the sequel, and I began to write *Ulysses*" (*JJ* 416). With the background of *A Portrait*, Stephen comes into *Ulysses* with an accumulated weight of identity, indispensable to the structure of the later novel, as "the universal, representative, archetypal artist,"[5] and even though *Ulysses* exploits the "new terminology" and "new personal experience" that Stephen predicted must follow the aesthetic experience of his youth (*P* 209), it depends on the earlier novel for comprehension. Bloom, who may be seen as the new experience of *Ulysses*, is not introduced, after all, until after Stephen has been situated in the novel in the first three episodes.

Ulysses is thus a sequel to *A Portrait of the Artist as a Young Man*, not just incidentally but essentially, and the status of *A Portrait* as an essential preliminary to the understanding of *Ulysses* is underscored by Joyce's reminder to Stanislaus in a 1925 letter that "I never give [translation rights for *Ulysses*] till *A Portrait* is first translated" (*Letters* 3:128). Thus, when Adolf Hoffmeister, the noted Czech artist and writer, presented Joyce with the first copy of the Czech translation of *Ulysses* in 1930, it was bound in four volumes, the first being a translation of *A Portrait of the Artist*.[6]

In an interview with Hoffmeister, Joyce told the Czech that his work, "from *Dubliners* on, goes in a straight line of development. It is almost indivisible, only the scale of expressiveness and writing technique rises somewhat steeply"; "*Portrait* was a picture of my spiritual self. *Ulysses* transformed individual impressions and emotions to give them general significance. 'Work in Progress' [which would become *Finnegans Wake*] has a significance completely above reality."[7] Joyce's first-person identification of *A Portrait* as "a picture of my spiritual self" strengthens the presumption of the primacy of the autobiographical base for the fiction, and his characterizations of the individual works in this interview support Ellmann's assertion that Joyce thought of his books as "way stations on a psychic journey."[8]

It is surely clear by now that Joyce's fiction, autobiographical though it is, is not in any important sense an attempt to describe the reality of the past; it is rather a restructuring of authentic memories of that past into a fiction that is also informed by the author's present view of himself and his aims as he constructs the fiction, a creative activity that is spelled out by Stephen in *Ulysses*: "So in the future, the sister of the past, I may see myself as I sit here now but by reflection from that which then I shall be" (*U* 9:383–85).[9] This kind of recollection and restructuring is, of course, basic to any kind of psychic history, whether it be called psychoanalysis or depth analysis, autobiography or fiction, and Joyce's structuring of his memories, directed toward a portrait of the artist that is a combination of autobiography and myth, is essentially a psychic history. Indeed, Morris Beja, in his recent brief biography of Joyce, asserts that "above all, [Joyce's] revolution was in the presentation of the psyche."[10] It is thus not surprising to discover, as I have, that the psychic transformations realized in the stages of Joyce's fictional portrait exhibit patterns that are congruent with Jung's theoretical descriptions of stages in the psychic transformation process he called individuation, the aim of which is the integration of the personality.[11]

THE *BILDUNGSROMAN* AND JUNGIAN INDIVIDUATION

In its broadest sense, the individuation process encompasses all the life experiences of an individual, from earliest infancy to death, a natural process. As a peculiarly Jungian concept, however, individuation refers to the attempt by the conscious personality to come to terms with unconscious aspects of the total personality, to establish a relationship with them, a psychic project that is initiated at the beginning of the second half of life. Jung's discussions of individuation tend to focus on this midlife undertaking, which he recognizes as an "extraordinary task," since it requires the individual to unite "two incongruous halves," that is, the conscious and unconscious halves of the psyche, into a whole (*CW* 9.1:287).[12] But Jung assumes as a necessary preliminary to any attempt to explore unconscious elements in the personality the prior development and socialization of the conscious personality in the first half of life (*CW* 6:449). The accommodation with the unconscious requires a strong ego and an established relationship to society to maintain stability through the process, as Jung himself discovered during his own journey through the unconscious in his mid thirties. "The unconscious contents could have driven me out of my wits," he admits in his autobiography, except that "my family and my profession remained the base to which I could always return, assuring me that I was an actually existing, ordinary person" (*MDR* 189).

Joyce's Dedalus novels encompass both halves, so to speak, of the Jungian individuation process, *A Portrait* serving as a prelude to *Ulysses*. *A Portrait*, which Joyce identified in a conversation with Arthur Power as "the book of my youth," traces psychic developments that are in Jung's view a necessary preliminary to the confrontation with the unconscious, a confrontation that is dramatized in *Ulysses*, "the book of my maturity."[13] Joyce's *Portrait* is often cited as an example of the traditional *Bildungsroman*,[14] and in fact Stephen's "I shall express myself as I am" (*P* 203) echoes the goal of Wilhelm Meister, Goethe's prototypical young hero, to "develop myself just as I am."[15] Such a categorization is further supported by a comparison of the course of events in Joyce's *Portrait* with Wilhelm Dilthey's nineteenth-century outline of the essentials of the classic conception of the *Bildungsroman*:

> A regular development is discerned in the individual's life; each of its stages has its own intrinsic value and is at the same time the basis for a higher stage. The dissonances and conflicts of life appear as the necessary growth points through which the individual must pass on his way towards maturity and harmony.[16]

A Portrait is clearly structured, as in Dilthey's outline, by levels of development. The narrative begins with a kind of collage of the hero as a child in the world of his family, then it moves directly to the next level of the child's schooling and his exposure to the norms of the world outside his family, as well as his development of ways of dealing with this world without sacrificing his own vision of himself. This conflict between socialization and self-determination is at the heart of his experience of "the dissonances and conflicts of life" and continues through his adolescent struggles to maintain an acceptable social posture without sacrificing his vision of self-determination. His self-nomination as an artist then, as the novel moves toward a conclusion, seems to promise a tenuous resolution to the struggle, a tenuous approach to "maturity and harmony."

But, as Gregory Castle points out, *A Portrait* "subverts" the traditional possibility of combining self-realization and social integration by presenting "the experience of a hero struggling to break free from an oppressive social system and the narratives of history that legitimize it."[17] Stephen's declaration for self-expression, in fact, appears in the context of his recognition of the "nets" that his country flings out to entrap the soul, making self-realization impossible (*P* 203), and a ruling assumption of the novel is, as Castle says, that "the hero's formation cannot be enacted in his native Ireland."[18] The young hero at novel's end is on the verge of "fly[ing] by" the "nets" of "nationality, language, religion" (*P* 203), rather than taking his place in the society of his birth.

Thus, whereas Goethe in eighteenth-century Germany could assume that individual development and achievement were compatible with the social integration that is the accepted goal of the novel of development, Joyce is perfectly clear that his young hero has no hope of expressing himself as he is unless he escapes Ireland. Furthermore, writing at the dawn of the twentieth century, a century that has thoroughly explored the reality of unconscious motivation, Joyce has reason to believe that Stephen cannot express himself "as I am" until he knows more about the dimensions of his personality, a psychic quest that is obviously closer to Jungian individuation than to the conventional *Bildungsroman*.

As early as 1904, in fact, long before there could be any question of his being influenced by Jung's theories, Joyce laid out in the opening paragraph of his unpublished "Portrait of the Artist" the pattern for his lifelong fictionalized presentation of the artist in terms that are tantalizingly close to Jung's later concept of individuation. Characterizing the portrait as "the curve of an emotion," rather than "an identificative paper," the odd little manifesto points to the past as "a fluid succession of presents" aiming at "the development of an entity of which our actual present is a phase only." The author counts himself among those "who seek . . . to liberate from the personalised lumps of matter that which is their individuating rhythm" (*FP* 60). And that "entity," that "individuating rhythm," hint at the conception Jung was to develop of the Self, the "wholeness that transcends consciousness" (*CW* 9.1:164), which is the goal of the individuation process (*MDR* 196).

JUNGIAN INDIVIDUATION IN OUTLINE

Before considering *A Portrait* in a Jungian frame as a fictional presentation of the development of the Ego and the construction of the Persona, as well as the corollary accumulation of the repressed contents that make up the Jungian Shadow, I should sketch in the dimensions of that frame. The following summary description of the characters and the psychic action of Jung's theoretical individuation process is offered for orientation, not for detailed understanding of Jung's psychology, which is well beyond the scope of this study. Individuation is the core of Jung's psychology, the basic components of which were consolidated by 1920. Although significant changes after that date were minimal,[19] relevant descriptions, fine-tuning these ideas, or simply bringing them into relation with the specific subject he was writing about are scattered through more than a dozen volumes of Jung's *Collected Works*, written over a period of forty years.

Further commentary on the individuation process and the personified psychic forces involved in it is also included in Jung's correspondence, and although my summary is informed by much of this material, I do not pretend to cover all the nuances that have accumulated through the years.

It is important to realize that we are dealing here with archetypal patterns and should remember Jung's warning about the impossibility of "clear-cut distinctions and strict formulations" in this kind of endeavor. When an archetype "takes shape in matter," as is the case in the fictional characters and situations with which this study is concerned, it changes shape. But even though "it is a well-nigh hopeless undertaking to tear a single archetype out of the living tissue of the psyche," the archetypes "do form units of meaning that can be apprehended intuitively" (*CW* 9.1:179). I recognize that, in presenting the parallels I see between "units of meaning" in Joyce's fiction and Jung's theory, I am necessarily simplifying Jung's theory somewhat, although I believe this simplification does not lead to distortion.

As I have earlier noted, Jung, defining the individuation process in terms of an interior drama, personifies the psychic forces that are involved in the process. The names he assigns to these forces, adopted from traditional concepts, have become a part of our common stock of psychic metaphors, with a more or less agreed-upon character and function for each, so that I shall provide here only a minimal explanation of Jung's use of them as characters in the interior drama of the relations between the Ego and the unconscious.

The Ego, of course, is the center of consciousness, and it is essentially equivalent to the Freudian Ego. Like Freud, Jung sees ego-consciousness as "grow[ing] out of unconscious life" (*CW* 8:347), and it is the task of the Ego, as the center of the conscious personality, to "hold the balance" between "the social consciousness"—"the world without" in Stephen's vocabulary—and the collective unconscious—the last frontier of Stephen's "world within" (*U* 9:1041–42). The Ego must remain "conscious of both at once" (*CW* 8:219), a mediating task that Joyce assigns to the artist of his myth from the beginning of his autobiographical fiction. In *Stephen Hero*, that is, Stephen imagines the artist as a "mediator between the world of his experience and the world of his dreams" (*SH* 77), a role that is assumed by Stephen himself as he leaves Bloom's house at the end of "Ithaca," "affirm[ing] his significance as . . . a conscious rational reagent between a micro and a macrocosm ineluctably constructed upon the incertitude of the void" (*U* 17:1013–15), the inner and the outer worlds.

The Persona, also a psychic construction of the first half of life, in part consciously developed and in part unconsciously accepted, is the mediator between the Ego and the outside world, a mask, Jung says, that "feigns individuality" (*CW* 7:155), helping a person to function in his society until he finds out who he really is, which, of course, he may never do. This "mask for the collective psyche" (*CW* 7:276) must be abandoned before self-realization can occur, and the "dissolution" of the Persona, an extraordinarily disorienting experience, is "absolutely essential for individuation" (*CW* 7:284).[20]

At the same time that the Persona is being constructed out of what is acceptable and/or appealing to the individual in the collective consciousness, a complementary process of repression—that is, putting unacceptable contents back into the unconscious—is also going on.[21] This process forms the Shadow, Jung's personification of all that the Ego has repressed or refused to acknowledge in himself, the contents of what Jung originally named the *personal unconscious* as opposed to the *collective unconscious*. It is thus roughly equivalent to Freud's concept of the unconscious as the repository of repressed material, but it is important to realize that this material is not entirely defined by social norms but is specific to the individual. Even though the process is largely unconscious, every man casts his own Shadow, which is composed of all that the ego-personality denies and represses and "habitually hides from himself" (*CW* 14:473). This may include traits of character that are perceived by the Ego as inferior but in actuality "are sometimes worse and sometimes better" (*CW* 9.1:261–62) than those the Ego values. Still, worse or better, they belong to the total inventory of the personality, which is incomplete without them, and the Shadow must be recovered and reintegrated to some degree for the Ego to approach wholeness.

In the case of excessive repression by the Ego, the Shadow may become "contaminated" with archaic contents of the collective unconscious that have never reached consciousness,[22] but for the most part, the contents personified in the Shadow have at some time and to some degree been conscious. It is thus the "most accessible" of the archetypes (*CW* 9.2:8), and its acknowledgment by the Ego is the necessary first step on the way to some apprehension of the archetypal figures of the collective unconscious—a "narrow door" through which the Ego must pass to reach the wholeness of the Self (*CW* 9.1:21–22). In particular, the realization of the Shadow, which Jung labels "the apprentice-piece" of mature psychic development, is an essential prerequisite to any conscious encounter with the female Anima, that is, the apprehension by the masculine Ego of her true nature as an aspect of his own personality. This is "the master-piece" of individuation (*CW* 9.1:29), but it is an encounter, Jung reminded one of his correspondents, that "not many can bring off."[23]

The Jungian Anima, "exclusively a figure that compensates the masculine consciousness" (*CW* 7:203–4), is a complex concept, comprising three elements: a man's experience of woman, his own femininity, and a collective image of woman that he inherits, like the rest of the archetypes, with his humanity (*CW* 7:186–88). She does not belong to the Ego in the same way the Shadow does and is experienced throughout life mainly through projection upon a woman. Thus, Jung says, "every mother and every beloved is forced to become the carrier and embodiment of this omnipresent and ageless image, which corresponds to the deepest reality in a man . . . this perilous image of Woman" (*CW* 9.2:13). He names four Anima images, each figuring a stage in a man's relationship to woman: Eve, Helen of Troy, the Virgin Mary, and Sophia. Again, Jung draws on traditional understandings, and each of these figures carries her traditional connotations, so that Eve is equated with the biological/instinctual reality of the mother; Helen with the Anima proper as erotic and romantic object; Mary with "spiritual motherhood"; and Sophia with the "eternal feminine" as "the alchemical Sapientia," or wisdom (*CW* 16:174). If these projections can be dissolved and the Anima understood as an aspect of a man's total psyche, she becomes what Jung calls "a function of relationship between conscious and unconscious . . . an archetypal image which, in its right place, functions to the advantage of the individual" (*CW* 16:293). But in any case, the primary function of the Anima is to give "relationship and relatedness to a man's consciousness" (*CW* 9.2:16).

There is a fifth character in Jung's hypothetical drama, and this is the Self, the "indescribable totality" (*CW* 14:107, note 66) that is the goal of the individuation process (*MDR* 196). In Jung's terminology, the Self is never an interchangeable term for the Ego, and it has no real equivalent in Freud's vocabulary.[24] Because it encompasses unconscious elements in the psyche as well as consciousness, it is a totality that cannot be fully known[25] and thus necessarily remains a hypothesis—but a necessary hypothesis for Jung's view of psychic development. "By definition greater than the ego-conscious personality" (*CW* 14:122), the Self is pictured by Jung as "that larger and greater personality maturing within us," indeed, "that other person who we also are and yet can never attain to completely" (*CW* 9.1:131).

The Ego thus can never comprehend the whole personality and still maintain its integrity *as* the conscious personality,[26] but an individual can significantly expand his sphere of consciousness, and to the degree that he assimilates the unconscious contents personified in the Shadow and actually achieves a synthesis of conscious and unconscious elements, he develops an apprehension of the dimensions of the totality of the Self. In the most fortunate case, this expanded awareness of the reality of the unconscious domain of the personality results in a wholesome humbling of the Ego and a "shifting of the centre of personality from the ego to the self" (*CW* 9.1:180–81). With this decentering of the Ego, linear development is replaced by "a circumambulation of the self," so that "everything points toward the center" (*MDR* 196–97).[27] This describes the happy ending, or at least the stabilized continuation of Jungian individuation.[28]

INDIVIDUATION IN *A PORTRAIT*

I turn from this summary of the characters and the course of the individuation process in theory to a consideration of the tacit rendering of this theory in Joyce's fiction. Of the personified psychic forces involved in the process—Ego, Persona, Shadow, Anima, Self—it is Stephen Dedalus as the Ego who is clearly the prime actor in *A Portrait*, his centrality becoming problematic only in *Ulysses*. The earlier novel carries the artist-hero through the development of the Ego as well as the choice and consolidation of his Persona, actually a series of choices. These choices necessarily result in an accumulation of repressed impulses and undeveloped aspects of his total personality, which come together in the Shadow. Stephen's adolescent experience of the eruption of the sexual impulses he has repressed, his first intimation of the Shadow, leads to excesses, which he dramatically rejects as not belonging to him, so that, instead of accommodating to the Shadow, he rebuilds and strengthens his Persona in the final chapter of the novel.

At the same time, the fiction follows, more or less at the edges of the action, the early stages of Stephen's relationship with the Anima as it is projected on the Anima figures of the mother, the Virgin Mary, the whores, the bird-girl, and Emma Cleary. In the fiction, these do not quite follow the order Jung names as typical for the "heterosexual Eros- or anima-figure" (*CW* 16:174), but Jung indicates that like other transferences, "the course they actually follow is subject to powerful modifications from the personality" (*CW* 16:173), and for the Irish Catholic Stephen the spiritualized relationship with Mary coexists with his flesh-bound relationship with the whores, a relationship that Jung considers an aspect of the "maternal significance of the anima" (*CW* 10:40). In the course of these developments, Stephen passes through the first two stages of the individuation process, identified by Jung as the *child archetype* and the *hero archetype*. In Jung's theoretical process, as in Joyce's fiction, these stages are recollected and to a degree reconstructed by the subject, and Jung's designation of them as archetypes points to the regularity of their appearance as the initial stages in individuation, whether the process is "spontaneous" or "therapeutically induced" (*CW* 9.1:180).

Joyce's 1904 "Portrait of the Artist" begins with a recognition that "the features of infancy are not commonly reproduced in the adolescent portrait" (*FP* 60), nor are they in this germinal essay. But by 1913, when *A Portrait* was ready to be set in type,[29] the "features of infancy" had become the dramatic opening of a two-page overture,[30] which begins, not with the birth of the child, as in the nineteenth-century David Copperfield's "I Am Born," but with the birth of the hero's ego-consciousness, his awareness that he is "baby tuckoo" (*P* 7). Even in the overture the Ego immediately begins widening his sphere of consciousness, taking in his father, then his mother (who is at the beginning, I think, to be equated with the "moocow") and, still in the world of his home, moving to Uncle Charles and Dante, as the overture traces Stephen's progress from infancy to early childhood and even to a rudimentary political awareness, focusing on Dante's brushes, one for Michael Davitt and the other for Parnell.

Stephen's awareness extends to the Vances, representatives of the world outside his home, and he even explores, apparently, the differences between the sexes. And at this point the overture takes note of the essential psychoanalytic fact of repression, as Stephen hides under the table, repeating to himself, "Apologise / Pull out his eyes / Pull out his eyes / Apologise" (*P* 8), a self-punishing litany that signals the repression that follows some kind of childish sexual research involving Stephen and the neighbor girl Eileen. Thus the Shadow, as well as the Ego, has its beginnings in the overture, as does the Anima, the feminine other projected on the mother, on Dante as an alternate mother, and, at a stage beyond the mother figure, on Eileen Vance.

Then, with Stephen's schooling, the construction of a Persona that will enable him to function in his society is also under way. The choices presented to Stephen are, of course, the stuff of the narrative throughout, but Stephen himself offers a surprisingly comprehensive summary list of the messages he receives from his society. Stephen's inner summary winds up a scene (*P* 75–84) that is a mix of present event, at the time of the Whitsuntide play at Belvedere, and past memories, which go back two years to his first term at the college when he was twelve. In the present of the Whitsuntide play, when Heron teases him about his relationship with Emma Cleary, Stephen turns off Heron's command to "Admit" with a mocking recitation of the *Confiteor* (*P* 78). But this encounter takes him back two years to the memory of an earlier attack by Heron and "his two attendants" (*P* 79) when Stephen's attempt to defend his position about the excellence of Byron's poetry against Heron's "Admit"—reinforced, as in the present, by strokes from Heron's cane—ended in physical pain and humiliation (*P* 82).[31] In these two years he has learned much about dealing with his school world, and he has developed a Persona of detachment that mediates his second encounter with Heron. The trigger word that brings back the earlier memory is "Admit," which should also trigger in the reader's mind the memory of Stephen's mother's "Apologise" in the overture, marking Stephen's first conscious recognition of the need for accommodation to the demands of the world outside.

Here at the end of his Belvedere days, recognizing the Persona of "quiet obedience," which has served him so well in the world of the Jesuits, Stephen considers the "constant voices" that urge him to one Persona or another. His father and masters urge him "to be a gentleman above all things" and "a good catholic above all things." In the gymnasium he is urged to be "strong and manly and healthy." Voices from the revival movement urge him to be "true to his country." He foresees that a worldly voice will urge him to rescue his father's fortunes, and always the voices of his "school comrades" urge him to be "a decent fellow," with all that this entails (*P* 83–84).

This early development of Ego and Persona in the first two chapters I connect with the child archetype, the "first identification" of the individuation process, which Jung describes as "typically an 'abandoned' or 'misunderstood' and unjustly treated" figure with "overweening pretensions" (*CW* 9.1:180). We have only to recall the cruel incident at Clongowes with Father Dolan and the pandybat (*P* 49–51), as well as Stephen's childishly heroic response to its injustice (*P* 54–58), to recognize both aspects of the archetype in *A Portrait*. And Simon Dedalus's deflating report of the rector's response to Stephen's heroic protest—"Father Dolan and I had a great laugh over it" (*P* 72)—adds yet another stroke to the picture of this misunderstood child.

The occurrence of the child motif, Jung says, ordinarily signifies "an anticipation of future developments" (*CW* 9.1:164), and in Cork with his father, Stephen, moving into adolescence, suddenly feels himself threatened with the loss of his childhood. He calls up representative events of that childhood, but the "little boy" who had experienced these events, although he "had not died," had "faded out like a film in the sun" and had been "lost or wandered out of existence" (*P* 93). This rather remarkable interpolation in the narrative, just a paragraph long, concludes with Stephen's vision of the child that is no more: "a little boy in a grey belted suit. His hands were in his sidepockets and his trousers were tucked in at the knees by elastic bands" (*P* 93). This vision dramatically marks the end of a stage of development for the artist-hero, with no immediate prospect for positive future developments, as Stephen confirms at the end of the visit to Cork: "Nothing stirred within his soul but a cold and cruel and loveless lust. His childhood was dead or lost and with it his soul capable of simple joys, and he was drifting amid life like the barren shell of the moon" (*P* 96). Although the figure of the child will reappear at moments in *Ulysses*, it disappears from *A Portrait* with Stephen's sexual initiation at the end of chapter 2.

This initiation effectively puts a temporary end to Stephen's struggles against the erupting Shadow, which has also been developing throughout his childhood, more or less by default, and is composed almost exclusively, it appears, of repressed sexual impulses. Stephen distances himself from these impulses by dehumanizing them. The word "Foetus" carved in a desk at the medical school in Cork sets him brooding over a "brutish and individual malady of his own mind," a "den of monstrous images" (*P* 89–90). And even when Stephen acts out these impulses with the prostitutes, they remain for him essentially bestial,[32] radically foreign to his concept of himself as well as contradicting his Persona. Although he discovers, contrary to his fears, that "no part of body or soul had been maimed," and "a dark peace had been established between them" (*P* 103), he lives in a dark, cold world, even before the retreat sermons shatter the dark peace. Using the imagery associated with the church beliefs that have been a dominant developmental guide through all his life, the sermons present to Stephen a vivid picture of his sin and its potential for everlasting punishment.

When, in his agony of repentance after the retreat, he is assailed by "the leprous company of his sins" (*P* 137), he has an overwhelming vision that is a contrasting parallel of sorts to his earlier vision of himself as a child. In contrast to the "little boy in a grey belted suit," he sees "goatish creatures with human faces" in "the hell reserved for his sins: stinking, bestial, malignant, a hell of lecherous goatish fiends" (*P* 137–38). The Shadow is here represented as inhuman, literally monstrous, certainly in no way a part of Stephen's personality.

His rejection extends even to his own body, to that "bestial part of the body able to understand bestially and desire bestially," and he questions whether it be "he or an inhuman thing moved by a lower soul than his soul . . . a torpid snaky life feeding itself out of the tender marrow of his life and fattening upon the slime of lust." Although he eventually admits to himself that "his own soul had sinned in thought and word and deed wilfully through his own body," he is confident that, through the magic of confession, he may rid himself of this foreign element and become "free and sinless again" (*P* 140). Even as he has reacted to his vision of the noisome junkyard of his sins by vomiting (*P* 138), he seeks an analogous purging when he goes to confession in response to his more or less rational consideration of the disease of his soul.

Stephen's repudiation of the personal reality of the eruption of unconscious contents into his conscious life is a not uncommon way station in individuation. Jung points out that one choice for patients who want to deny any value to the unconscious and "go on living reasonably" is to "reconstitute" the Persona and try "to forget if possible that one has an unconscious at all" (*CW* 7:279). And Stephen's confession, which concludes chapter 3, is the first step in his determined effort to reconstitute the Persona he had abandoned—the remembered "habit of quiet obedience" (*P* 156)—at a different level. His aggressive individual program of "resolute piety" (*P* 147) and mortification of the senses, which leads only to a kind of "spiritual dryness" (*P* 150–51), is succeeded by his consideration, under the prodding of the director, of a possible vocation to the priesthood. The lure of this call for Stephen, with its promise of "awful power" (*P* 158), is beautifully and convincingly presented, but it is countered by his vision of the "grave and ordered and passionless life that awaited him," and "an instinct subtle and hostile . . . armed him against acquiescence" (*P* 160–61). He thus rejects this vocational Persona and turns toward home, recognizing that "it was this disorder, the misrule and confusion of his father's house . . . which was to win the day" (*P* 162). For a priest not only has to promise chastity but, as an inevitable corollary, gives up a family. And the pomp and power of Stephen's vision of the priesthood is replaced by the moving scene with his brothers and sisters as they are transformed into a "choir of voices" in the squalor of the Dedalus kitchen, "*giving utterance, like the voice of Nature herself*," Stephen thinks, borrowing from Cardinal Newman, "*to that pain and weariness yet hope of better things which has been the experience of her children in every time*" (*P* 164).

The priestly Persona refused, Stephen moves on to another—the Persona of The Artist, which at the same time is hardly separable from his identity as a university student. Again, a vision—or rather a pair of visions—marks this "solution," both revealed to Stephen on the "day of dappled seaborne clouds" (*P* 166). This section of the chapter begins with Stephen's joyful recognition of the freedom promised by his escape from the schoolboy world of the Jesuits into the world of the university, his freedom doubly ensured through his rejection of membership in the order (*P* 165). This joy is sustained throughout the day, lighting up Stephen's vision of Daedalus, the "fabulous artificer," whose "winged form" is for him "a symbol of the artist" (*P* 169), opening the way for a rebirth for Stephen, whose "soul had arisen from the grave of boyhood" to "create proudly out of [its] freedom and power" (*P* 170). And like a confirmation of this vision of "the end he had been born to serve and had been following through the mists of childhood and boyhood" (*P* 169) comes another, the vision of the girl on the strand.

Stephen's silent, ecstatic communion with the figure of the girl echoes, in tone at least, his boyhood yearning to "meet in the real world the unsubstantial image which his soul so constantly beheld." As a boy, he has had a "premonition" that "this image would, without any overt act of his, encounter him," as indeed the girl on the strand has. And "in that moment of supreme tenderness," Stephen foresees, "he would be transfigured. . . . Weakness and timidity and inexperience would fall from him in that magic moment" (*P* 65). To be sure, this "premonition" apparently has been fulfilled in the encounter with the prostitute who initiates Stephen at the end of chapter 2. Whatever the differences in circumstances, the tone of this earlier climactic scene with the prostitute is surprisingly similar to Stephen's boyhood vision and also to the vision on the strand. In the arms of the prostitute, Stephen feels himself transfigured—"strong and fearless and sure of himself" (*P* 101), leaving behind in parallel sequence the "weakness and timidity and inexperience" of his boyhood. This sexual initiation, tainted though it is by the incubus of sin, is surely an essential stage in the development of Stephen's relationship to women.

The vision of the girl on the strand, however, goes beyond the sexual to merge with the vision of his artistic vocation, and Stephen's transfiguration here encompasses both life and art. He feels that the girl has called him "to live, to err, to fall, to triumph, to recreate life out of life" (*P* 172), this last phrase a restatement of his vision of Daedalus, the artist, "forging anew . . . out of the sluggish matter of the earth a new soaring impalpable being" (*P* 169).[33] He sees the girl as an "envoy from the fair courts of life," who throws open before him "in an instant of ecstasy the gates of all the ways of error and glory" (*P* 172). These are grand words, and they echo, both in tone and in substance, the somewhat overblown apostrophe in Joyce's 1904 "Portrait" to an unnamed woman, also "an envoy from the fair courts of life." Addressed as "Dearest of mortals!" and "Beneficent one!" this early Anima figure is assumed to have been in some kind of communication with the young artist even "in all that ardent adventure of lust," (*FP* 65), which may be equated with Stephen's adventure in Nighttown. Like the Jungian Anima, "whose significance oscillates between the extremes of goddess and whore" (*CW* 9.1:199), Stephen's vision of the bird-girl calls him both to "error" and to "glory."

Inspired by these two passionate visions, Stephen reconstitutes his Persona to a new, stronger level, which determines his stance in chapter 5 of *A Portrait*, and with his construction of this new Persona, Stephen moves into a stage in his development that parallels the second stage of the individuation process, Jung's hero archetype, an "identification" that dominates the final chapter of *A Portrait*. Like the child archetype, the hero archetype or the "epiphany of the hero" is characterized by opposing convictions. Even as the first stage pictures a "misunderstood" child who nevertheless has "overweening pretensions," so in the second stage, when these pretensions have grown into "a conviction that one is something extraordinary," they are counterbalanced by equally strong feelings of inferiority. The fear that the pretensions can never be fulfilled is "favourable," Jung says, "to the role of the heroic sufferer" (*CW* 9.1:180). And the picture of Stephen in the final chapter of *A Portrait*, which encapsulates his university experience, exhibits this kind of alternation between contradictory feelings, both equally real.

In the 1904 "Portrait," it is clear that when the unnamed artist enters the university, he consciously adopts a Persona as a protective mask—"an enigma of manner . . . put up at all comers to protect the crisis"—and to permit him to "disentangle his affairs in secrecy" (*FP* 61). The Stephen of *Stephen Hero* is also explicitly aware that the "boldnesses" of his essays are "defence-works" he erects "while he [is] busy constructing the enigma of a manner" (*SH* 27). The text of the published novel is much less open about Stephen's adoption of this final Persona through most of chapter 5 as a conscious disguise or defense, but the clues are there at the beginning of the chapter when Stephen is shown at home and in the diary that concludes the chapter and the novel. In both these segments Stephen appears without his "enigma of a manner."

The scene in the Dedalus kitchen that opens chapter 5 is a jolting contrast to the rhapsodic conclusion to chapter 4. The "crusts of fried bread" that Stephen chews on; the pawn tickets in the box at his elbow, whose lid is "speckled with louse-marks"; the "old washingglove" with which he allows his mother "to scrub his neck and root into the folds of his ears and into the interstices at the wings of his nose" (*P* 174–75): all these give the lie to his grandiose visions on the strand and threaten "to humble the pride of his youth" (*P* 176). As he makes his way to the university, having missed his first lecture, he characterizes his thinking as "a dusk of doubt and selfmistrust lit up at moments by the lightnings of intuition," but he nevertheless believes that these lightnings are "of so clear a splendour that in those moments the world perished about his feet" (*P* 177). And, although he is afraid of being nothing but "a shy guest at the feast of the world's culture" (*P* 180), his conversation with the dean of studies is replete with proffered evidence of the superiority of his independent learning, and his inward judgments of this "half-brother of the clergy" (*P* 190) are tinged with contempt.

Among his fellow students, only Cranly, who publicly identifies Stephen as "the only man in this institution that has an independent mind" (*P* 201), appears to be accepted as an equal by Stephen, and it is only Cranly that Stephen allows into his personal feeling life. Indeed, he admits that Cranly has "made me confess the fears that I have," and as Cranly presses his arm "with an elder's affection," he is "thrilled by his touch" (*P* 247). But he knows also that this "friendship [is] coming to an end" (*P* 245), and he evades Cranly's implied offer in their final meeting to be "more than a friend," even though he recognizes the "cold sadness" and "loneliness" out of which Cranly speaks (*P* 247). Cranly serves in *A Portrait* as the precursor for Mulligan in *Ulysses*, both of them embodying the function of the Persona in Stephen's development and both of them insistently connected with the threat of homosexuality.[34]

With the other students, however, Stephen's conversations are carefully distanced. He talks to Davin, for example, in the mildly condescending tone of an elder brother, to which Davin responds with appropriate humility. Lynch, for his part, serves as a convenient sounding board for Stephen's intellectually heroic lectures on art, contributing only a series of irrelevant one-liners. He is in fact almost incredibly patient with Stephen's sustained monologue, which has always been of great interest to Joyce critics, but is all too clearly of no intrinsic interest to Lynch, who appears to admire Stephen *as* a hero and to be willing to act as an audience simply to be with him.

INTIMATIONS OF THE ANIMA

As Stephen winds up his peripatetic lecture on Aquinas and art near the library with the grandiloquence of the often-quoted comparison of the artist to "the God of the Creation," the other part of the dual vision on the strand enters the text, as Lynch whispers to Stephen, "Your beloved is here" (*P* 215). And through the rest of the novel the image of Emma Cleary hovers over the text, never really a part of the action and identified throughout only by feminine pronouns—*she* and *her*. In this final chapter Stephen's perspective on this image begins to shift. Like Helen of Troy, as Jung names the second stage of the Anima figure, her image for Stephen is "still dominated by the sexual Eros, but on an aesthetic and romantic level where woman has already acquired some value as an individual"; in fact, as the novel moves to a close, Emma appears to Stephen as a person with feelings and needs.

Here on the steps of the library, though still nursing his grudge about her flirtation with the young priest, Stephen asks himself if he has "judged her harshly" and actually considers what her life may be like, quite apart from its effect on him (*P* 216). After writing out the villanelle, an "aesthetic and romantic" endeavor that clearly springs from his relationship with her and reinforces her participation in his vision of himself as an artist, he goes over his fairly meager store of memories of their encounters, including the one on the tram steps ten years before, which also had inspired a poem (*P* 220–22, 70–71). These memories are accompanied by a rekindling of the confused feelings of anger and insecurity aroused by the experiences he treasures in memory, but again he has a sense of having "wronged her," and again he considers her life as an individual, a woman, different from him and yet linked to him. He equates her first experience of menstruation—when "the strange humiliation of her nature had first come upon her"—with his own first experience of sin, both events marking the birth of their souls, and "a tender compassion filled his heart" (*P* 222). And although "a glow of desire kindled again his soul and fired and fulfilled all his body" as he thinks of her (*P* 223), he later distinguishes between her image and the images of lust with which he is familiar. "Her image was not entangled by them. It was not the way to think of her. It was not even the way in which he thought of her" (*P* 233).

"She" is on Stephen's mind throughout the time covered by the entries in the diary that concludes *A Portrait*, with some reference to "her," her absence as well as her presence, on every page. And, as has often been noted, the tone and substance of these diary entries present a marked and sometimes bewildering contrast to what has gone before.[35] Like the opening scene of this final chapter, the diary presents Stephen without his mask. He still has his heroic pretensions, but the "enigma of manner" that has characterized his speech and even to a degree his unspoken thoughts through most of the chapter is absent. His diary account of his final meeting with Emma in Grafton Street is relatively straightforward and includes once again a recognition of her feelings as he reports feeling "sorry and mean" for having contributed to her confusion with his personally directed response to her question about his poetry.

True, he admits to "open[ing] the spiritual-heroic refrigerating apparatus, invented and patented in all countries by Dante Alighieri" (*P* 252), which has caused some critical confusion: apparently following Don Gifford's *Joyce Annotated*, critics continue to identify this invention as some general allusion to "Dante's delicately controlled platonic admiration for Beatrice in *La Vita Nuova*."[36] But surely it is more direct and much more specific than this. In fact, it calls up one of the most arresting sights in the *Inferno*: Satan in the frozen center of hell where the "engine" of his constantly beating wings creates the everlasting cold. The final canto of the *Inferno* opens with Virgil's directing Dante's attention to the figure of "the King of Hell" fixed "at the core of the frozen shell." From a distance the figure looks "like a whirling windmill," which "stir[s] up such a wild and bitter wind" that Dante hides behind Virgil for protection. On closer view, this apparatus turns out to be Lucifer himself, stuck up to his chest in ice. Three heads he has, with two "terrible wings," "like a bat's wings," beneath each head, "and he beat them so / that three winds blew from him in one great storm: / it is these winds that freeze all Cocytus."[37]

This is a tremendous picture, and it fits the context in *A Portrait*, where it is, however, playfully used. For when Stephen figuratively turns on his "spiritual-heroic refrigerating apparatus," what he literally does is let loose a gale of talk about his plans, apparently complete with gestures because he reports "a sudden gesture of a revolutionary nature . . . like a fellow throwing a handful of peas into the air" (*P* 252). This flurry, since "people began to look at us," appears to prompt Emma to remove herself from the scene, to shake hands and wish him well. Stephen has earlier identified himself with Lucifer in his portentous assurance to Cranly that "I will not serve" (*P* 239), and he will reiterate this identification in *Ulysses* (*U* 15:4228), but here the tone of his allusion to the great rebel is self-mocking and in no way heroic.

And when he assesses his own feelings about the meeting with Emma, he calls it "friendly." "I liked her and it seems a new feeling to me" (*P* 252). *Friendly* and *like* are surprisingly neutral words for a wordsmith like Stephen, and they do describe a new feeling. This is the only time in *A Portrait* that *friendly* describes a woman or her actions, and the word echoes Gabriel Conroy's feeling about Gretta at the end of "The Dead." As Gabriel watches the sleeping Gretta, "a strange friendly pity for her entered his soul," a pity that leads to his "generous" tears and marks a real turning point in his understanding of his wife and himself (*D* 222–23).[38] Stephen's recognition of his new, almost everyday feeling about his relationship with Emma appears to mark a truce in his struggle with himself about the place of woman in his life, which is reinforced by his return in the next to last diary entry to the prosaic description of his mother packing his clothes and giving him motherly advice. Stephen's "Amen. So be it" (*P* 252) extends this truce to his mother.

To be sure, this general acceptance of the everyday is countered by the extravagance of Stephen's poetic paragraph that comes between these acknowledgments of the women in his life and ends with his "kinsmen" "shaking the wings of their exultant and terrible youth." And *A Portrait of the Artist as a Young Man* concludes on the very high note of Stephen's apostrophe to life and to Daedalus: "Welcome, O life! I go to encounter for the millionth time the reality of experience and to forge in the smithy of my soul the uncreated conscience of my race." This is followed by his cry to Daedalus—"Old father, old artificer, stand me now and ever in good stead" (*P* 252–53)—which is less a plea for help than a demand by the hero for his mythological inheritance.

But the gifts of Daedalus are not unequivocally beneficial; and although Stephen's grandiose statement of purpose—"to forge in the smithy of my soul the uncreated conscience of my race"—calls up the heroic figure of Siegfried, the "artist-smith,"[39] his call to Daedalus as "old father" necessarily brings into the picture Icarus, the son of Daedalus, who is the prototypical failure with delusions of grandeur. Siegfried and Icarus, hero and failure, here image the contradictory nature of Jung's view of the hero archetype, that "dangerous" stage of individuation, in which "conscious megalomania is balanced by unconscious compensatory inferiority . . . (you never get one without the other)" (*CW* 9.1:180). And it is this contradictory vision that sets the stage for *Ulysses* and for Stephen in his Icarus identification: "Seabedabbled, fallen, weltering" (*U* 9:954).

PART TWO

Confrontation with the Unconscious

FOUR

Realization of the Shadow

The life history of the artist who is the hero of *A Portrait of the Artist as a Young Man* is continued in its sequel. But more than a year has elapsed between the ending of *A Portrait* and the beginning of *Ulysses*, and Stephen, the exultant young artist-hero of the closing sentences of the earlier novel, has undergone a crippling metamorphosis. His heroic self-exile to Paris has been annulled by the death of his mother, which has turned his psychic economy upside down, and he is now painfully conscious of the enormous gap between his heroic pretensions and the possibility of their realization. The wise and loving mother, who put his "new secondhand clothes in order" on the eve of his departure and prayed that he might learn "what the heart is and what it feels" (*P* 252), has turned into the "ghostwoman" (*U* 3:46) who haunts his dreams in *Ulysses* and communicates only through "mute secret words" (*U* 1:272). As the novel opens, he is standing on a tower that he himself later identifies as a tower of death, "a silent tower entombing their blind bodies" (*U* 3:277).[1]

The Stephen who appears in "Telemachus" embodies what Jung sees as the inevitable counter face of the "megalomania" characteristic of the "epiphany of the hero," Jung's label for the second stage in the individuation process (*CW* 9.1:180). The highflown consciousness of his artistic mission, which informed the ending of *A Portrait*, is balanced by compensatory and resentful feelings of inferiority as *Ulysses* begins. For although the hero identification is "attractive," Jung says, it is often "dangerous to the psychic equilibrium," and the conscious hero must be "reduced to human proportions" before he can get on with his psychic journey (*CW* 9.1:180). And, we may note, there are no human organs listed in Stuart Gilbert's schema[2] for the first three episodes of *Ulysses*. These enter the schema only with Bloom.

The setting of the first episode of *Ulysses* at the edge of the sea harmonizes with Jung's figure for this second stage of individuation as a "reef" which the hero must "circumnavigate" to reach the next level of development. Jung's theory promises that, once beyond the reef of the hero identification, "conscious processes can be cleanly separated from the unconscious," making possible "an accommodation with the unconscious" and thus "a possible synthesis of the conscious and unconscious elements of knowledge and action." The end result is "a shifting of the centre of personality from the ego to the self" (*CW* 9.1:180–81), which is, of course, the goal of the individuation process. Jung here states a psychic agenda that is realized, on one level at least, in *Ulysses*.

The next stage in Stephen's journey toward the psychic wholeness necessary for him to become a productive artist is the recognition and acceptance of the unconscious dimension of his personality that Jung personifies as the Shadow and Joyce embodies in Bloom: the "realization of the shadow," in Jung's phrase. Jung acknowledges that this designation is poetic rather than scientific, but he points out that the process it describes is not an "intellectual activity." Indeed, "the essence of that which has to be realized and assimilated [in this stage of individuation] has been expressed so trenchantly and so plastically in poetic language by the word 'shadow' that it would be almost presumptuous not to avail oneself of this linguistic heritage" (*CW* 8:208).

INTIMATIONS OF THE SHADOW

This realization is a gradual process, but in the text of *Ulysses* it starts immediately. The first intimation of the confrontation to come, in fact, appears the first time Stephen is alone, when Mulligan exits down the stairs and Stephen becomes aware of the cloud that Bloom will also observe in "Calypso" as Bloomsday begins over again. Stephen's sighting of the cloud that "began to cover the sun slowly, wholly" (*U* 1:248) is matched rhetorically by Bloom's sighting of the cloud, which in "Calypso," too, "began to cover the sun slowly, wholly" (*U* 4:218). This is the first of the textual correspondences between Stephen and Bloom that prefigure their meeting and underscore their relationship.

These textual correspondences, both verbal and situational, are almost literally innumerable and operate on more than one level of significance.[3] On the most superficial level, the only apparent function of the correspondences is simply to confirm that there *is* a relationship. In "Proteus," for example, Stephen's association of the "trailing navelcord" with a telephone call to "Edenville" (*U* 3:36–40) is paralleled in the cemetery when Bloom notices the "coffinband. His navelcord" (*U* 6:914), which he follows shortly afterwards with the idea of the gramophone as a means of remembering the dead: "Put on poor old greatgrandfather. Kraahraark! Hellohellohello" (*U* 6:964–65). Similarly, Stephen's experiment in "Proteus"—"Shut your eyes and see" (*U* 3:9)—is matched by Bloom's experiment in "Lestrygonians," as he tries to imagine being blind and feels his belly to see if it is the "feeling of white" (*U* 8:1131–42). In themselves, these parallels, often not exact matches, are hardly noticeable, and their significance is perhaps debatable, but once a reader becomes aware of their existence, they pop up on all sides.

Here at the beginning of the novel, however, the textual correspondence is exact, and the parallel continues, setting up a pattern for a textual play between light and darkness, which operates through the "Telemachiad" as a prefiguring device for the embodiment of Bloom in "Calypso" and Stephen's eventual encounter with him. In "Telemachus," for example, the "sunlight now radiant on the sea" is reflected in Mulligan's shaving mirror (*U* 1:131), but it is blotted out by the cloud, "shadowing the bay" (*U* 1:248) and plunging Stephen into memories of his mother's death. With Mulligan's cry of "Kinch ahoy!" however, Stephen escapes from the darkness and "hear[s] warm running sunlight" (*U* 1:282–83).

In "Calypso," then, Bloom repeats this alternation of light and darkness. He walks to Dlugacz's shop on "the bright side" of the street "in happy warmth" (*U* 4:77, 81), but on his return trip, when the cloud turns the brightness to darkness, Bloom's thoughts, like Stephen's, turn to death, "dead sea in a dead land . . . the grey sunken cunt of the world" (*U* 4:223–28), thoughts so depressing to him that "grey horror seared his flesh" (*U* 4:230). But coincident with his reviving thought of Molly's "ample bedwarmed flesh," the sunlight returns in a phrase that substantially duplicates the description of the sunlight's return for Stephen: "Quick warm sunlight came running from Berkeley road" (*U* 4:238–41).

Leading up to Bloom's embodiment in "Calypso," verbal intimations of the relationship between the two men, signaled by the counterposing of brightness and darkness, continue for Stephen in "Nestor." Remembering the library of Saint Genevieve in Paris, Stephen opposes the "tranquil brightness" of thought to "my mind's darkness," where "a sloth of the underworld, reluctant, shy of brightness [is] shifting her dragonscaly folds" (*U* 2:74, 72–73). As he helps Cyril Sargent with his sums and ponders the "secrets" that "sit in the dark palaces of both our hearts" (*U* 170–71), he thinks of the Moors as the originators of numerals, "dark men in mien and movement," among whom he places the Jewish philosopher Maimonides, and, playing with reverse echoes of St. John's gospel, he identifies the dark men with "a darkness shining in brightness which brightness could not comprehend" (*U* 2:160).[4] The textual interplay of darkness and brightness climaxes in "Nestor" with Mr. Deasy's equating the darkness with the Jews. "They sinned against the light," he reminds Stephen. "And you can see the darkness in their eyes. And that is why they are wanderers on the earth to this day" (*U* 2:361–63).[5] Stephen's inner musing about the Jews—"goldskinned men" at the Paris stock exchange—dwells on their eyes, which "knew their years of wandering and, patient, knew the dishonours of their flesh," but his overt response is to only the first term of Deasy's charge—"They sinned against the light." "Who has not?" Stephen asks (*U* 2:364–73).

In "Proteus," then, the "darkness/brightness" opposition again appears, this time in the context of Stephen's hope for immortality through his art. Bending over the rocks, he sees his "ended" shadow and asks himself, "Why not endless till the farthest star? Darkly they are there behind this light, darkness shining in the brightness" (*U* 3:408–10). And as the episode draws to a close and Stephen becomes aware that the sky is again "clouding over," he identifies himself with the Christ of the crucifixion—"I thirst" (*U* 3:485)—and, thinking of the possibility of a thunderstorm, calls up the "proud lightning of the intellect, Lucifer," the great archetypal Shadow of the Christ image who is here paradoxically "Allbright" (*U* 3:485–86).[6] The real nature of Stephen's Shadow, however, has been revealed in his dream of Haroun al Raschid, first recalled in "Proteus" (*U* 3:365–69), for in this dream the promise the Shadow holds for the sensual enrichment of Stephen's life and for the restoration of the whole man is prefigured. It is the man with the "creamfruit melon" to offer, the friendly foreigner, who will provide the corrective for Stephen's one-sidedness—the regular and natural function of the unconscious in the Jungian perspective.[7]

DISSOLUTION OF THE PERSONA

But before the promised beneficence can be realized, before he can even confront the Shadow, Stephen must "distinguish between what he is and how he appears to himself and others" (*CW* 7:193): he must abandon his Persona. Stephen has adopted yet another Persona in *Ulysses*. And Buck Mulligan, who succeeds Cranly as Stephen's alter ego, is associated with this new Persona in the same way that Cranly was associated with the Persona of the detached, ironic university student and self-conscious artist that masked Stephen in the final chapter of *A Portrait*.

The Persona that Stephen hides behind in *Ulysses* is again a combination figure, as it apparently was for the young Joyce of the period dramatized in *Ulysses*. According to Oliver St. John Gogarty, the model for Buck Mulligan and a shrewd observer of Joyce, his artist friend "was the best example of a medical student's pal Dublin produced," a role that "by virtue of the glamour that surrounded a student of medicine was almost a profession in itself."[8] Gogarty amends this perception to suggest that Joyce was perhaps instead "the best example of the type, extinct since the Middle Ages, of a Goliard, a wandering scholar,"[9] an identity that Gogarty also assumed. And this ambiguous friend, himself a medical student, completes his description of the amalgam that made up Joyce's Persona with the label of "artist"—but an entirely different kind of artist from that of *A Portrait*: "a great artist," in the Dublin sense of "a quaint fellow or a great cod." And again we may note that Mulligan, who is himself identified by Stephen as "a lubber jester" (*U* 9:1110), also fits Gogarty's description of the Dublin "artist": "a pleasant and unhypocritical poseur, one who sacrifices his own dignity for his friends' diversion."[10] These identities, alternating or combined, may be glimpsed whenever Stephen occupies center stage in *Ulysses*.

As the day begins in "Telemachus," Stephen is beginning to consider separating himself from Mulligan, a separation that parallels the necessary dissolution of the Persona in Jungian individuation. The preparation in the text for the abandonment of Mulligan circles around possession of the key to the Tower, "a very large copper key about ten inches long," according to Gogarty's account,[11] which is in Stephen's possession as the day begins (*U* 1:322–23). Stephen locks the door and retains the key when they leave the Tower with the Englishman Haines (*U* 1:533) but senses that Mulligan will ask for it (*U* 1:630–32), as he does, "to keep my chemise flat" (*U* 1:721). The twopence "for a pint," which he also demands,

Stephen tosses on Mulligan's heaped clothes (*U* 1:724–25). But as he leaves Mulligan at the swimming hole, Stephen determines, "I will not sleep here tonight" (*U* 1:740).

Stephen repeats this vow in "Proteus" as he pictures the other two men "entombed" in the Tower: "He has the key. I will not sleep there when this night comes" (*U* 3:276). Stephen then characterizes the "entombed" men, Haines and Mulligan, as "the panthersahib and his pointer" (*U* 3:277–78), recalling the incident that has in part triggered Stephen's decision to leave the Tower. Haines, Stephen has complained, was "raving and moaning to himself [all night] about shooting a black panther," prompting Stephen to notify Mulligan that, if Haines stays, he is off (*U* 1:61–63). The phrase thus calls up a picture of the Englishman as a hunter and Mulligan as his trusted hunting dog, clarifying Stephen's characterization of Mulligan in the opening scene as a servant.[12]

For as Stephen picks up the shaving bowl, which Mulligan has left on the parapet, and debates about taking it down to him, he sees himself as "a server of a servant" (*U* 1:312). This is the first indication of his understanding of his relationship to Mulligan as a form of servitude, and it is also a hint of his understanding that Mulligan, for all his lighthearted deprecation of the "oxy chap" (*U* 1:154), is himself subservient to the English visitor. Mulligan comes when Haines calls him (*U* 1:229) and prepares "morning rashers" (*U* 1:232) for the Englishman in a microcosm of the national relation of servant and master between the Irish and the British. When Stephen later identifies himself to Haines as "a servant of two masters . . . the imperial British state . . . and the holy Roman catholic and apostolic church" (*U* 1:638–43), he adds "a third . . . who wants me for odd jobs" (*U* 1:641). These three masters—the British state, the Catholic Church, and Mulligan—are all present in his initial vision of himself as "a server of a servant." For the shaving bowl reminds Stephen that he "carried the boat of incense then at Clongowes" (*U* 1:310–11) in the service of the Jesuits, even as he now carries the bowl for Mulligan, who in turn is in a kind of servitude to Haines.

The image of the child he was at Clongowes is thus connected to Stephen's decision to separate himself from Mulligan, a decision that is gradually actualized through the day as Stephen approaches his encounter with Bloom—also gradually. This movement in the text is consonant with Jung's assertion that in the individuation process "the child paves the way for a future change of personality," anticipating "the figure that comes from the synthesis of conscious and unconscious elements in the personality" (*CW* 9.1:164), prefiguring, that is, the Jungian Self, which must be approached through a prior realization of the Shadow. The child will reappear in *Ulysses* as Stephen moves farther from the prefabricated mediator represented by the Persona and closer to a true understanding of his identity, which must include the Shadow as well as the Ego.

Stephen faces a new psychic task with his decision to part from Mulligan. Up to now in his development, his task has been to become socialized, to relate to the collective consciousness, and for this the Persona is invaluable. Stephen has to a degree, in fact, asserted his individuality in his "selection of the particular elements of the collective psyche which serve to constitute his persona" (*CW* 7:283). To develop his true individuality, however, he must cast aside the accustomed mask of the Persona, which, Jung says, only "simulates individuality," only pretends that "it is individual" (*CW* 7:276).

And as a matter of fact, Stephen does not again see Mulligan until they come together in the National Library, where he identifies Mulligan as "mine enemy" (*U* 9:483). Otherwise occupied during the morning hours, Stephen has reneged on the earlier arrangement to meet Mulligan and Haines for lunch at The Ship, bringing his teaching salary with him, and Mulligan complains mockingly in "Scylla and Charybdis" about the telegram Stephen has sent announcing his defection (*U* 9:548–55). To be sure, Stephen does follow Mulligan out of the librarians' office, apparently anticipating, though glumly, another "Irish nights entertainment" (*U* 9:1105) in Mulligan's company. He is clearly resentful of the relationship, a relationship he establishes as that of peasant to courtier, through an allusion to *Hamlet*: "I gall his kibe" (*U* 9:1109).[13] Having performed as a Dublin "artist" for his audience in the library, Stephen is now a "mournful mummer" in Mulligan's phrase (*U* 9:1155).

As they reach the foot of the stairs, however, Stephen finds his determination to separate from Mulligan renewed. "About to pass through the doorway, feeling one behind, he stood aside." As he does so, he reminds himself of his vow of the morning: "Part. The moment is now," and asks himself, "Where then?" answering, "If Socrates leave his house today, if Judas go forth tonight" (*U* 9:1197–1200). He is alluding to the line from Maeterlinck that he has earlier paraphrased: "*If Socrates leave his house today he will find the sage seated on his doorstep. If Judas go forth tonight it is to Judas his steps will tend*" (*U* 9:1042–44).[14] Earlier Stephen followed this paraphrase with his observation that "life is many days, day after day. We walk through ourselves, meeting . . . [all kinds of people], but always meeting ourselves" (*U* 9:1044–46). And at the doorway he concludes, "That lies in space which I in time must come to, ineluctably" (*U* 9:1200–1201), that is, himself. He acknowledges the conflict between himself and Mulligan—"My will: his will that fronts me. Seas between" (*U* 9:1202), providing an almost irresistible image for Scylla and Charybdis, the title assigned to this episode and the great Homeric choice point.[15] At this moment, "a man passed out between them, bowing, greeting" (*U* 9:1203). And the man is Bloom.

In Homeric terms, Stephen here faces his own Scylla and Charybdis, a crucial choice; in Jungian terms, the Shadow has come between the Ego and the Persona, also presenting a crucial choice; and in terms of the narrative of *Ulysses*, Bloom is here offering himself as an alternative to Mulligan. That Stephen makes the choice that is offered him is explicitly indicated through a textual correspondence in *Ulysses*. In "Hades," that is, Bloom, riding in the carriage with Simon Dedalus, sees Stephen near the tram lines and tells Simon that his "son and heir" has just gone by. Simon asks, "—Was that Mulligan cad with him? His *fidus Achates*! —No, Mr Bloom said. He was alone" (*U* 6:39–50).

Achates, Thornton reminds us, was the faithful friend of Achilles,[16] and in

"Eumaeus," this same designation has become attached to Bloom, who in the early morning hours is "acting as [Stephen's] *fidus Achates*" (*U* 16:55), warning Stephen that he "wouldn't personally repose much trust in that boon companion of yours" (*U* 16:279–80), who "is what they call picking your brains" (*U* 16:298–99). As they leave the cabman's shelter, in fact, he is planning to advise Stephen "to sever his connection with [this] budding practitioner," who is "prone to disparage" Stephen in his absence (*U* 16:1868–71).[17] It is at least suggestive that Bloom's acknowledgment here in "Eumaeus" that Mulligan is "a versatile allround man" (*U* 16:288) echoes Lenehan's description in "Wandering Rocks" of Bloom himself as "a cultured allroundman" (*U* 10:581), reinforcing the textual parallel between these alternative "faithful friends."[18]

Thus, between Hades and Ithaca, which marked the limits of the homeward journey of Homer's Odysseus, Stephen, who in this reading parallels the Jungian Ego, has accomplished the essential shift from an accommodation with the Persona to the beginnings of an accommodation with the Shadow. This psychic shift, like the Odyssean voyage, though it does result in a genuine homecoming, though it "gives rise to truth and meaning" (*CW* 9.1:132), is fraught along the way with pain and peril and disorientation—as Jung describes it and as it is dramatized in *Ulysses*. For with the dissolution of the Persona, "one no longer knows who one is" (*CW* 7:277). And throughout the day Stephen exhibits the effects of this disorientation, heightened, of course, by his drunkenness in later episodes.

Indeed, Stephen, the Ego in a Jungian scenario for *Ulysses*, is through much of the novel in a state of eclipse, to borrow a metaphor from Fredric Jameson's discussion of Wyndham Lewis's *Tarr*, a metaphor that is unusually apt for Stephen's state in *Ulysses*, even as Jameson's view of Lewis's novel as "a virtual allegory of the fragmented psyche itself" is consonant with my own view of the relationship between Stephen and Bloom.[19] An eclipse in nature, after all, refers to a relationship between two bodies, in which one partially or wholly blots out the other, as Bloom at least partially blots out Stephen in *Ulysses*. For in contrast to Stephen, who has been fully developed in *A Portrait*, Bloom enters *Ulysses* with no fictional past, and Joyce builds up his world in its entirety, so that in sheer bulk he does indeed "overshadow them all," as Joyce said to Budgen.[20] But like an eclipse in nature, Stephen's minimalization in *Ulysses* is gradually accomplished and then is gradually reversed. It is not a permanent darkening.

I AND NOT-I

Although the looming meeting with the Shadow intensifies the disorientation resulting from the Ego's abandonment of the Persona, Stephen is sustained by a conviction that holds in the face of the threat of permanent eclipse, a conviction that "I am I." From the beginnings of Joyce's autobiographical fiction, his artist-hero is convinced of a central personal identity that has much in common with Jung's concept of the Self.[21] The unnamed artist of the first "Portrait," seeing the past as "a fluid succession of presents," identifies the goal of this succession as "the development of an entity of which our actual present is a phase only" (*FP* 60). And he links his autobiographical endeavor to "that ineradicable egoism which he was afterwards to call redeemer" (*FP* 61), a phrase that appears unchanged in *Stephen Hero* (*SH* 34). In *Ulysses* Stephen affirms that this "I" remains constant over time and changing circumstances,[22] an affirmation that is a new development on Bloomsday. For in *A Portrait*, when Cranly asks Stephen if he had been happier as a believing schoolboy, Stephen answers, "I was someone else then. . . . I was not myself as I am now, as I had to become" (*P* 240). As *Ulysses* begins, however, and Stephen remembers himself as a child at Clongowes, he recognizes that "I am another now and yet the same" (*U* 1:311–12), a recognition that he reiterates in "Proteus." Recalling his activities in Paris, he half-jokingly claims, "Other fellow did it: other me," but refutes this claim with the admission that "*Lui, c'est moi*" (*U* 3:182–83).

And it is on the strand in "Proteus," in a garbled little paragraph (*U* 3:288–93), that Stephen first sees the possibilities for revealing this unchanging identity in a fiction, for redeeming his experience through his art. The sand becomes a metaphor for language, in which he can hide the "gold" of his experience. "Try it," he tells himself. "You have some. Sands and stones. Heavy of the past." Stephen then identifies these "sands and stones" as "Sir Lout's toys." When Budgen questioned Joyce about the passage, Joyce affirmed that Sir Lout was, as Budgen surmised, a giant who was making a world.[23] It is not unreasonable then, though it requires some free translation, to see this passage as Stephen's tentative vision of himself as a giant, creating a world in his own image—the image of an Irishman—which can be his "steppingstone" to eternity. He thus fantasizes an affirmative answer to his question at the beginning of the episode—"Am I walking into eternity along Sandymount strand?" (*U* 3:18–19)—and foreshadows his claim for the immortality of Shakespeare, who "passes on towards eternity in undiminished personality," living forever in the world he built in his own image, "the son consubstantial with the father" (*U* 9:476–77).

In "Scylla and Charybdis," Stephen continues his investigation of the continuity of his identity through changes in circumstances and again links it to his artistic ambitions. He expands on his first statement of identity—"I am another now and yet the same"—as he carries on a debate with himself about the pound he has borrowed from Æ five months before and answers his own suggestion that "I am other I now" with the reminder that "I, entelechy, form of forms, am I by memory. I that sinned and prayed and fasted. A child Conmee saved from pandies. I, I and I. I." And he thus concludes his debate with the acknowledgment that "A.E.I.O.U." (*U* 9:205–13). There is no "other I."

Later in the episode, in the course of his lecture on Shakespeare, he makes a public declaration of his conviction of the continuity of his personal identity over time. He delivers this declaration to his audience in the library in the context of the artist "weaving and unweaving his image."[24] Prefacing his declaration with a physical analogy to "the mole on my right breast [which] is where it was when I was born, though all my body has been woven of new stuff time after time" (*U*

9:378–80), Stephen pronounces: "In the intense instant of the imagination . . . that which I was is that which I am and that which in possibility I may come to be" (*U* 9:381–83). And he immediately goes on to spell out what this fusion of past, present, and future in the artist's consciousness means to him as he reconstructs his experience in the artwork: "So in the future, the sister of the past, I may see myself as I sit here now but by reflection from that which then I shall be" (*U* 9:376–85), that is, the mature artist of the future.

This hypothesized artist, the presumed author of *Ulysses*, who will see his younger self "by reflection" from his own present time, exists in Stephen's present time largely as a wish for the future, as does the portrait he will create. What Stephen is putting into words is thus essentially a recurring daydream in which he duplicates Shakespeare's achievement in *Hamlet*, writing his own "book of himself" (*U* 9:115), the "ghoststory" (*U* 9:141) that will immortalize him. And in all the shifting of times implied in Stephen's statement, the first person remains: *I was*, *I am*, *I may come to be*, *I shall see myself*, pointing to the assumption that is basic to his artistic ambitions: the stability of the artist's image through time and thus the validity of the artist's re-creation of that image in his work.[25] "I, I and I. I."

Bloom, in contrast, cannot attain to this affirmation of identity. Like the Shadow of Jung's theory, which personifies the dark side of the psyche, what the Ego does not know he is, Bloom embodies the non-Ego, the "not-I" of the artist's personality in a variety of ways. Despite the piling up of detail about his life and his thoughts, there is a real and continuing uncertainty about Bloom's identity, an uncertainty that Joyce underlines in his appellations "Entity and nonentity," "Everyman or Noman" (*U* 17:2006–8). Early in the critical history of *Ulysses*, Gogarty dismissed Bloom's connection to the real world of Dublin: "The Bloom that never was on sea or land. He is quite unconvincing. A mere chorus to Joyce."[26] Although Gogarty is perhaps suspect as a critic of Joyce, he saw immediately and holistically the anomalies in Bloom's characterization that led Scholes in a later generation of critics to create the "cybernetic" label for Bloom and to conclude that the "characterization of Bloom is remarkable . . . because it shows us an autobiographical characterization without egocentricity."[27]

For Bloom shares the uncertainty about his identity. "A dark man in some perplexity" on Molly's cards (*U* 18:1429–30), Bloom, in contrast to Stephen, cannot affirm an enduring identity through time and change. Remembering himself and Molly of ten years before, he can in fact affirm nothing. "I was happier then. Or was that I? Or am I now I? . . . Can't bring back time. Like holding water in your hand" (*U* 8:608–11). On the strand at dusk, Bloom makes another attempt to arrive at his identity, when he thinks of writing a message for Gerty in the sand. He starts his message: "I." Then he thinks, "Useless. Washed away." Attempting to finish the message, however, he follows the "I" with "AM. A.," then thinks, "No room. Let it go." And "Mr Bloom effaced the letters with his slow boot. Hopeless thing sand. Nothing grows in it. All fades" (*U* 13:1258–67). This scene, of course, parallels Stephen's metaphoric contemplation of the sand as language in "Proteus," and Mr. Bloom's conclusion that "all fades" is a direct contrast to Stephen's vision of creating from the sands of language a world in his own image.

Bloom is throughout *Ulysses* unable to say who he is. Although he is identified as a Jew by most of those with whom he has contact during the day,[28] he tells the citizen at Barney Kiernan's pub that Ireland is his nation—"I was born here" (*U* 12:1431). Immediately thereafter, however, he points out that he "belong[s] to a race . . . that is hated and persecuted" (*U* 12:1467), reclaiming his Jewish heritage. At the cabman's shelter, turning a "long you are wrong gaze on Stephen of timorous dark pride" (*U* 16:1088–89), Bloom narrates his exchange with the citizen, claiming to be "as good an Irishman as that rude person" (*U* 16:1132), although he has reported to Stephen that the citizen "called me a jew . . . so I . . . told him his God, I mean Christ, was a jew too and all his family like me though in reality I'm not" (*U* 16:1082–85). By his own account, then, Bloom is an Irishman, "a typical and perfect Dubliner," Mary Colum says, "so real that no Dubliner can fail to recognize in him a father or an uncle."[29] He also identifies himself as a Jew (but not really),[30] and the text establishes that he has been baptized both Protestant and Catholic (*U* 17:542–47). He is indeed a real "anythingarian" as charged in "Circe" (*U* 15:1712), and Ned Lambert's question in "Cyclops" is very much to the point: "Is he a jew or a gentile or a holy Roman or a swaddler or what the hell is he?" (*U* 12:1631–32).

Bloom does not clearly belong anywhere. His relation to the Dublin world is, in fact, reminiscent of Jung's commentary on the archetypes of transformation, of which the Shadow is one. These archetypes, Jung writes, are "singular beings whom one would like to endow with ego-consciousness" but cannot because "there is nothing in their behaviour to suggest that they have an ego-consciousness as we know it." "Fragmentary personalities," they remain, like Bloom, "strangers in the world of consciousness, unwelcome intruders saturating the atmosphere with uncanny forebodings" (*CW* 9.1:286).[31] The uncertainty about Bloom's past and present identity is reinforced by a number of otherwise unconnected oddities about him that do indeed fragment the entity—or nonentity—presented as Bloom. Adams, for example, points to a string of "inconsistencies . . . which create a tangled image of Bloom's personal history" with regard to his residences and his "muddled" employment record, as well as a peculiar selectivity in his memory.[32]

Clive Hart and Leo Knuth, too, in their detailed examination of space and time in *Ulysses*, detect in Joyce's handling of the details of Bloom's life in Dublin a striking departure from his usual method, a "reluctance to be specific or to accommodate the fictional materials to documentary truth [which] reveals a difference not merely of working method but also of conceptual approach."[33] In "Wandering Rocks," for example, where, according to Hart and Knuth, "the physical movements of virtually everyone else . . . can be followed through time and space with great precision, those of Bloom seem designed to be mysterious," and he is only "hazily located at the centre of the chapter."[34] The "aura of vagueness which surrounds Bloom's movements" continues in "Sirens" and also extends to the time before Bloomsday, for Joyce "chose to ignore the historical facts when recreating Bloom's past"; there are no house numbers, for example, for any of Bloom's residences prior to 1904.[35] And though his residence on Bloomsday does have a number and until a few years ago was an actual house on an actual street in Dublin—Number 7 Eccles Street—in 1904, Adams notes, this house was vacant.[36] The fact is, as I have suggested in chapter 2, however we may interpret this character, Joyce is well aware that there was no Leopold Bloom living in Dublin in 1904; Bloom and his story originate in 1909, and Joyce thus honors Bloom's absence from the Dublin scene of the earlier time.

Perhaps the most striking of the anomalies in Joyce's portrait of Bloom is the absolutely zany list of measurements assigned to him in "Ithaca" (*U* 17:1817–19), buried, to be sure, in the miscellaneous facts and figures of that graceless chapter, even more deeply buried among the contents of Bloom's "first drawer" (*U* 17:1774), but undeniably there. Adams appears to have been the first to notice publicly the "absurd and impossible dimensions" included in this "chart of the measurements of Leopold Bloom compiled before, during and after 2 months' consecutive use of Sandow-Whiteley's pulley exerciser" (*U* 17:1815–17), for which Adams finds "no evident reason."[37] Clive Hart, considering only the "28 in." chest measurement in his 1968 study of *Ulysses*, dismissed it as a "discrepancy" overlooked by Joyce,[38] while Hugh Kenner, a decade later, elaborated on possible reasons for the admittedly impossible dimension, which, he pointed out, is not necessarily "an unlikely error . . . for a distracted half-blind man in a hurry."[39]

We may recognize that Joyce from time to time makes mistakes of fact, but he is certainly not careless about patterns, and Bloom's chest measurement is part of a sustained pattern of anomaly that does indeed, as Adams says, impute "a physical impossibility to Bloom as a physical organism."[40] For the chest measurement is only one item in the total catalogue of the "absurd and impossible dimensions" objected to by Adams. Besides the before-and-after list, which is presumably Bloom's work, there are other measurements offered by the narrator in "Ithaca" that, when they are brought together, do not add up to a believable human figure.

In "Ithaca," Bloom removes a size 17 collar, which is exerting "inhibitory pressure," but unbuttons at the same time a waistcoat, which is presumably a size 28 (*U* 17:1431–37). A Sears, Roebuck & Co. catalogue lists 17 as the largest available neck size, whereas the smallest chest measurement given for men's sizes is a "teen male" 32–33 ½ inches, with a corresponding neck size of 13–13 ½ inches (the twenty-eight-inch chest measurement belongs to a boy's size 10 in the catalogue). Bloom, of course, is no teenager, but a "gent about 40" with a "full build" (*U* 17:2002–3). This full build, in turn, quarrels not only with the chest measurement but also with the figures for Bloom's height and weight, which are given as "5 ft. 9 ½ inches" (*U* 17:2002) and "eleven stone and four pounds" (*U* 17:91), or 158 pounds, which surely is not heavy for this height. The height and weight, in fact, are the actual figures for Byrne in August 1909, when he and Joyce, before returning to Number 7 Eccles Street, weighed themselves on what Byrne calls "a pennyin-the-slot weighing machine"[41] and the narrator of "Ithaca" describes as a "graduated machine for periodic selfweighing" (*U* 17:92). The familiar picture of Byrne with Joyce and George Clancy (*JJ* 110, Plate V) shows him to be the epitome of trim youth, a far cry from the Bloom whose size 17 collar is too tight.

Bloom's overall dimensions are thus at the very least questionable, and the proportions given in the before-and-after list for the less familiar measurements are beyond belief. When Bloom starts Sandow's exercises, his biceps measure nine inches and his forearm eight and one-half inches, only half an inch smaller than the biceps. His ten-inch thigh, only an inch larger than the biceps, balloons into an eleven-inch calf, an inch *larger* than the thigh. One person to whom I presented these measurements observed thoughtfully, "He would look like Popeye." This is not one anomalous measurement, or two, or three, but a deliberate pattern, which is itself part of the larger pattern of questionable identity that surrounds Bloom. These measurements fit the Bloom who lives in a house that was vacant on Bloomsday; who identifies himself as a Jew, "though in reality I'm not"; who asks himself, "Was that I? Or am I now I?" and never answers.

Adams speculates that in assigning the impossible dimensions to Bloom, Joyce may have "wished to emphasize the extent to which he must be seen from within,"[42] suggesting that Bloom is created in a different dimension from that which underlies the creation of Stephen. Scholes's recognition in the seventies that "Stephen 'is' Joyce in a different way from the way Bloom 'is' Joyce"[43] points to a similar conclusion. And my own perception that Stephen's role in *Ulysses* parallels that of the Ego in the Jungian drama of individuation, while Bloom's role is a rough match for the Jungian Shadow, the non-Ego, assumes the same kind of difference in conception.

Stephen comes into *Ulysses* out of a fictional world that has been specified in detail in *A Portrait* and in *Dubliners* as well, a world that is in addition subject to the constraints of the facts of Joyce's own life. Stephen represents a piece of Joyce's history, a chaotic time in 1904 when Joyce was living in Dublin and grieving in his own fashion over the death of his mother, and the character is thus very strictly bound to that time. This constraint is surely a part of what Joyce meant when he told Budgen that Stephen "has a shape that can't be changed."[44] In traditional autobiographical fashion, Stephen duplicates his creator's chronology, up to and through the historical date of 16 June 1904, the fictional day of *Ulysses*, and probably we could all agree with William Noon that, so far as Stephen is concerned, despite minor anachronistic details from Joyce's return trips to Dublin in 1909 and 1912,[45] Joyce in effect "stopped his own clock somewhere between 1902 and 1904."[46]

For Bloom, however, who has no fictional history before he comes into *Ulysses* and is not rigidly tied to any actual time in Joyce's life, Joyce's clock kept running—right up to the final page proofs for *Ulysses*, according to Danis Rose, who reminds us that there are always "two distinct time-frames holding together the world of Leopold Bloom," that of the fictional Bloomsday and a second, which "begins some time in 1917 and ends a few days before February 2, 1922."[47] I would expand that time frame backwards to cover all the time in Joyce's life after 1904, and especially the experience of jealousy in 1909, during which Joyce discovered the subpersonality in himself that ultimately entered his autobiographical fiction as Bloom. But even though Bloom has his origins in James Joyce's world, this was a world that, after Joyce's self-imposed exile from Dublin in 1904, had no fictional counterpart. Thus, besides not being bound by historical time, neither is Bloom contained in the fiction by historical space, so to speak, and he comes into *Ulysses* from a world of his own, a world very close to that of the unconscious.

The accumulation of anomalies in the portrait of Bloom is suggestively congruent with the "trickster," a "collective shadow figure" that Jung comments on in "The Psychology of the Trickster-Figure" (*CW* 9.1:255–72).[48] The trickster, Jung points out, "is both subhuman and superhuman, a bestial and divine being, whose chief and most alarming characteristic is his unconsciousness. . . . He is so unconscious of himself that his body is not a unity," a disunity that is suggested in the measurements assigned to Bloom in "Ithaca." "Even his sex is optional, despite its phallic qualities," Jung says. "He can turn himself into a woman and bear children" (*CW* 9.1:262–63), which Bloom "actually" does in "Circe." Having been pronounced "a finished example of the new womanly man" by Dr. Dixon (*U* 15:1798), Bloom cries, "O, I so want to be a mother" (*U* 15:1817), and "*bears eight male yellow and white children*" (*U* 15:1821–22).

To say that Bloom embodies the non-Ego is not to deny that he dominates the novel. He does. *Ulysses* is the Book of the Shadow, even as *A Portrait* was the Book of the Child and the Hero. Nevertheless, the point of *Ulysses* remains what it was for *A Portrait*, the fate of the conscious artist, who remains Stephen.[49] For, as Jung reminds us, "the decisive factor is always consciousness, which can understand the manifestations of the unconscious and take up a position toward them" (*MDR* 187).[50] In the final analysis, this is Stephen's task in *Ulysses*: to understand Bloom and to take up a position toward him. Bloom cannot be seen in any sensible way as a development of Stephen: since they are opposites, there is no real basis for development from one to the other. At the same time, Bloom is equally essential to that "expression of myself" that Joyce identified as the motivating force for his work from *Chamber Music* (1907) onward (*JJ* 240), and he arises as surely as does Stephen out of the events of Joyce's life. Even as the Shadow personifies a vital stage in the development of the conscious personality, Bloom's character is crucially determining for the fully developed portrait of the artist that is the overall aim of Joyce's fiction. For with the advent of Bloom in Stephen's life, the fiction faces up to the unconscious as an integral part of the portrait of the artist.

THE REALIZATION

The Jungian Shadow encompasses a variety of unwelcome and unacknowledged personal facts. "Inferior traits of character and other incompatible tendencies" (*CW* 9.1:285) and "childish fantasies and resentments" (*CW* 14:473) are attached to the Shadow, as are the psychic functions that have not been brought under the control of the conscious will, especially the "inferior function," which is the polar opposite of the ego-personality's dominant conscious attitude.[51] This designation does not necessarily carry any moral connotations,[52] and certainly Bloom does not exhibit the evil that is traditionally associated with the darkness of the Shadow. What he does exhibit in archaic, amorphous form, are characteristics that Stephen has rejected or simply failed to develop. To confront this darkness and reintegrate some of its components requires the Ego to recognize the existence of an autonomous and, in terms of ego-consciousness, inferior part of the psyche, which, in contrast to the Persona, has grown without conscious direction and in ways that present "a fundamental contrast to the conscious personality" (*CW* 14:497).

Since this "split-off personality" (*CW* 9.1:261) personifies "everything that the [conscious man] refuses to acknowledge about himself" (*CW* 9.1:284), it is almost inevitably "just as one-sided in one way as the ego is in another" (*CW* 9.1:132), and one area of agreement among critics of *Ulysses* has been that Bloom represents in some way the other side of Stephen. Furthermore, there is considerable critical agreement with the Jungian corollary, as applied to Bloom and Stephen, that the Shadow is "that part of the personality which still has to be added to the conscious man in order to make him whole" (*CW* 14:128). For what the Ego has rejected nevertheless belongs to the "inventory" of the total personality, a "loss to consciousness" which must be restored (*CW* 7:133). And by embodying what Stephen has denied and repressed, Bloom makes possible this restoration.

The physical facts of the way Bloom lives, for instance, are not really different from the unacknowledged squalor of Stephen's own background,[53] the "houses of decay" that he sets against his remembered pretensions to the "Clongowes gentry" about "an uncle a judge and an uncle a general" (*U* 3:105–6). In contrast, the details of the Blooms' disorderly abode are almost joyously exploited in "Calypso": the "stale smell" of the bedroom, "like foul flowerwater" (*U* 4:315–16), Molly's "soiled drawers" (*U* 4:321), and the discarded book "sprawled against the orangekeyed chamberpot" (*U* 4:329–30) in the "broken commode" (*U* 4:383). And outside the house Bloom contemplates complacently the "scabby soil," "household slops," and chicken droppings from the "next garden" (*U* 4:477–79) before opening "the crazy door of the jakes" with its "stench of mouldy limewash and stale cobwebs" (*U* 4:494–97).

Furthermore, those "incompatible tendencies," which Jung in his earliest inventory of the Shadow side of the personality assumed were related to "sexuality in all its various manifestations,"[54] and which the younger Stephen rejected as evidences of "a brutish . . . malady," "monstrous images" alien to his humanity (*P* 90), are also recaptured through Bloom, who carries the burden of a notable variety of these manifestations *for* Stephen. For while it is Stephen, the Ego, who chooses to go to Bella Cohen's, it is Bloom, the Shadow, who does all the sexual acting out.

This kind of standing in for Stephen is further related to Bloom's compensation for Stephen's psychic one-sidedness as he embodies Stephen's "inferior function."

Of the four psychic functions postulated by Jung—the rational functions of thinking and feeling and the nonrational intuition and sensation—the dominant function for Stephen is, by common agreement, thinking, a function so undeveloped in Bloom that he appears a living example of Jung's reminder that the Shadow "has its own peculiar intellect and its own logic. . . . Everything that the darkness thinks, grasps, and comprehends by itself is dark" (*CW* 14:255). Indeed Jung's description calls to mind Robert Adams's question about Stephen and Bloom: "How can that lean and predatory mind, which is common to Stephen and Joyce, come to terms with the blurred six-inch margins of Bloom's brain?"[55]

Bloom is instead dominated by "an almost inseparable amalgam of feeling and sensation," which Jung identifies as characteristically the inferior function in the introverted thinking type. And this is the inferior function for Stephen, having the character of "something inimical and foreign" (*CW* 6:98), so undeveloped in Stephen that it has become archaic and "inaccessible to [the conscious] will" and "comes and goes of its own volition" (*CW* 9.1:238), beyond the control of the Ego. Bloom is the embodiment of this function for Stephen. "At the mercy of his senses," in James Maddox's phrase,[56] even as Stephen is sensually deprived and at the mercy of his intellect, Bloom "comes and goes" in Stephen's world on Bloomsday.

If the paths of the wanderings of both these characters are traced on a map of Dublin, such as the map that Michael Seidel provides in his *Epic Geography* for the streets of the major actions of *Ulysses*,[57] the lines tend to run parallel, even though the times may be different. Stephen begins his day in the southeast corner of the map, and Bloom's day begins in the northwest, and through the first six episodes, except for Bloom's seeing Stephen from the carriage (*U* 6:39–50), the coming meeting is signaled only through textual correspondences, although both are moving toward the center of Dublin. In "Aeolus," then, Bloom and Stephen play a textual hide-and-seek, with Bloom hurrying out of the newspaper office, the "capering newsboys" in his wake (*U* 7:436), only minutes before Stephen enters as a "suppliant" for Deasy's letter (*U* 7:505–9). While Stephen is in the newspaper office, Burke mentions Bloom in connection with "the gentle art of advertisement" (*U* 7:608), and there is a telephone call from Bloom, which Myles Crawford, engrossed in the details of the Phoenix Park murders, refuses to take (*U* 7:671–72), but Stephen has left the office with MacHugh (*U* 915) before Bloom returns and again tries to get Crawford's attention (*U* 7:963–65). Here again Bloom sees Stephen and wonders, "is that young Dedalus the moving spirit" for the drinking party, noting also the quality of the boots Mulligan has given Stephen (*U* 7:984–85). But Stephen has not yet seen Bloom.

In "Scylla and Charybdis," Bloom appears as "a patient silhouette," waiting and listening at the librarians' door (*U* 9:597), a "bowing dark figure" following Mr. Lyster's "hasty heels" (*U* 9:602–3). He is immediately identified as "the sheeny . . . Bloom" (*U* 9:605–7) by Mulligan, who also tells Stephen, "He knows you. He knows your old fellow," following this information with his insinuation that Bloom is homosexual, "Greeker than the Greeks" (*U* 9:614–15), an insinuation that he will repeat as the episode concludes (*U* 9:1210).[58] But Stephen still has not seen Bloom. Only at the close of the episode when Bloom passes between Stephen and Mulligan does Stephen come face to face with Bloom. And he immediately remembers his dream of the night before: "I flew. Easily flew. . . . A creamfruit melon he held to me. In. You will see" (*U* 9:1207–8). As Stephen and Mulligan follow Bloom "out by the gateway, under portcullis barbs," Stephen declares a truce: "Cease to strive" (*U* 9:1215–21). But this truce, like any truce, is temporary.

In a Jungian frame, when Bloom passes between Stephen and Mulligan, the Shadow has separated the Ego from his Persona, and the "terrors" of this "psychic strait," Jung says, are known only to the man "who has passed through it" (*CW* 14:233). By the time Stephen next appears in "Wandering Rocks," standing across from the powerhouse, these terrors are already evident. He sees his psychic situation in terms that duplicate Jung's descriptions of the reaction to the confrontation with the Shadow, which "produces at first a dead balance, a standstill that hampers moral decisions and makes convictions ineffective or even impossible" (*CW* 14:497). At first "the only thing that is at all clear is the incompatibility of the demands coming from without and from within, with the ego standing between them, as between hammer and anvil . . . tossed like a shuttlecock between the outer and inner demands" (*CW* 7:194). And in "Wandering Rocks" Stephen says to himself, "Stop!" Aware of the "Throb always without you and the throb always within," he is also aware of his precarious position: "I between them. Where? Between two roaring worlds," whose conflicting demands may "shatter" him. And he reacts by temporizing: "Not yet awhile" (*U* 10:822–26).

For the confrontation with the Shadow is not, Jung reminds us, "a harmless affair that can be settled by 'reason,' " as Freud had assumed (*CW* 14:253). In Jung's view, the Shadow carries much more than the repressed contents of the personal unconscious, since it brings with it the "uncanny influence" of the "archetypal contents of the collective unconscious" with which it is contaminated (*CW* 12:32), thus causing "confusion and mental darkness" (*CW* 14:520), even the "fear of 'going mad' " (*CW* 12:32). And the disequilibrium pictured in the little vignette in "Wandering Rocks" builds up for Stephen through "Oxen of the Sun," climaxing in "Circe," as the progressive darkening of the conscious personality by the influence of the Shadow is matched by the increasing confusion of the narrative structure. The style of the narrative in these two episodes thus reproduces the violence of the confusion threatening the Ego.

"Everything becomes doubtful," Jung says, "which is why the alchemists called this stage *nigredo*, *tenebrositas*, chaos, melancholia" (*CW* 14:497), and "as the influence of the collective unconscious increases, so the conscious mind loses its power of leadership," while the unconscious "gradually takes control" (*CW* 7:159). This shift in power gradually takes place in "Oxen of the Sun" and "Circe" as Bloom moves into Stephen's life. In "Oxen of the Sun," where Stephen complains of the "tenebrosity of the interior" that afflicts him (*U* 14:380), Bloom takes a seat beside him at the table in the "high hall of Horne's house" (*U* 14:1201,

1216–18). He follows the drunken Stephen to Bella Cohen's, where he takes over the management of Stephen's money (*U* 15:3600), deals with Bella over the broken lampshade (*U* 15:4268–313), and as "*Incog Haroun al Raschid*" (*U* 15:4325), the friendly foreigner of Stephen's dream, rescues Stephen from the consequences of his quarrel with Privates Carr and Compton (*U* 15:4422–30). By the end of the episode, then, the Ego has been "ousted from its central and dominating position," becoming "a passive observer" (*CW* 8:224), and Stephen groggily recognizes, "My centre of gravity is displaced" (*U* 15:4432).

What has happened in "Circe" is the actualization, in the indeterminate actuality of this episode, of Stephen's generalization in the library about walking "through ourselves . . . always meeting ourselves" (*U* 9:1045–46), a meeting that Jung says "is, first, the meeting with one's own shadow" (*CW* 9.1:21). Stephen's generalization is echoed by Bloom in a characteristic version as "Life, love, voyage round your own little world. . . . Think you're escaping and run into yourself" (*U* 13:1093–94). In "Circe" Bloom's reverie is in turn picked up by Stephen as he struggles drunkenly with a brief lecture to "The Cap," which stands in for Lynch in "Circe" and has pronounced: "Jewgreek is greekjew. Extremes meet" (*U* 15:2097–98). Stephen attempts to explain, in musical terms, how "extremes meet" when the fundamental and dominant tones of the chord unite in the harmonic series that resolves into the octave, the "ultimate return" (*U* 15:2105–12). This explanation has obvious psychological overtones, which Stephen reinforces as he switches to his version of Bloom's "voyage round your own little world": "What went forth to the ends of the world to traverse not itself . . . having itself traversed in reality itself, becomes that self . . . which it . . . was ineluctably preconditioned to become" (*U* 15:2117–21), or, in Bloom's words, "Think you're escaping and run into yourself."

It is apparent in "Circe" that Stephen and Bloom do indeed run into themselves, and the collision is resounding. The verbal echoes here move into the sphere of a psychological identity, a literal "reduplication of personality" (*U* 15:2523), and during this episode the two appear to exchange pieces of their separate selves. Stephen's memory of trying to cash his mother's money order at the Paris post office, just past closing time, "the banging door of the post office slammed in your face by the usher" (*U* 3:185–86), is echoed by Bloom's "I stand, so to speak . . . before the too late box of the general postoffice of human life" (*U* 15:2778–80). When Zoe is reading palms, Bloom points to his hand and says, "That weal there is an accident. Fell and cut it twentytwo years ago. I was sixteen" (*U* 15:3713–14). Stephen immediately links Bloom's fall with his own, which, when the mishmash of numbers is untangled, appears to be the traumatic incident at Clongowes, when Stephen, at the age of six, broke his glasses and was punished with the pandybat. Thus, when Stephen "winces" and says, "Hurt my hand somewhere" (*U* 15:3720–21), he is referring both to the pandying of sixteen years before and to some kind of identity with Bloom.[59]

The nature of the identity is suggested by the appearance of the "Siamese twins, Philip Drunk and Philip Sober," both of whom are "masked with Matthew

Arnold's face" (*U* 15:2512–14), thus adding the prestige of Arnold's Hebraic/Hellenic dichotomy to this chaotic exposition of the pronouncement "Jewgreek is greekjew." Philip Sober, the Hebraic twin, immediately begins to make an accounting of Philip Drunk's salary, with the reminder, "I am watching you" (*U* 15:2519–20), the whole action anticipating the sober Bloom telling Stephen, "You had better hand over that cash to me to take care of," and promptly counting it (*U* 15:3601–7). Philip Drunk, on the other hand, with the characteristically Hellenic "desire after the things of the mind,"[60] says, "If I could only find out about octaves. Reduplication of personality (*U* 15:2522–23), a reprise of Stephen's dialogue with Lynch's Cap.

The Siamese twins have appeared before, hypothetically at least, at the maternity hospital, where, a "heated argument having arisen . . . regarding the juridical and theological dilemma in the event of one Siamese twin predeceasing the other, the difficulty . . . was referred to Mr Canvasser Bloom for instant submittal to Mr Coadjutor Deacon Dedalus" (*U* 14:1000–1004). Stephen at the hospital "delivered briefly . . . the ecclesiastical ordinance forbidding man to put asunder what God has joined" (*U* 14:1007–9). This opinion is much more than the feeble joke it might appear, for the possible impossible separation of the Siamese twins presents with painful sharpness the dilemma of the psyche divided between two entities, neither of which can be denied or destroyed without denying or destroying the self, a reprise of Stephen's perception of himself "between two roaring worlds" in "Wandering Rocks": "Shatter them, one and both. But stun myself too in the blow" (*U* 10:824–25).

Neither can be denied, but the nightmare of "Circe," the climactic confrontation of the conscious and the unconscious, demonstrates vividly that the consequences of their being completely confused with one another may also be destruction. The nightmare, however, is not the end; the climax in "Circe" is followed by a dénouement, the extended dialogue between Stephen and Bloom in "Eumaeus" and "Ithaca," which, with its progressively indirect and removed quality, has all the marks of the "inner dialogue" that Jung identifies as "an essential part of the technique for coming to terms with the unconscious" (*CW* 12:274). In this dialogue the Ego and the Shadow communicate with each other, and the encounter between them moves toward a resolution. The "centre of gravity of the total personality shifts its position" from the Ego to "the hypothetical point between conscious and unconscious," a "new centre [which] might be called the self" (*CW* 13:45). And the flatness of the narrative in these two episodes reproduces the consequent dissipation of the threat to the Ego. The "loss of balance" (which Stephen literally experiences in "Circe" [*U* 15:4748–49]) Jung sees as "purposive," aiming at the "creation of a new balance" (*CW* 7:160), *with* the "collaboration" of the Shadow, which is "compensatory in an intelligent way, as if it were trying to restore the lost balance" (*CW* 9.1:282). And Bloom, "in orthodox Samaritan fashion" (*U* 16:3), does everything he can to restore Stephen's balance.

Stephen, for his part, does what the Ego must to establish the new balance. He grants Bloom, as the Shadow, his "rightful personality" (*CW* 9.1:132): "*Christus* or Bloom his name is." He really looks at him, "their two or four eyes conversing" (16:1091–92); he really talks with him, whatever the quality of the talk, a "real colloquy [which] becomes possible only when the ego acknowledges the existence of a partner to the discussion" (*CW* 9.1:132). He even accepts Bloom's offer to "lean on me," though "uncertainly," because the autonomy of this "alien 'other' in oneself" (*CW* 13:348) is "a most uncomfortable thing to reconcile oneself to" (*MDR* 187), a discomfort that is reflected in Stephen's awareness of "a strange kind of flesh of a different man, sinewless and wobbly and all that" (*U* 16:1720–24). But in the course of these two episodes the Ego realizes his Shadow, sees who he really is, and to a degree comes to terms with the unconscious. Stephen has communion with Bloom.

Because "the shadow is a living part of the personality and therefore wants to live with it in some form" (*CW* 9.1:20), Bloom asks Stephen to stay, an invitation that Stephen declines, "inexplicably" (*U* 17:955), but wisely. For, although "consciousness is renewed through its descent into the unconscious" (*CW* 14:369), the Ego cannot stay with the Shadow. He must leave "the wonder kingdom of the inner world" or he will "become for the world above a phantom." There is "a dangerous moment," Jung says, "in which the decision takes place between annihilation and new life" (*PU* 330), and Stephen chooses life. He makes his "exodus from the house of bondage to the wilderness of inhabitation" (*U* 17:1021–22), intoning to himself the "commemorative psalm" of deliverance that Dante's pilgrims sang in canto 2 of the *Purgatorio* as they were ferried over to the shore of Purgatory, having escaped hell: "*In exitu Israel de Egypto*" (When Israel out of Egypt came [*U* 17:1029–31]).

In a Jungian frame of reference, Stephen as the Ego has met his Shadow. He has seen the full dimensions of "his own image," and he goes back to the world of consciousness, "knowing" in some undefined way that his relationship with that world does not circumscribe the whole of his personality. Having expanded his awareness of the nature of the world and his part in it, he has become someone other than the Dublin "artist" who descended into Bloom's kitchen. For the connection with the collective unconscious, which the Shadow makes available to the Ego, "means an extension of man beyond himself . . . a rebirth in a new dimension" (*CW* 10:10). And in the text of *Ulysses*, both Stephen and Bloom participate in this rebirth. When Bloom unlocks the garden gate for Stephen, Joyce uses an explicitly sexual image—the male key inserted in the female lock—for this action; the "aperture for free egress and free ingress" is equally explicit (*U* 17:1215–19), and the total image may be considered a comprehensive symbol for the entire birth process—the "artistic conception, artistic gestation and artistic reproduction" that the Stephen of *A Portrait* said would require "a new personal experience" (*P* 209). Stephen is thus reborn into the world, and Bloom, of course, returning to the house, becomes "the manchild in the womb" as "Ithaca" closes, sinking back into unconsciousness but, at the same time, sharing in the promise of rebirth.

The pattern of the relationship between Stephen and Bloom, beginning with unawareness, moving through confusion, and culminating in the paradox of union with separation, is reproduced in a mirror image that runs through *Ulysses*. In the opening episode, Mulligan holds the mirror up for Stephen: "Look at yourself," he says, "you dreadful bard," and the mirror into which Stephen looks is "cleft by a crooked crack (*U* 1:134–36). Bloom, alone on the strand, tries to "see my face" in the "dark mirror" of the pool left by the tide but sees no reflection at all—"all these rocks with lines and scars and letters. O, those transparent!" (*U* 13:1260–62). In "Circe," Stephen and Bloom look into the mirror together and see Shakespeare but a paralyzed Shakespeare (*U* 15:3821–22). When, finally, both are in Bloom's garden, both look at Molly's lighted window and then look at each other, "each contemplating the other in both mirrors of the reciprocal flesh of theirhisnothis fellowfaces" (*U* 17:1183–84). This final mirror image of the relationship presents the paradoxical union of the opposites of Ego and Shadow in the Self. And it is significant that this image involves Molly, for only with the realization of the Shadow does the encounter with the Anima become possible. Although this encounter does not happen in *Ulysses*, what it may mean for the artist will be revealed in Molly's episode, "Penelope."

It is "Ithaca," identified by Joyce as "in reality the end" of *Ulysses* (*Letters* 1:172), however, that brings the curtain down on the psychic drama of the realization of the Shadow. Stephen, having seen the full dimensions of "his own image," becomes the "centrifugal departer" and Bloom the "centripetal remainer" (*U* 17:1214); as the schematic Telemachus, he "exchanges unity," in Joyce's phrase,[61] with the schematic Ulysses. But then, as W. B. Stanford pointed out some thirty years ago, Stephen throughout *Ulysses* (and even before) has represented one element in the Ulysses tradition, the "rebellious, home-abandoning" Ulysses of the line that descends from Dante's view of the hero in the *Inferno*. In fact, Stephen explicitly identifies himself with Ulysses in "Oxen of the Sun," boasting of his power to call the phantoms of the past into life "across the waters of Lethe" (*U* 14:1113–15), even as Odysseus did in Hades.[62] Joyce has thus "used Dedalus-Telemachus as a means of solving a radical antimony in the tradition—the conflict between the conceptions of Ulysses as a home-deserter and as a home-seeker."[63] In Joyce's treatment of the Ulysses theme, in a word, Telemachus and Ulysses are both Ulysses, the "son consubstantial with the father" (*U* 9:481). And Ulysses, in this reading, is equated with the productive artist of the future, who parallels the Self in Jung's individuation process.

The final view of this consubstantial father and son is in the elaborated context of "the heaventree of stars" (*U* 17:1039), and it is surely not irrelevant that a century before Joyce's *Ulysses*, Samuel Taylor Coleridge had used "a metaphor borrowed from astronomy" to characterize "the two opposite and counteracting forces" in "the process of self-construction" as "the centrifugal and centripetal forces." These "contrarieties" are in turn embraced by the principle Coleridge called "the I AM,"[64] a principle that is hardly distinguishable from the Self in the "process of self-construction" that Jung called individuation. As "Ithaca" comes to a close, Stephen, having assimilated "as much of [the unconscious] as [he] can stand" (*CW* 9.1:288),[65] is freed from his "mind's bondage" (*U* 9:1016) and reborn into the world. Bloom returns to the house and sees in the mirror a "composite asymmetrical image. . . . of a solitary (ipsorelative) mutable (aliorelative) man" (*U* 17:1348–50). The reconciliation of the "world within" ("ipsorelative") and the "world without" ("aliorelative") extends somehow to Bloom; he becomes a part of a larger unity. For with the Ego's realization of the Shadow, both are embraced by "a figure that somehow dwarfs the ego in scope and intensity" (*CW* 8:224), the Jungian Self. And "Ithaca" closes with a vision of this wholeness, "the hypothetical summation of an indescribable totality . . . bright and dark and yet neither" (*CW* 14:107–8, note 66). This paradoxical unity is presented in *Ulysses* as the "square round Sinbad the Sailor roc's auk's egg in the night of the bed of . . . Darkinbad the Brightdayler" (*U* 17:2328–30).

Jung became convinced that the essence of this indescribable totality is regularly presented in dreams and in art in what he called the *mandala* (*MDR* 195–97).[66] And here at the close of "Ithaca" the picture of Darkinbad the Brightdayler includes the essential features of the Jungian *mandala*: first, the squared circle, which is the essence of the hypothetical and indescribable and is regularly associated with the revelation of the Self;[67] second, the Joycean hero-self Ulysses as Sinbad the Sailor; and finally, the Jungian conjunction of opposites, "expressing the divine nature of the self," "at once bright as day and dark as night" (*CW* 14:148). This Joycean *mandala* in fact duplicates the components of two other significant *mandalas*, widely separated in time: the dream that Jung reports as revealing to him "a first inkling of my personal myth" (*MDR* 199) and, six hundred years before, the final vision of Dante's "personal myth," *The Divine Comedy*, in the concluding lines of the *Paradiso*.[68] In these two *mandalas*, as in Joyce's, there is a traveler, a conjunction of opposites, and the squaring of the circle.

Jung dreamed that he found himself a traveler in the dark square of a strange city with a round pool in the middle of the square. And in the middle of that dark pool was an island with a tree of light. And "through this dream," he wrote, "I understood that the self is the principle and archetype of orientation and meaning" (*MDR* 199), an understanding that underlies his conclusion that "spontaneous symbols of the self or of wholeness cannot, in practice, be distinguished from a God image" (*CW* 9.2:40).

For Dante, of course, the image *is* God. Himself the traveler,[69] grappling with the absolute conjunction of opposites—God and man in the individual's participation in the incarnation—Dante is "like a geometer wholly dedicated / to squaring the circle." And at the point of comprehension which is yet not comprehension, "I could feel my being turned— / instinct and intellect balanced equally / as in a wheel whose motion nothing jars— / by the Love that moves the Sun and the other stars," the most lyrical expression imaginable of the "centring process" (*CW* 8:203), in which "the whole of the conscious man is surrendered to the self, to the new centre of personality which replaces the former ego" (*CW* 14:494).

There is no lyricism in Joyce's *mandala*; even the positive affirmation of Jung's response to his dream of individuation is only ambiguously suggested in *Ulysses* by the tone of the parting between Stephen and Bloom in "Ithaca" and by Molly's soliloquy that follows in "Penelope."[70] But the archetypal nature of the transformation imaged here receives confirmation from its essential agreement with Dante's vision and Jung's and, beyond that, from its very ambiguity. For the symbols of transformation, of which the realization of the Shadow is one, are "genuine symbols precisely because they are ambiguous, full of half-glimpsed meanings" (*CW* 9.1:38). The "ultimate core of meaning" of an archetypal content, which "may be circumscribed but not described," expresses itself, "first and foremost, in metaphors," and "even the best attempts at explanation are only more or less successful translations into another metaphorical language" (*CW* 9.1:156–57, 160).

In attempting to explain the transformation process by which the Ego comes to terms with the unconscious, Jung borrowed from literature the metaphor of the Shadow. And Joyce, in another translation of the realization of the Shadow, which provides an underlying psychic structure for his *Ulysses*, has embodied that Shadow in Leopold Bloom. Bloom thus carries the weight of an archetypal content, which "is altered by becoming conscious and being perceived and . . . takes its colour from the individual consciousness in which it happens to appear" (*CW* 9.1:5). In a very literal sense, of course, Bloom takes his color from Joyce's own experience. He confronts the equally autobiographical Stephen Dedalus within the framework of the fiction and compels him to come to terms with the dimensions of his total personality. Whether the confrontation and resolution represent a personal psychic experience for Joyce we cannot know, but through their presentation in *Ulysses*, Joyce has preserved this archetypal experience for his own time, accomplishing what Jung says is "the most we can do, which is to "*dream the myth onwards* and give it a modern dress" (*CW* 9.1:160, Jung's emphasis).

FIVE

Flight from the Mother

In a 1920 letter to Carlo Linati, Joyce explained that *Ulysses*, besides being "an epic of two races (Israelite-Irish)" and "the cycle of the human body," was "a little story of a day (life)." Small wonder that he spoke in the same letter of the "more than enormous complexity of my three times blasted novel" (*Letters* 1:146).[1] For in the day of *Ulysses*, as in any day, let alone any life, many things happen, and many of these happenings are interconnected, appearing in the novel as integrated figures in a tapestry that is woven, however, of many continuous strands. Stephen's metaphor of the artist as a weaver, who "weave[s] and unweave[s] his image" (*U* 9:378), owes something, of course, to Walter Pater's reference to "that strange, perpetual weaving and unweaving of ourselves,"[2] in the conclusion to *The Renaissance*. But whatever its source, the figure is an apt one for the way *Ulysses* is put together, and any attempt to follow separate aspects of the image through the novel inevitably involves a measure of unweaving, a process that obviously does some violence to the effect of the totality but is just as obviously necessary for analysis.[3]

From the perspective of the relationship between the two protagonists—who in this reading embody the divided self of the artist—the essential action of *Ulysses* is the confrontation by the conscious personality—Stephen—of the hitherto unrecognized part of his total personality, which Jung personifies as the Shadow and I identify with Bloom. This gradual process, paralleling the "realization of the shadow" in Jungian individuation, involves as a necessary preliminary the "dissolution" of the Persona, that pseudoindividuality that mediates the relationship of the Ego to the "world without," the world of the collective consciousness. In chapter 4, I have traced this process in somewhat summary fashion, from foreshadowings of the confrontation in the first episodes of *Ulysses* through to its figurative resolution at the close of "Ithaca." This resolution, however, is not the end of the individuation process. The encounter with the Anima, the third personified force in Jung's psychic drama of the relations between the Ego and the unconscious, has yet to be reckoned with.

Without the realization of the Shadow, a recognition of the Anima is "impossible," Jung says (*CW* 9.2:22). But even when the conscious personality has taken in the existence of the Shadow and has begun to recognize the dimensions of the larger personality that Jung calls the Self, the conscious encounter with the Anima—the apprehension by the Ego of *her* true nature as an aspect of the totality of *his* personality—may not happen. And in *Ulysses*, this conscious encounter, though dimly visible as a potentiality at the close of the novel, does not take place. Still, prefigured in *A Portrait* in the peripheral development of Stephen's relationships with his mother and Dante, with the whores and Emma Cleary, the Anima, as she is experienced through projection, plays a significant role in *Ulysses*.

Projected in Stephen's dead mother as the day begins and in Molly Bloom at the end of the novel, the Anima is a dynamic factor throughout the novel in the psychic development of the male artist. These two Anima figures in *Ulysses* parallel Jung's personifications of the first two stages in a heterosexual male's developing relationship with woman, which is, he points out, "subject to powerful modifications coming from the personality itself" (*CW* 16:173).[4] The first stage Jung personifies as Eve and defines as the purely instinctual, biological relation in which "woman is equated with the mother"; and the second, which is "still dominated by the sexual Eros, but on an aesthetic and romantic level," he personifies in Helen of Troy (*CW* 16:174). Although both the mother and Molly are in a curiously literal way outside the action (the mother dead and Molly in a special way confined to her bed on Bloomsday), each is a controlling preoccupation for one of the protagonists of *Ulysses*. For even as the psychology of the male artist is split in *Ulysses*, so also is there a split in the female reality which is an aspect of that psychology. At the beginning of the novel, Stephen's mother is the dominant female reality for him, while Molly is paired with Bloom. By the end of the novel, Stephen's mother has disappeared, and Molly's voice is heard alone. Stephen's fate is involved with both female figures, in contrast to Bloom, for whom only Molly has personal meaning.

Stephen in fact moves between these two stages of the Anima projection, freeing himself from the dead mother and progressing at least to the threshold of the second stage, projected in Molly. Like the textual shift from Persona to Shadow, Stephen's movement between the Eve and the Helen projections of the Anima is a gradual, almost back-and-forth process, as the accomplishment of the psychic shift is foreshadowed by textual intimations of the coming change. To be sure, it is only after the mother has disappeared from the text, having been dispatched by Stephen's ashplant-sword at the climax of "Circe," that Stephen is free to consider what Empson many years ago called the "Bloom Offer," that is, Bloom's offer "to put Stephen to bed with his wife." But, as Empson also pointed out, the offer, first suggested by Bloom in "Eumaeus," is prefigured in Stephen's dream of Haroun al Raschid and the "creamfruit melon,"[5] a dream that appears in the text before Bloom does and competes with the dream of Stephen's dead mother throughout the day. The escape from the mother and the approach to the Anima proper are thus woven together through the novel.

In my analysis of Stephen's psychic development as it relates to the Anima, however, I have to a degree unwoven them. Stephen's most obvious and most pressing psychic task on Bloomsday is to free himself from his obsession with his dead mother, and in this chapter I consider this aspect of Stephen's movement between the two stages of the Anima figure separate from the promise of development beyond the mother, despite the textual melding of the two tasks. The progression itself I trace in my consideration of the positive movement toward the Anima in chapter 6. For, to a degree, the escape from the mother is a necessary preliminary to any movement at all.

Jung presents the son's efforts to renounce his dependence on the mother as a uniquely difficult psychic undertaking, as does, for that matter, Joyce in *Ulysses*. The mother is, after all, the "first incarnation of the anima archetype" (*CW* 5:330), and, Jung says, "the numinous qualities which make the mother-imago so dangerously powerful derive from the collective archetype of the anima, which is incarnated anew in every male child" (*CW* 9.2:14). Thus, separation from her, though "of the greatest educational significance," is at the same time extraordinarily difficult because it means separation from childhood (*CW* 7:195). Because Stephen's mother is dead, she appears in *Ulysses* only in Stephen's mind, as an insubstantial image, a haunt, and Joyce's presentation of Stephen's flight from that image owes a good deal, I believe, to Jung's vision of "the loving and the terrible mother" in his 1912 *Transformations and Symbols of the Libido*.

ECHOES FROM *TRANSFORMATIONS*

Transformations was first published in two parts in successive issues of the 1911–12 volume of the *Yearbook for Psychoanalytic and Psychopathological Research*, edited by Jung and received by the library in Zurich, and we may suppose that Joyce became acquainted with the work as it appeared in the *Yearbook*. His complaint to Budgen after the family's return to Trieste in 1919 that Ottocaro Weiss had reneged on his promise to send him the published volume of Jung's *Transformations* testifies to the fact that the work had made an impression on him. Joyce had, in fact, already planted echoes of this work in episodes of *Ulysses* published before he left Zurich and his library resources there. This use need not mean that Joyce had carefully read and analyzed *Transformations*; I doubt that he had. During the Zurich years, however, he knew German well enough to be paid as a translator, and he was amply subsidized by Harriet Shaw Weaver and Edith Rockefeller McCormick[6] so that he had no need to work for money. He thus had time to be a full-time writer, an occupation that for Joyce involved a measure of research, and the early psychoanalytic writings were a natural hunting ground for him. With his powerful intuition for analogy, he selects phrases from Jung's work that, more often than not, bring significant contextual content with them, content that is congruent with Joyce's own fictional agenda to begin with. In the following paragraphs, I examine in some detail two examples of Joyce's inclusion of echoes from Jung's *Transformations*, one in "Proteus" and the other in "Scylla and Charybdis."

In the strangely garbled paragraph in "Proteus" that I have considered in the preceding chapter, Stephen ponders the possibility of securing his immortality by constructing a world made in his own image—the image of "an Iridzman" (*U* 3:293). I noted there that Joyce's "Sir Lout's toys" echoes a phrase Jung uses in his *Transformations*: "toys of giants." The echo is assonant at best, but the context in both passages sets up additional resonances. Jung, interpreting Longfellow's "Song of Hiawatha" in psychoanalytic terms, mentions "the 'toys of giants' " in connection with the common "infantile phantasy" of taking the place of the parents (*PU* 363–64). Hiawatha's first deed, Jung recalls, was to kill a magic roebuck, from whose hide he made himself gloves and moccasins that bestowed superhuman powers on him. "By enwrapping himself in the buck's skin," Jung writes, "he really became a giant," a magical phenomenon that introduces into this fantasy the parents, "whose gigantic proportions as compared with the child are of great significance in the unconscious" (*PU* 363).

It is a fact of the text of *Ulysses* that even before Stephen proposes to become a "bloody well gigant" (*U* 3:292) and create a world in his own image, he has downgraded, if not denied, the creative power of his parents, who "clasped and sundered, did the coupler's will," but who have been superseded for Stephen by the coupler Himself, for "from before the ages He willed me and may not will me away or ever" (*U* 3:47–48). This muted denial becomes more open, if less personal, as the day progresses and Stephen first casts doubt on the reality of paternity in "Scylla and Charybdis" and then suggests in "Oxen of the Sun" that the artist may appropriate and surpass the creative power of the mother in "the word that shall not pass away" (*U* 14:295). Thus the fantasy of taking the place of the parents, which Jung sees in the Hiawatha legend, enters *Ulysses* in Stephen's fantasy in "Proteus" of becoming a self-perpetuating giant.

To be sure, the allusion is all but undetectable, but Joyce, in transferring and transforming Jung's image of the toys of giants into his own structure, ties it in with a more readily identifiable allusion to the ogre of the old folk tale, whose "Fee, fie, foh, fum. / I smell the blood of an Englishman. / Be he alive or be he dead, / I'll grind his bones to butter my bread" is abbreviated and revised in Joyce's text to "Feefawfum. I zmellz de bloodz odz an Iridzman" (*U* 3:293). But it still calls up for me, and I suspect for others as well, the fearsome giant Jack found at the top of his bean stalk in the old tale, in whom an alert psychoanalytic critic could surely see a parent figure.

It is through such layering of kindred allusions that Joyce characteristically adds density to his text, and in "Scylla and Charybdis," where the phrase "himself his own father" becomes a leitmotif and where psychoanalytic echoes abound, an allusion to Jung's *Transformations* combines with others to add resonance to Stephen's statement on fatherhood. Eglinton says, "We have it on high authority that a man's worst enemies shall be those of his own house and family" (*U* 9:812–13), while Stephen later points out that the son "is a new male: his growth is his father's decline" (*U* 9:855–56). Together these echo Jung's comment, which in his own text is a commonsense psychic explanation for a patient's "renunciation of the erotic wish":

> To be fruitful means, indeed, to destroy one's self, because with the rise of the succeeding generation the previous one has passed beyond its highest point; thus our descendants are our most dangerous enemies, whom we cannot overcome, for they will outlive us, and, therefore, without fail, will take the power from our enfeebled hands. (*PU* 117)

Thus, in the library discussion Joyce alludes to Jung's observation in combination with similar statements by other psychoanalytic writers, as well as quotations from William Blake and the Bible, to deepen Stephen's presentation of the ambivalence of the father-son relationship.[7]

THE "TERRIBLE MOTHER"

Almost certainly, then, Joyce's acquaintance with Jung's *Transformations* had been considerably more than casual when he complained to Budgen about not receiving a promised copy of the work from Weiss. Jung's depiction in *Transformations* of the mother imago as a paralyzing psychic reality to be feared and rejected finds an echo in Stephen's reaction to the memories of his mother that haunt him from the beginning of the day. To become a man, Jung points out, "the growing youth must be able to free himself from the anima-fascination of his mother" (*CW* 9.1:71). To the degree that he fails in this developmental task, "the son throws all the burden of the guilt on the mother, from which arises the idea of the 'terrible mother.' " He accuses his mother as if she were to blame for his failure, and the "deep animosity" that Jung attributes to the son in the archetypal situation (*PU* 267) is a striking feature of Stephen's feeling toward his dead mother, starting somewhat mildly with his inner cry of the morning—"No, mother! Let me be and let me live" (*U* 1:279)—and climaxing in his frantic rejection of the horrible specter in "Circe."

Jung's *Transformations* is thus strikingly relevant to Stephen's overwhelming anxiety in the face of his memories of the death of his mother and also to the structuring of the young artist's flight from the mother. More than half of its pages are devoted to a mythologically tinged account of the archetypal hero's "battle" to liberate his creative energy, the "libido," from its entanglement in the mother, an endeavor that is analogous to the struggle of the artist-hero in *Ulysses* to free himself from his dead mother. Much has been made of the dating of *Ulysses* as a celebration of Joyce's commitment to Nora Barnacle, and so it should be and so it was. But the celebration is a double one since the commitment itself marked Joyce's release from the period of mourning for his mother.

Joyce's grief and sense of desolation at the death of his mother is the great autobiographical fact underlying Stephen's individual story in *Ulysses*, even as Joyce's relation with Nora underlies Bloom's story. The acknowledged favorite of his mother, Joyce depended on her "completely," in his sister Eileen's judgment,[8] a dependence that was both practical and emotional. It is true that she engaged in a "bitter and painful conflict" with him over his rejection of the church, as Stanislaus reports, asserting, however, that such a personalized opposition "was necessary to Joyce; it was breath to his nostrils."[9] Equally essential was her faithful service to him in practical ways and her wholehearted emotional support for this much-loved firstborn son, all of which is evident in her letters to him during his stay in Paris. With her death, he lost his psychic bearings, a disorientation that was obvious not only to the ever-observant Stanislaus but to Joyce's friend Constantine Curran, who saw in Joyce's behavior during the period after his mother's death a "plain contradiction with his life before and after."[10] Gogarty's characterization of Joyce as "the greatest schizophrene who ever wrote this side of an insane asylum"[11] also dates from this period. During this time the young Joyce appeared to be without workable defenses against his pain, and the memory of his desperate need for release surely would make excruciatingly real for him Jung's insistence in the 1912 work that "the relation to the mother must cease, *must die, which itself almost causes man's death*" (*PU* 346, Jung's emphasis).

Jung's view of the nature and significance of the mother-son relationship in *Transformations* is very close to Freud's reconstruction of Leonardo da Vinci's destructive relationship with his mother in his 1910 monograph, *Leonardo da Vinci and a Memory of His Childhood*, which Joyce owned. Freud's insistence on the Oedipus story as the master plot of neurosis and on the centrality of the father-son relationship in the legend and complex later became a shibboleth of psychoanalysis. It is thus an irony that in *Leonardo*, his only venture into psychobiography, he focuses on the son's "mother-complex" even as Jung does in *Transformations*. Freud views Leonardo's mother, that is, not as the disputed object of desire in the oedipal triangle but as a threat to her son's full sexual development—specifically, a threat to his escape from the limitations of homosexuality into a heterosexual relationship. Thus Freud sees in Mona Lisa's famous smile a "double meaning"—"the promise of unbounded tenderness and at the same time sinister menace"—which he attributes to the artist's feeling about his mother, concluding that her tenderness was "fateful" for him (*SE* 11:115).

Jung's emphasis on the threat from the mother is not specifically concerned with the homosexual block to development but more generally with the son's reluctance to turn his back on the "pampering sweetness of childhood" (*PU* 335) and get on with his life.[12] Jung's statement in *Transformations* of the threat from the mother, however, which, as in Freud's view, combines tenderness and menace, is equally dire, as he asserts, with a nod to both Homer's Penelope and Sophocles's Jocasta, that "the mother can be the all-consuming passion of the son, which perhaps undermines his whole life and tragically destroys it" (*PU* 4).

Joyce had been in Trieste for two months when he wrote to Budgen with his complaint about Weiss's failure to send him Jung's work and, although he does not mention "Circe" in his letter, he had already begun to compose the episode before he left Zurich in October 1919, motivated, Budgen says, by a visit the two of them made in May 1919 to a twentieth-century Circe, "who owned two of the islands in the Lago Maggiore." This "Lady of the Lake," who actually was called Circe, gave Joyce "a packet of letters and a valise of books on the theme of erotic perversion," which she felt might be useful "as documentation for his writings." Joyce began to write "Circe" "a month or two later," Budgen says,[13] and the earliest known draft of the episode—which includes the essentials of the encounter with The Mother—was written, according to Phillip Herring, "during Joyce's post–World War I stay in Trieste" (October 1919 to July 1920).[14]

It is thus reasonable to assume that, when Joyce wrote to Budgen in December, the materials for "Circe" were coming together in his mind, both in the way of conscious planning and in whatever mysterious way the unconscious works in this process, and Jung's work on the mother complex provides associations that clearly could serve the novelist's purpose. Since the work was not available to Joyce in Trieste, however, traces of *Transformations* in later episodes do not appear as specific echoes. What I see, rather, is an impressionistic transfer to Joyce's text of Jung's vision of the "terrible mother."[15] Jung provides a number of baleful identifications for the terrible mother, equating her, for example, with the Sphinx, the "fear animal" (*PU* 204); with the "great whore" of Revelation (17:1–5), the "mother of all abominations" (*PU* 241–42); and with Hecate, who, "as nightmare, appears . . . in a vampire role, or as Lamia, the devourer of men" (*PU* 405). The mother is not only "terrible" (*furchtbar*, *schrecklich*[16] [*PU* 202, 427]) but also "devouring" (*verschlingend* [*PU* 364]), a "malicious pursuer" (*heimtückischen Verfolgerin* [*PU* 335]), a "death-bringing demon" (*totbringenden Dämon* [*PU* 388]), and "the mother of death" (*Todesmutter* [*PU* 396]).

To be sure, Jung also points to the other face of the mother, the "nourishing [*ernährend*] mother," the "smiling love- and life-giving mother" (*die lächelnde liebe- und lebenspendende Mutter* [*PU* 427]).[17] But he makes clear that this loving aspect of the "dual mother" may be equally threatening to the developing son, whose energy, Jung says, is "paralyzed" by the "consuming poison of the stealthy retrospective longing" for the loving mother (*PU* 427). The contradictory image of the loving and the terrible mother, the mother of life and the mother of death, is consistently a feature in the appearances of Stephen's mother throughout the novel. And nowhere is the terrible mother more terrible than in the climactic confrontation between mother and son in "Circe."

THE HOMOSEXUAL CONNECTION

Like all the encounters in "Circe," this confrontation appears to operate in accord with Freud's outline of the dreamwork, condensing and distorting conscious events of the day. It is thus Mulligan who announces "the afflicted mother" in "Circe" (*U* 15:4170), even as he has introduced Stephen's mother into the novel with his report that "The aunt thinks you killed your mother" (*U* 1:88). And the echoes from "Telemachus" are thick as Mulligan in "Circe" repeats his pronouncement, so offensive to Stephen in "Telemachus" (*U* 1:198–99), that "She's beastly dead" (*U* 15:4170) and accuses Stephen in her death. Epithets he has used for Stephen in the morning reappear in "Circe," as does his comment on "the mockery" of Stephen's wearing black. And again he produces his figure of the sea as mother (*U* 1:55, 122, 80): "The mockery of it! Kinch dogsbody killed her bitchbody. . . . Our great sweet mother! *Epi oinopa ponton*" (*U* 15:4178–80). These explicit correspondences within the text point to a thematically significant context, a pattern throughout the novel that links the mother with the threat of homosexuality.

Admittedly this pattern is directly associated with Freud's hypothesis about "a causal connection between Leonardo's relation with his mother in childhood and his later manifest, if ideal, homosexuality" (*SE* 11:98) and thus is more reminiscent of Freud's threatening mother than Jung's. But this connection between mother love and homosexuality is more or less a given in the early psychoanalytic view,[18] and it is clearly significant for Joyce's portrait of the artist in *A Portrait* as well as in *Ulysses*. It is worth remarking that when *Leonardo* was published, Jung pronounced it "wonderful" and admitted that it was "the first essay of [Freud's] with whose inner development I felt perfectly in tune from the start."[19] Thus, it is reasonable to suppose that Jung's approach to the mother-son relationship was built on Freud's view; and if Joyce combined impressions from Freud's *Leonardo* with impressions from Jung's *Transformations* in developing this aspect of the threat from the mother, it would seem a natural combination.

In "Telemachus," Stephen's preoccupation with his dead mother, which is introduced in the context of Mulligan's raptures about the sea, the source of all life, as "our great sweet mother" and "Our mighty mother" (*U* 1:80, 85), is played off against his problematic, potentially threatening relationship with Mulligan, which is itself shadowed by the ghost of Oscar Wilde's "love that dare not speak its name." Introduced into *Ulysses* in "Telemachus," this pattern carries over from *A Portrait*, where Cranly, Mulligan's precursor, lectures Stephen on "a mother's love" (*P* 240–42), a lecture that informs Stephen's own comments on *amor matris* in *Ulysses*. And in *Ulysses*, Cranly is associated, though circuitously, with Mulligan and with Wilde. In "Telemachus," as Mulligan links arms with him and walks with him around the tower, Stephen comments inwardly, "Cranly's arm. His arm" (*U* 1:159). This unexplained comment is then picked up in "Proteus," where Stephen thinks, "Staunch friend, a brother soul: Wilde's love that dare not speak its name. His arm: Cranly's arm" (*U* 3:450–51), completing the chiastic structure and identifying both friends with Wilde. Stephen's following thought—"He now will leave me" (*U* 3:451–52)—refers in *Ulysses* to his decision to part from Mulligan but, at the same time, harks back to his final talk with Cranly in *A Portrait*, during which Cranly, too, had taken Stephen's arm "in a strong grip" (*P* 238).[20] At the conclusion of the earlier scene, Stephen had silently rejected Cranly's implied offer to be "more than a friend, more even than the noblest and truest friend a man ever had" (*P* 247). And in *Ulysses* Stephen's inner question and answer—"And the blame? As I am. As I am. All or not at all" (*U* 3:452)—brands both these relationships as incomplete and rejects both.[21]

Snatches from "Telemachus" that are echoed in other episodes reinforce the homosexual relation as a problem for Stephen. Mulligan's assurance as the novel opens that Stephen has "the real Oxford manner" (*U* 1:54) surfaces in "Scylla and

Charybdis" as "Manner of Oxenford" (*U* 9:1212) in a context that explicitly identifies the phrase with homosexuality; and Mulligan's laughing taunt in "Telemachus," "If Wilde were only alive to see you" (*U* 1:143–44), is sandwiched between allusions to Wilde's *Dorian Gray* and "The Decay of Lying,"[22] which is one of the "Platonic dialogues Wilde wrote" (*U* 9:1069), to which Best refers in the library scene. Mulligan's response in "Telemachus" to Stephen's question about Haines—"Yes, my love?" (*U* 1:48)—is echoed in "Scylla and Charybdis" by Stephen's reference to Shakespeare's "dearmylove," followed by his inner association: "Love that dare not speak its name" (*U* 9:658–59). This phrase also comes into Stephen's mind in "Proteus" as he contemplates "his broadtoed boots, a buck's castoffs" (*U* 3:446)—Mulligan's discarded boots, which he wears on Bloomsday and which replace the fetishistic symbol in *A Portrait* of his mother's "jewelly slippers" (*P* 10). And, of course, he is wearing the "secondhand breeks" that Mulligan has asked about in "Telemachus" (*U* 1:113), immediately following Stephen's recollection of his dream of his mother in death (*U* 1:102–5).

The link between the threat from the mother and from the homosexual relationship is also confirmed and intensified through correspondences in "Scylla and Charybdis," in which Stephen's brooding upon his dead mother merges with his speculations about Shakespeare's love life, including, of course, the love that underlies the Sonnets. Stephen's mother appears in death, both in "Telemachus" and in "Scylla and Charybdis," but in the later episode her living influence is projected onto Ann Hathaway, Shakespeare's wife, whom Stephen oddly conflates with his own mother, beginning with his reminder that Ann "saw [Shakespeare] into and out of the world," that is, "took his first embraces" and "laid pennies on his eyes . . . when he lay on his deathbed" (*U* 9:216–20). To be sure, Stephen, like Joyce himself, equates a man's "first embraces" with a second birth,[23] and his description of Ann's relationship with Shakespeare is immediately succeeded by an inward vision of his mother in death: "Who brought me into this world lies there" (*U* 9:221–22). Then, as he describes how Shakespeare was "chosen" by the twenty-six-year-old Ann, who "tumble[d] in a cornfield a lover younger than herself" (*U* 9:256–60), the hostility of his description bleeds into his feeling about his mother. Mark Shechner early commented that "in Stephen's mind, the death of his mother and the sexual undoing of Shakespeare are significantly related,"[24] while William Schutte, also noting the identification of Ann Hathaway with May Dedalus, has suggested a comparison of Stephen's relationship with his mother to "the relationship between a pair of lovers of whom the older is a woman."[25]

Stephen, at any rate, charges Ann with responsibility for Shakespeare's sexual malaise in an argument that runs over many pages with multiple digressions and interruptions (*U* 9:257–464) and comes to a climax in the context of Shakespeare's Sonnets, returning through allusion to the connection between the mother and homosexuality. For Stephen's reference to Shakespeare as "a lord of language" (*U* 9:454) echoes Oscar Wilde's description of himself in *De Profundis* as "a lord of language" made wordless by his mother's death when he was in Reading Gaol.[26] And Stephen's summation of the charge against Ann—"Belief in himself has been untimely killed . . . and he will never . . . play victoriously the game of laugh and lie down" (*U* 9:455–58)—bears clear traces of Freud's picture of Leonardo's mother, who, "by the too early maturing of his erotism robbed him of a part of his masculinity" (*SE* 11:117). Stephen's comment, apparently a transition back to the circumstances of King Hamlet's murder, may also suggest the submerged, unconscious character of the early maternal influence: "The soul has been before stricken mortally, a poison poured in the porch of the sleeping ear" (*U* 9:466–67). And as Stephen concludes his case against Ann, linking the effects of Shakespeare's "undoing" with his "unhappy relation with the dark lady of the sonnets" (*U* 9:442), Mulligan appears in the librarians' office. The introduction of the Sonnets throws over the discussion the shadow of the homosexual threat, regularly associated with Mulligan, whose reference to "the charge of pederasty brought against the bard" prompts Stephen's unspoken epithet, "Catamite" (*U* 9:732–34). And the context of homosexuality dominates the final pas de deux with Mulligan (*U* 9:1101–1212).

Thus, when The Mother arises in "Circe," it is artistically logical that Buck Mulligan, "*in particoloured jester's dress of puce and yellow*" with "*a smoking buttered split scone in his hand*," should provide commentary on the apparition, repeating phrases from the morning conversation with Stephen. For Mulligan represents one of the relationships that Stephen must abandon to become a fully developed adult man and an artist: the quasi-loving relationship of male to male, which cannot become a relationship of the flesh without threatening the family continuity that Stephen focuses on in his discussion of Shakespeare's life and work. The other relationship that must be abandoned is, of course, that of child to mother. These two relationships, each of which represents an obstacle to Stephen's full development, to his making a life, are intertwined in the novel, though the dominant threat remains the mother.

THE "DUAL MOTHER"

The pattern in *Ulysses* of Stephen's obsession with his dead mother, lightened at times by tenderness, but progressively darkened by fear, anger, and guilt over the relationship, parallels Jung's description in *Transformations* of the archetypal hero's intensely ambivalent relationship with the "dual mother," at once loving and terrible. Jung introduces the loving and the terrible mother in his chapter on "The Unconscious Origins of the Hero" (*PU* 196, 202), and in his melodramatic recital of the course of the relationship between mother and son, Jung documents the dangerous power of the mother, making it clear that the crucial problem is the son's refusal to give up his infantile personality, his childhood, and the loving, nurturing mother at its center. Through this refusal, he cripples himself in his development toward adulthood at the same time that he shifts the blame for this failure onto the mother. The mother thus, because of his own anxiety about his own failure, becomes "terrible" for him, "a spectre of anxiety, a nightmare," indeed "the symbol of death" (*PU* 267, 346).

This same kind of intense ambivalence attaches itself to all of Stephen's memories of his mother, starting in "Telemachus" with the recall of his recurring dream of her in her "loose brown graveclothes" (*U* 1:103–4), which draws from him his initial plea for release—"let me live"—and reminds us that the mother of the hero in Jung's account, whose "garment is the garment of death" (*PU* 385), appears to her son as a "malicious pursuer" (*PU* 335). But the extended image of the mother as the symbol of the terrors of death in the opening episode is set off against the equally extended image of the mother as the giver and sustainer of life in "Nestor," the episode that follows.

Stephen's vision in "Telemachus" of his mother's "glazing eyes, staring out of death, to shake and bend my soul. . . . to strike me down" (*U* 1:273–76), brings from him the most dramatic evocation of the terrible mother in *Ulysses*: "Ghoul! Chewer of corpses!" (*U* 1:278), an expression of rejection that is emphatically confirmed in "Circe" at the appearance of The Mother. The initial vision of the terrible mother in "Telemachus," however, is immediately counterbalanced in "Nestor" by the case Stephen makes for "*amor matris*," the son's relation to the nurturing mother, as possibly "the only true thing in life." Stephen's interior presentation of the mother who shelters and nourishes her son with her body, her blood, her "wheysour milk," who saves him from "being trampled underfoot" by the outside world (*U* 2:141–47, 166–67), echoes Jung's emphasis on the nurturing, nourishing, and protecting qualities of the "good" aspect of the dual mother imago (*PU* 387).

This pattern of alternation between the loving and terrible aspects of the mother, established in the first two episodes of *Ulysses*, is reprised in snatches of memory any time Stephen's mother appears in the text, until in "Oxen of the Sun," the birth chapter, Stephen declares his release from the mother's threat through his proposed appropriation, as an artist, of her creative power: "In woman's womb word is made flesh, but in the spirit of the maker all flesh that passes becomes the word that shall not pass away. This is the postcreation" (*U* 14:292–94). Like many of "young Boasthard's" declarations in "Oxen of the Sun," Stephen's arrogant pronouncement has no discernible prospect of immediate realization, but it marks the end of a conscious development. Pursued throughout the day by the memories of his mother in death and in life, Stephen has moved from his desolation of the morning, coupled with his inner plea to his mother to release him—"Let me be and let me live"—to this declaration of purpose at the maternity hospital. And this declaration leaps beyond the not-yet-accomplished release to his claim to a creative power that surpasses that of the mother.

In "Circe," then, The Mother confronts Stephen directly, costumed indeed in this "costume episode"[27] and lavishly made up as well, as the terrible mother, in her "leper grey," with her "bluecircled hollow eyesockets" in her "noseless" face, "green with gravemould" (*U* 15:4156–60). And here in the brothel, the release from the mother—which is necessary for Stephen to become the godlike creator of his proclamation—is accomplished in the unconscious, which is the ruling principle of "Circe."

The dialogue between mother and son basically reprises Stephen's encounters with her memory through the day, more or less distorted, but maintaining the same odd balance between the loving and the terrible that is characteristic of the conscious memories. For although The Mother delivers a message of death—"All must go through it, Stephen. . . . You too" (*U* 15:4182–83)—she retains powerful intimations of the loving mother. As Stephen frantically denies responsibility for her death—"Cancer did it, not I" (*U* 15:4187)—The Mother reminds him, "You sang that song to me. *Love's bitter mystery*" (*U* 15:4189–90). This line from Yeats's "Who Goes with Fergus?" has been heard earlier, in "Telemachus," as Mulligan leaves the parapet, droning:

> —*And no more turn aside and brood*
> *Upon love's bitter mystery*
> *For Fergus rules the brazen cars.* (*U* 1:239–41)[28]

The paradox implied in "love's bitter mystery" colors The Mother's response to Stephen's plea, "Tell me the word, mother, if you know now. The word known to all men" (*U* 15:4192–93). Twice before Stephen has put the same question to himself about "the word known to all men": in "Proteus" (*U* 3:435) and in "Scylla and Charybdis" (*U* 9:429–30). In all the episodes in which the question arises, the context is the *fact* of the loving mother's death, and in only one is a direct answer given.

The answer, in fact, had never been in the published text of *Ulysses* until Hans Walter Gabler's 1984 *Critical and Synoptic Edition* restored five lines in "Scylla and Charybdis" (*U* 9:427–31)—forty-three words, eleven of them in Latin. This text, restored to one of the most examined segments in *Ulysses*, the source of favorite quotations about art and life, about fathers and sons, about mothers and sons, identified *love* as the "word known to all men." The most publicized of the five thousand changes in the Gabler edition, "the love passage" as it came to be called, was also the most controversial. Richard Ellmann, in his 1984 presentation address to the Ninth International James Joyce Symposium in Frankfurt, reminded the audience of his own unequivocal and prescient identification (1972, in *Ulysses on the Liffey*) of the word known to all men as *love*, contrasting this with Hugh Kenner's suggestion in his *Ulysses*, which was published in 1980, that the word was "perhaps" *death*.[29] Kenner's view that it might be *death* is much more than suggested in his 1956 *Dublin's Joyce*, where he rings changes on Dublin as "the Kingdom of the Dead" and characterizes Molly's final "yes" as "the 'Yes' of authority: authority over this animal kingdom of the dead."[30] But, as I argue in considerable detail in a 1987 essay,[31] mother love, as Stephen presents it, is true *because* it is of the flesh. The mother thus embodies the "bitter mystery" that the complete answer to the question Stephen asks about the "word known to all men" is not "love" *or* "death" but "love" *and* "death"—*liebestod*—for whatever is born of the flesh through love will die.[32] "The love passage," though it does not alter the substance of what is already in the text, does make clearer a textual pattern that insistently juxtaposes love and death, sometimes to the point of fusion, a pattern that, so far as Stephen's mother is concerned, is virtually indistinguishable from the Jungian alternation between the "loving" and the "terrible" mother.

In "Circe," The Mother responds to Stephen's demand with a contradictory blending of the loving and the terrible mother, the loving aspect drawn from Stephen's own musings about *amor matris* in "Nestor" and also from Joyce's dream-epiphany of his mother, written, we may remember, during his 1902–3 sojourn in Paris—before his mother's death and also before he had discovered in Jung's work confirmation of his own experience of the "terrible" aspects of mother love:

> She comes at night when the city is still; invisible, inaudible, all unsummoned. She comes from her ancient seat to visit the least of her children, mother most venerable, as though he had never been alien to her. She knows the inmost heart; therefore she is gentle, nothing exacting; saying, I am susceptible of change, an imaginative influence in the hearts of my children. Who has pity for you when you are sad among the strangers? Years and years I loved you when you lay in my womb.[33]

But The Mother in "Circe" is by no means "gentle." True, she offers evidences of her love for him—*amor matris*—in terms that echo Stephen's own reminder to himself in "Nestor" that his mother "had saved him from being trampled underfoot" (*U* 2:146–47): "Who saved you . . . ? Who had pity for you?" (*U* 15:4195–96). But when she calls for Stephen's repentance, she becomes for him "The ghoul! Hyena!" (*U* 15:4198–4200). And as she continues to offer assurances of her love and concern—"I pray for you . . . Get Dilly to make you that boiled rice. . . . Years and years I loved you" (*U* 15:4202–3)—her simultaneous threat of "the fire of hell" brings from him the cry, "The corpsechewer! Raw head and bloody bones" (*U* 15:4212–14), completing the echo in "Circe" of his rejection in "Telemachus": "Ghoul! Chewer of corpses!: (*U* 1:278).

Up to this point in the encounter with The Mother, although mother and son speak to one another, like Odysseus and his mother in Hades, they do not touch. But with Stephen's frantic rejection of The Mother's final demand for repentance, a crab suddenly appears, and mother and son touch through the crab. This "*green crab with malignant red eyes*," although apparently autonomous and freestanding, so to speak, is nevertheless mysteriously, ambiguously attached to The Mother, who "*raises her blackened withered right arm slowly towards Stephen's breast with outstretched finger*," saying, "*Beware God's hand!*"[34] as the crab "*sticks deep its grinning claws in Stephen's heart*" (*U* 15:4217–21). This crab is an actual presence for Stephen, and whatever its traditional connections with the disease that has killed Stephen's mother—"Cancer did it, not I" (*U* 15:4187)—it has all the earmarks of an archetypal creature from the murky depths of his unconscious.

Just such a crab appears in a dream reported by Jung in his chapter on "Symbolism of the Mother and of Rebirth," where it is explicitly connected—as is Stephen's image of the crab—to a strong attachment to a dead mother (*PU* 275–76). The crab dream is only briefly explained in the 1912 volume, but Jung's 1917 *Psychology of the Unconscious Processes*, also available in the Zentralbibliothek Zurich, includes a full-scale amplification and interpretation of this same dream, and especially of the archetypal crab image,[35] which is significantly relevant to Stephen's hallucination. This amplified analysis of the crab dream points out that, besides the association with cancer—the cause of death for both mothers and in German, of course, the same word: *Krebs*—the crab is "an animal that walks backwards,"[36] connecting this characteristic with the dreamer's "overpowering infantile craving" for love,[37] naturally associated with the mother, a craving that surely finds an echo in Stephen's remarks about mother love as "the only true thing in life." The crab is thus not a representation of the mother herself or of her memory but a fact of the dreamer's own psyche, as it is for Stephen, I think: "the symbol of the unconscious contents"[38] that pull the dreamer backwards.

Jung notes the similarity of this crab dream to "the typical combat of the hero with the monster,"[39] which he considers in some detail in *Transformations of the Libido* in connection with the Siegfried legend (*PU* 392–410), that is, with Siegfried's combat with Fafnir, the "cave dragon." Not surprisingly Jung identifies Fafnir as the terrible mother (*PU* 396, note 67), who guards the "incomparable treasure" of the son's libido, so that the son is forced to do battle with the mother dragon to gain this "source of life and power" (*PU* 397). The crab, in Jung's dream analysis, is thus another manifestation of the mother dragon, and so it becomes for Stephen.

As his confrontation with The Mother in "Circe" draws to a close, Stephen slips almost imperceptibly from an identification with Lucifer to one with Siegfried, while his hallucinated crab appears to turn into a dragon through an allusion to the Norse epic. "Strangled with rage" (*U* 15:4223) in the wake of the crab mother's attack, Stephen delivers Lucifer's famous line, which he has already made his own in *A Portrait*: "*Non serviam*!" (*U* 15:4228; *P* 239). This denial is addressed to the attachment to his dead mother and also to mother church, since The Mother identifies herself with Christ—"expiring with love, grief and agony on Mount Calvary" (*U* 15:4239–40).[40] And his "all or not at all" (*U* 15:4227), which is a textual echo of his rejection in "Proteus" of the partial love relationship represented by homosexuality (*U* 3:452), extends the denial also to the relationship with Mulligan. Then, as Stephen lifts his ashplant over his head, he calls out the name of Siegfried's sword—"*Nothung*!" (*U* 15:4242). This is the sword Siegfried used to slay Fafnir, a sword that Jung, in his discussion of the Siegfried legend, equates with "the word, or the procreative Logos" (*PU* 393). And with his ashplant-sword, Stephen prepares to slay the mother-crab-dragon, thus acting out his claim in the maternity hospital for the ultimate victory of the artist's word over mortality, the "flesh that passes," which is the domain of the mother.

Stephen's crab is not visible to others, and his dragon is not necessarily visible even to him, but the horrible apparition with whom both crab and dragon are associated remains—for the reader and for Stephen himself—Stephen's mother, whatever her textual metamorphoses. Of course, Stephen's ashplant is not a sword, and it does not touch crab, dragon, or mother; as it turns out, it hardly even damages the chandelier (*U* 15:4284–91). But Stephen's blow is followed in the text by the annihilation of time and space (*U* 15:4243–45) and the disappearance of the mother from *Ulysses*.

SACRIFICE AND REBIRTH

Stephen's confrontation with The Mother in "Circe" is as close to a climax as *Ulysses* provides,[41] and it leads to a significant psychic outcome for Stephen. From the perspective of the psychic development that Jung calls individuation, Stephen's aggressive separation of himself from the mother imago represents a crucial liberation, a step toward adulthood and thus toward the achievement of his central goal, to become a productive artist. This is a very large claim, which admittedly is not demonstrated by any explicit narrative event. To be sure, the scene with The Mother takes place in "Circe," in which events are uniquely difficult to pinpoint,[42] but we can be sure of some things that happen in the closing pages of "Circe." We know that, after striking the chandelier with his ashplant, Stephen abandons this accessory and rushes out the door (*U* 15:4255–57), leaving Bloom to retrieve his ashplant and to deal with Bella Cohen, which Bloom does with considerable aplomb (*U* 15:4270–4313). Outside the brothel, to borrow from Kenner's summary of "bare happenings" in "Circe," Stephen "runs afoul of drunken soldiers, one of whom knocks him unconscious; and Bloom stands by him till he comes to."[43]

The text, separate from narrative incident, provides a good deal more support for the significance of Stephen's conquest of his mother, requiring, however, a sensitivity to allusion and a return to earlier episodes to retrieve the connections that are suggested through allusion. As Stephen smashes the chandelier with his ashplant, "*Time's livid final flame*" and the "*ruin of all space*" (*U* 15:4243–45) bring into this context the quotation from Blake that provides a base for Stephen's claim in "Oxen of the Sun" for the artist's immortality through his works. "Every Mortal loss is an Immortal Gain," Blake wrote. "The Ruins of Time builds Mansions in Eternity."[44] In his Shakespeare lecture, Stephen has already proposed that Shakespeare's immortality rests on the fact that "loss is his gain" (*U* 9:476), and at the maternity hospital he prefaces his own claim to artistic immortality with a condensation of Blake's reminder. "Know all men, he said, time's ruins build eternity's mansions," following this with his assertion that the artist's creative power surpasses the mother's, since "in the spirit of the maker all flesh that passes becomes the word that shall not pass away. This is the postcreation. *Omnis caro ad te veniet*" (*U* 14:289–94).

Stephen repeats here in the hospital the phrase from the Requiem Mass that he earlier associated with the death of his mother: "Unto thee shall all flesh come" (*U* 3:396–97).[45] He thus underlines the analogy between God and the creative artist, to whom also all flesh comes for transformation into the eternally living word. Thus in "Circe," when the text announces "Time's livid final flame" and the "ruin of all space," it invests Stephen's rejection of the hallucination of The Mother with the promise of realizing his grandiloquent affirmation in "Oxen of the Sun" of the power of the artist's word over the "flesh that passes." Stephen has, in Jung's vocabulary, "sacrificed" his mother for his future growth, and when he does, the stage is set for his rebirth.

"The world arises," Jung says, "when man discovers it. He discovers it when he sacrifices the mother" (*PU* 458). Jung indeed equates the "separation from the mother-imago"—and this does happen for Stephen in "Circe"—with "the birth out of one's self" (*PU* 337), and this event also occurs for Stephen in the text of *Ulysses*, though in stages. Even before his confrontation with The Mother, Stephen has announced his birthday as "Thursday. Today" (*U* 15:3685). Then, toward the end of "Circe," after his collapse outside the brothel, he first lies with "his face to the sky" (*U* 15:4748–49) then shifts into a fetal position, "doubling himself together" and "curl[ing] his body" (*U* 15:4934, 4944), as he prepares—in the text at least—for rebirth, a rebirth, however, that is not accomplished until he leaves Bloom's garden, freed to the "world of inhabitation." The final picture of Stephen in "Circe" thus parallels the final picture associated with Bloom in "Ithaca": "the childman weary, the manchild in the womb" (*U* 17:2317–18). Stephen has accomplished a crucial developmental task, though not the only one, essential to his rebirth in a new dimension. Like the archetypal hero of Jung's psychoanalytic tale, like the legendary hero Siegfried, he has done battle with the loving and the terrible mother, and he has won his deliverance.

SIX

Approach to the Anima

Even though Stephen has delivered himself from the dangerous power of the mother in the climactic confrontation in "Circe," this deliverance represents only part of the resolution of his psychic task in relation to the Anima. As "Circe" comes to a close and Bloom looks down at Stephen, curled up on the ground and murmuring snatches from Yeats's "Who Goes with Fergus?" he attempts to decipher Stephen's murmurings: "Ferguson, I think I caught. A girl. Some girl. Best thing could happen him" (*U* 15:4950–51). Despite the fact that Bloom misconstrues the words he hears, he has identified the problem that is a corollary to Stephen's need to escape from his dependence upon his mother. Stephen's perception of the threat from his mother and his flight from her image, which I have to a degree separated out in chapter 5, are interwoven in the text with his fear of being himself abandoned and, even more, his anxiety about who is to replace the mother. For the mother, dead though she is, is presented in *Ulysses* as a psychic reality in Stephen's life, which, though it must be abandoned, performs functions that are so vital that it must be replaced. Stephen must find a woman to "take over the magical role of the mother" (*CW* 7:196).

Of course, as the text makes ever clearer, Bloom is promoting a candidate for this takeover in Molly, a female figure that carries strong traces of the experiential, psychological, and collective elements of the Anima proper, which Jung personifies as Helen of Troy. Helen is a powerful image for our culture, the "paradigmatic female,"[1] far more dramatic and glamorous than Penelope, who is the Homeric equivalent for Molly in *Ulysses*. Mr. Deasy introduces Helen as "the runaway wife of Menelaus" and compares her with Eve, who "brought sin into the world" (*U* 2:390–91), a comparison that Stephen echoes in the newspaper office (*U* 7:536–37). More significant for the Odyssean structure in *Ulysses* is MacHugh's pairing of Helen with Penelope when he tells Stephen that Antisthenes "wrote a book in which he took away the palm of beauty from Argive Helen and handed it to poor Penelope" (*U* 7:1038–39). In the library, when Eglinton compares "Mrs S" to Penelope, Stephen repeats MacHugh's information, adding his own description of "Argive Helen" as "the wooden mare of Troy in whom a score of heroes slept" (*U* 9:622–23), thus reminding us that the list of Molly's lovers, however dubious, numbers just over a score, and making it reasonable to suppose that Molly takes on Helen's power along with Penelope's patience.

Molly's unmediated voice, however, is not heard until the final episode; she is instead perceived through Bloom's eyes and ears or entangled with his thoughts. Except for fragmented hints like the "whistling within" and the "generous" arm that throws a coin to the one-legged sailor in "Wandering Rocks" (*U* 10:249–53), her actual appearances in the text are mediated, both for Stephen and for the reader, by Bloom. Even in "Calypso," where the reader is given what David Hayman calls "fleeting impressions" of an actual woman, she is presented, as he points out, "in terms of objects, sensations, and actions that make her accessible to her man." Hayman, who is writing a brief for "The Empirical Molly," sees this figure as "Bloom's version of Molly" and "only a footnote to the chapter,"[2] as, indeed, she is in the seventeen episodes before "Penelope."[3] In this final episode, however, which Joyce described to Budgen as "perfectly sane full amoral fertilisable untrustworthy engaging shrewd limited prudent indifferent *Weib*" (*Letters* 1:170), Molly's point of view is given free rein. The famous list of adjectives has been regularly applied to Molly, but, like Joyce's equally familiar designation of this episode as "the indispensable countersign" (*Letters* 1:160), these adjectives describe the essence of the episode itself rather than Molly as a person or character—a distinction that is not frivolous or accidental.

ANIMA AS COMPLEMENT

Molly's monologue,[4] for a variety of reasons, has always been a prime focus of interest for readers of *Ulysses*, and one reason, whether recognized or not, is that it is relatively easy to comprehend. There is no other voice than Molly's, and it is singularly uninterrupted, either by punctuation or by outward sense impressions. Furthermore, she is hiding nothing from herself; she does not, as Stephen and Bloom both do, put unidentified things out of her mind or think *around* them, an openness that gives her monologue some of the unquestioned veracity of a deathbed confession. Thus, the content of "Penelope" is relatively straightforward and uncomplicated, except for the purely artificial device of the omitted punctuation, which in most cases can be supplied with a fair degree of certainty.[5] Even more significant for the undiluted effect of the episode is the fact that the voice in "Penelope" has no overlay of the parody that dominates and deforms the voice of Gerty MacDowell, "the first extended delineation of a female psyche" in *Ulysses*, as Fritz Senn puts it.[6] The "last word" in *Ulysses* (*Letters* 1:160) thus appears to have the full assent of the author.

Indeed, more than one critic has suggested that the author speaks through or with the voice of "Penelope." Kimberly Devlin considers it obvious that Molly is "really a male female impersonation";[7] while Anne Robinson Taylor sees Molly as "a female masquerade," through whom Joyce "imaginatively fuses the voice of the male author with the voice of the woman," and she suggests that it is "the ambiguous quality of this voice [that] has polarized her critics."[8] On a more negative note, Frances Restuccia claims that "Joyce uses Molly as a cipher" through whom he realizes his own masochistic desires, with Molly herself functioning as his "literary Venus in Furs" who "wields the pen" as a whip.[9] Colin MacCabe, viewing *Ulysses* from a Lacanian perspective, considers "the female voice within the male" in "Penelope" a "radical refusal of position," which signals the abandonment of "the world of representation."[10]

The "female voice within the male," identified in "Penelope" by all these critics, whatever their differences in emphasis, brings into the discussion the Jungian Anima. Like this female archetype, which Jung assumes every man carries in his unconscious as a complement and compensation for his consciously masculine personality, the female voice in this final episode complements and compensates for the predominantly male reality of the episodes that precede it. And Joyce's designation of the episode as the "indispensable countersign," the female "*Yes*," which affirms and completes the male artist's self-realization, is very close to Jung's assumptions about the radical complementarity of masculine and feminine principles in the human psyche. In Jung's view, these opposing principles, though they define separately the psychology of each sex (*CW* 10:123), are indispensable to each other for the psychic balance of either a male or a female individual. Like biological sex, male or female psychology is a matter not of exclusion of its opposite but simply of "the predominance of the corresponding genes." Thus in a man's psyche—which is clearly what we are concerned with in *Ulysses*—"it is only the conscious mind . . . that has the masculine sign, while the unconscious is by nature feminine." "All I have done in my anima theory," Jung points out, "is to rediscover and reformulate this fact. It had long been known" (*CW* 9.1:175).

Certainly Joyce seems to have known it intuitively long before Jung personified the feminine component in a man as the Anima. For Joyce's insights in *Ulysses* about the place of woman in the artist's life have their origins in the earliest versions of his self-portrait. The central pronouncement in *Ulysses* about the masculine-feminine opposition—"In woman's womb word is made flesh but in the spirit of the maker all flesh that passes becomes the word that shall not pass away" (*U* 14:292–294)[11]—builds on Stephen's "theory of dualism" in *Stephen Hero*, which "would symbolise the twin eternities of spirit and nature as the twin eternities of male and female" (*SH* 210), but goes beyond this theory to suggest the complementarity that Jung sees in masculine and feminine principles as balancing elements in the psyche. Stephen's pronouncement also goes beyond Jung to outline a functional complementarity between male and female in the creation of the artist and in his subsequent re-creation of himself in the artwork.

Likewise, Joyce's complicated approach to the Anima in *Ulysses* is prefigured in his earliest "Portrait of the Artist," in the apostrophe to an unnamed woman[12] who is an unmistakable Anima figure. This "dearest of mortals" shares with Jung's theoretical Anima a number of qualities. Like the Anima, this "Lady of the Apple Trees, Kind Wisdom, Sweet Flower of Dusk" (*FP* 66), can be said to have "a peculiar relation to *time*," as well as a significance that "oscillates between the extremes of goddess and whore" (*CW* 9.1:199). She has always been "sacramental" to the young artist, bringing to him, even in his boyhood, an "enrichment of soul" (*FP* 66). During "that ardent adventure of lust," which we may assume bears some resemblance to Stephen's Nighttown adventures in *A Portrait*, she has come to him "as a witch to the agony of the self devourer, an envoy from the fair courts of life" (*FP* 65–66). Like the Jungian Anima, who "gives relationship and relatedness to a man's consciousness" (*CW* 9.2:16), this "Beneficent One" has "revealed [the young artist] to himself" and has at the same time facilitated his relationship with the world outside himself, setting him on the path to "the measurable world and the broad expanse of activity." In this one florid paragraph (*FP* 65–66) the young Joyce has laid the groundwork for his immeasurably more convoluted presentation of the Anima in *Ulysses*.

A DOUBLE PROBLEM: DREAM, CLOUD, AND STAR

In *Ulysses*, of course, Joyce is dealing with two manifestations of the Anima and is presenting Stephen's progress from one to the other, indeed the possibility of his replacing one with the other. For however threatening Stephen's attachment to his mother is for him, the threat does not nullify her vital, dependable contribution to his life. The pain of the necessary separation from this first Anima image is compounded for Stephen by the fact that his mother is dead. *She* has left *him*, taking with her his assurance of being related to the world and to himself. Added to his anxiety about the psychic separation from his mother is the desperate realization that there is no physical woman to take the mother's place. This is the double problem that Stephen faces in *Ulysses* as he moves between the two stages of the Anima figure represented by his mother and Molly Bloom.

These two manifestations of the Anima, through their alternating appearances in the text, demonstrate the vital function of woman in the artist's total psychic/physical makeup, and this is the function of relationship, the gift of the feminine principle personified in the Jungian Anima.[13] Woman in *Ulysses* is shown, first and last, as providing for the artist's relationship to physical reality, to the flesh and the world. But she is also shown as involved in the other reality, the relationship between his conscious personality and the unconscious and, as an extension of this, in his relationship to the eternal: God's power and his own immortality. To be sure, as we have come to expect in *Ulysses*, none of this is realized through narrative action but rather through the almost autonomous interaction of words and images, often widely separated in the text.

Stephen's inward movement between the two Anima figures, through which the female reality in *Ulysses* is realized, follows the complementary progress through the novel of three intricately interwoven motifs, all of which signal the shift from the dead mother to the living Molly, from the "purely instinctual relationship" that Jung personifies as Eve to the Anima proper, personified in Helen of Troy (*CW* 16:174). The first of these motifs is the two dreams, one of the dead mother and the other of Haroun al Raschid's gift of the "creamfruit melon." These two dreams compete for Stephen's attention throughout the day until the dream of the mother is supplanted by the "reality" of Bloom as Haroun al Raschid and Molly as the "creamfruit melon." The second motif is the cloud, which appears with the mother in "Telemachus" and moves through the day, merging with the "pillar of the cloud"[14] and its Exodus-derived promise of deliverance from bondage. And the third motif is the star, the "recumbent neversetting constellation of Cassiopeia" (*U* 17:1122–23), which is associated with Stephen's hope for artistic immortality.

The tracing of these motifs tends to become somewhat circular because of Joyce's characteristic cross-referencing, but the pattern in its broad outlines is clear. The motifs attach to Stephen. All are introduced in the first three episodes and reprised in "Scylla and Charybdis" where Stephen is in focus, appearing in Bloom's episodes only as amplification. They again cluster in the later episodes, which include both Bloom and Stephen, especially in "Oxen of the Sun" and "Circe," while the final episode provides confirmation of the pattern's implications.

Although Stephen's dream of his dead mother appears only synecdochically in later episodes, in "Telemachus," it is described in detail and is dominated by the smells of death: "an odour of wax and rosewood" and "a faint odour of wetted ashes" (*U* 1:104–5). The memory of the dream in turn brings back to Stephen the physical facts of her dying—"the green sluggish bile which she had torn up from her rotting liver by fits of loud groaning vomiting" (*U* 1:109–10), a memory that is set against his view of the "dull green mass" of the sea, "hailed as a great sweet mother by the wellfed voice beside him" (*U* 1:106–7). For Mulligan's earlier reference to the sea as the "great sweet mother" (*U* 1:77–78) has triggered Stephen's memory of the dream. If we accept Jung's identification of the sea as the natural image of the collective unconscious,[15] we may note that the mother in her first appearance is linked both with the vast unknown of the collective unconscious and with immediate physical reality in its most terrible aspect.

Then, as the cloud covers the sun, the same dual connection with the unconscious and with physical reality appears in Stephen's memories of his mother, memories that counter and complement the earlier vision of death. His "awe and pity" for her in her suffering and his sympathy for the meagerness of her life, the "secrets" of her "locked drawer" (*U* 1:251–63), are rare expressions of feeling, a function normally so repressed in Stephen as to be virtually unconscious. In contrast to the terrible facts of her dying, he recalls "her glass of water from the kitchen tap when she had approached the sacrament" and calls up the wholesome image of "a cored apple, filled with brown sugar roasting for her at the hob on a dark autumn evening." He also remembers the concrete evidence of her concern for the physical well-being of her children: "her shapely fingernails reddened by the blood of squashed lice from the children's shirts" (*U* 1:266–69). Stephen, however, turns back from these memories to the dream and the death itself, which draw from him his cry for release—"No, mother! Let me be and let me live" (*U* 1:279). For with the death of the mother who has given him life, Stephen is himself pulled toward death. His cry is thus directed to the memories of both the dead mother and the living, to the whole relation with the mother, which must be abandoned so that the youth may move from the unthinking security of childhood to the creative responsibility of adulthood—so that, as Stephen pleads, he may "live."

In "Calypso," when Bloom sees the same cloud at the same time, his amplifying response provides the essential clue for Stephen's release from the entangling relationship with his mother, though Stephen has no access to this amplification since Bloom is not yet a part of his life. In "Calypso" the cloud interrupts Bloom's semidaydream, which associates the fertility of "immense melonfields north of Jaffa" (*U* 4:194) with his memory of "Molly in Citron's basketchair." Bloom's daydream continues, "Nice to hold, cool waxen fruit, hold in the hand, lift to the nostrils and smell the perfume . . . heavy, sweet, wild perfume" (*U* 4:206–8), a memory that not only counters the smells of death in Stephen's dream of his mother but also goes far to identify Molly with the "creamfruit melon" of Stephen's *Arabian Nights* dream. Both Bloom and Molly thus enter Stephen's life from the unconscious, through the dream, and his apprehension of them throughout *Ulysses* has a peculiarly undefined quality that suggests their origins in that other world.

Although the amplification in "Calypso" of the cloud motif originating in "Telemachus" points the direction for Stephen away from the memory of the dead mother to the promise of the living Molly, Stephen, despite his plea for release, is not yet ready to change direction. In "Nestor," as he contemplates the "ugly and futile" Cyril Sargent (*U* 2:139), he makes a full-blown case for the son's relation to the loving, nurturing mother as possibly "the only true thing in life" (*U* 2:143). Stephen's case, if not derived from Aristotle, certainly agrees with the philosopher's point that a man should love his mother more than his father because she "gives the body."[16] The mother shares her own flesh and blood with her son before birth and protects him from the harshness of the outer world after she has brought him into that world. Stephen's mother, introduced through the "odour of rosewood and wetted ashes," has done this for him; she has "saved him from being trampled underfoot and . . . gone, scarcely having been" (*U* 2:145–47). Moreover, the mother's domain includes the other face of reality, the inner world of the unconscious, as Jung has recognized in assigning to the mother the function of protecting her son "against the dangers that threaten from the darkness of his psyche" (*CW* 7:195). Stephen sees that he and the schoolboy Cyril have "secrets" that "sit in the dark palaces of both our hearts: secrets weary of their tyranny: tyrants willing to be dethroned" (*U* 2:170–72).

In this image of tyranny, Stephen first suggests the inner bondage that comes up again in "Scylla and Charybdis" when he laughs "to free his mind from his mind's bondage" (*U* 9:1016), a bondage that is not finally resolved in the text until he makes his "exodus from the house of bondage" after his colloquy with Bloom (*U* 17:1021–22). In turn, "his mind's bondage" in "Scylla and Charybdis" is connected with "my mind's darkness" in "Nestor" (*U* 2:72–73), which Stephen acknowledges just before he first considers the dimensions of *amor matris*. The motif of bondage is thus initially associated with the mother—the powerful Anima figure of childhood—even as the sign of escape from bondage, the pillar of the cloud, will finally be associated with Molly, the Anima figure that can replace the mother.

Here in "Nestor," the ruler of his mind's darkness appears to be "a sloth of the underworld . . . shifting her dragonscaly folds" (*U* 2:73–74). Although this creature is not unambiguously identified with the mother—or with anything else—Jung points out that "in mythology the dragon *is* the mother," is in fact called "the mother dragon" (*CW* 18:91).[17] Just such a dragon appears in "Circe," by allusion at least, when Stephen confronts his mother for the last time. Christening his ashplant-sword *Nothung*, the name of Siegfried's sword, Stephen reenacts Siegfried's slaying of Fafnir, a creature Jung identifies as the mother transformed into a "death-dealing dragon" through Siegfried's yearning for the mother imago of his childhood (*CW* 5:363). Stephen, like Siegfried, must destroy this mother imago if he is to leave the dependency of the infantile relationship and move to the interdependence of the adult love relationship.

The necessary changeover from mother to beloved is at least prefigured in "Proteus," the episode of metamorphoses, where Stephen's hope for the ultimate metamorphosis, for personal immortality through art, is also introduced. Early in the episode, a wispy echo of the dream of the "ghostwoman with ashes on her breath" (*U* 3:46–47) adds another aspect to the mother's function in Stephen's relation to physical reality, as the link to his father and his own conception. This link to physical reality is at the same time linked to a reality beyond the physical, to the eternal; for though Stephen acknowledges that he was conceived in the flesh—"made not begotten"—he also suggests that, since his parents "did the coupler's will," his existence has been willed "from before the ages" (*U* 3:47–48).

Stephen, however, as he meditates on the strand, is interested in the far side of eternity, in immortality beyond his physical existence, and the project he outlines for achieving this immortality (*U* 3:286–93) presents a claim, however imperfectly articulated, to the absolutely personal immortality of artistic creation, a vision of creating a world in his own image, his "steppingstone" to eternity. "Try it," he tells himself (*U* 3:290), but makes no move to act on his vision, continuing instead to brood on his mother's death—"I could not save her. Waters: bitter death: lost" (*U* 3:329–30). Idly he follows the circlings of the cockle pickers' dog in one of the most remarkable descriptive passages in *Ulysses*, a description that is an extraordinary example of the transformation process that turns the mortal reality of the "flesh that passes" into "the word that shall not pass away." As Stephen watches, the live dog comes upon the dead dog, the "poor dogsbody's body" (*U* 3:351–52) that initially prompted Stephen's vision of creating a world in words from the reality of the past. Stephen then recalls Mr. Deasy's reminder that "All human history moves towards one great goal, the manifestation of God" (*U* 2:381). He repeats to himself, "moves to one great goal" (*U* 3:351), in this context surely *death*, which, as Ellmann himself acknowledged, is the other "word known to all men."[18] Stephen, however, is looking beyond death to the eternal word as the goal of his human history at least.

And as Stephen sees the dog "root[ing] in the sand . . . vulturing the dead" (*U* 3:361–64), a phrase that also describes his own brooding, he remembers his dream of Haroun al Raschid, a dream that functions as a counterweight to Stephen's obsession with his dead mother. In Stephen's dream, Haroun al Raschid has offered him a melon with a "creamfruit smell" and told him, "You will see who" (*U* 3:367–69), a most promising omen. For Haroun al Raschid is the Caliph of Baghdad in the *Arabian Nights*, where he is shown, according to Yeats, as "the greatest of all traditional images of generosity and magnanimity." Indeed, his fabled generosity is expressed at least once in a gift to a friend, Kusta ben Luka, of a bride from his own harem.[19] The dream thus provides a ready-made answer of sorts to Stephen's inner question, "She, she, she. What she?" (*U* 3:426), and a response to his plea, "O, touch me soon, now." It also suggests the answer to his next question—"What is that word known to all men?" (*U* 3:434–35)—for the answer here must be *love*, as it is in "Scylla and Charybdis." This is indeed the promise of the dream, for even as the melon is identified with Molly in the text, the Caliph is revealed as Leopold Bloom, who, "*Incog Haroun al Raschid*" (*U* 15:4325), follows Stephen out of the brothel in "Circe," carrying his ashplant. The promise of the dream is that the Caliph—or Bloom—will provide a woman for Stephen.

In "Scylla and Charybdis," Stephen has branded Shakespeare "bawd and cuckold" (*U* 9:1021) because the poet willed his own betrayal by the dark lady of the Sonnets. And "bawd and cuckold" is one of a list of labels indicting Bloom in "Circe" (*U* 15:1159), a label, we might note, that could also be applied to Haroun al Raschid, who after all provides for his friend from his own harem. Bloom, putting into action Stephen's decree that "Greater love than this . . . no man hath that a man lay down his wife for his friend" (*U* 14:360–62), offers Molly to his new friend Stephen. Bloom instigates his own cuckolding; he is, in fact, fairly organized and insistent about it, beginning by exhibiting Molly's photograph to Stephen in the cabman's shelter (*U* 16:1425–38).

Molly's reaction to Bloom's recital of this part of his day—"showing him my photo . . . I wonder he didnt make him a present of it altogether and me too after all why not" (*U* 18:1302–5)—echoes Bloom's inner comment in the shelter about "matrimonial tangle[s]": "And why not?" Bloom's further note that "an awful lot of makebelieve went on about that sort of thing . . . instead of being open and aboveboard about the whole business" (*U* 16:1480–83) is echoed in turn by Molly's "Why cant we remain friends over it instead of quarreling" (*U* 18:1392–93). This mutually accepting attitude, though conventionally atypical, fits in with Jung's view of the psychic triad of Ego, Shadow, and Anima, in which the Shadow, like the Caliph of Stephen's dream, is the gift giver and the Anima is the gift. And like the Jungian Shadow, whose function is to lead the conscious personality to the Anima, to serve as a "bridge" (*CW* 14:107–8, note 66), Bloom picks Stephen up outside the brothel "in orthodox Samaritan fashion (*U* 16:3) and eventually takes him home to Molly, thus actualizing the promise of the *Arabian Nights* dream.

Stephen attributes his collapse to "the reapparition of a matutinal cloud . . . at first no bigger than a woman's hand" (*U* 17:40–42), a rewording of 1 Kings 18:44, where Elijah's servant, sent for the seventh time to see whether any cloud has appeared to fulfill Elijah's promise of a drought-breaking rain as a manifestation of God's power, reports: "Behold, there ariseth a little cloud out of the sea, like a man's hand."[20] In the morning at the Martello Tower, the cloud that covered the sun has turned Stephen's brooding thoughts to his mother and her death. And in the brothel, Stephen's hallucination of his mother, who threatens him with "God's hand" (*U* 15:4219), is, like Elijah's cloud, a manifestation of God, a promise (or a threat) of his power, and specifically a reminder to Stephen that he is also mortal—"You too" (*U* 15:4183).

But Stephen has already considered his own death and rejected it. The "matutinal cloud" has been, like Elijah's "little cloud," a portent of rain, and the thunder of the storm it brings by ten o'clock frightens Stephen into facing the fact that he is "in the land of Phenomenon where he must for a certain one day die." But Stephen refuses to "accept to die like the rest and pass away." Nor will he "make more shows according as men do with wives which Phenomenon has commanded them to do by the book Law" (*U* 14:438–43), which in the first chapter of Genesis exhorts male and female to "be fruitful and multiply."[21] Stephen refuses to settle either for the practical immortality of sexual propagation or for the collective immortality of heaven—"that other land which is called Believe-on-Me" (*U* 14:444).[22] Continuing to entertain the illusion that he can deny the demands of life with others, especially a wife and children,[23] he appears to opt for the status of "glorified man, an androgynous angel . . . a wife unto himself" (*U* 9:1052). He thus stakes his claim to immortality on his power as an artist over "the past and its phantoms," declaring himself "lord and giver of their life" (*U* 14:1112–16). He has determined to become the "maker" in whose spirit "all flesh that passes becomes the word that shall not pass away" (*U* 14:293–94).

Stephen winds up his manifesto about the "postcreation" with the line from the Requiem Mass that translates "Unto thee shall all flesh come." In the context of Stephen's boast about his power over the phantoms of the past, the phrase clearly refers to the artist, as it does, though more ambiguously, in "Proteus," where it also refers quite clearly to Stephen's dead mother: "Bridebed, childbed, bed of death, ghostcandled. *Omnis caro ad te veniet*" (*U* 3:396–97). On the strand, apparently in some way freed by the promise of the melon dream, which he has just remembered, Stephen begins to write a poem, which, though it circles around an unknown "woman to her lover clinging" (*U* 3:422–23), clearly springs from the vision of his mother and Death: "mouth to her mouth's kiss" (*U* 3:400). However derivative this poem may be,[24] with his first creative act of the day, Stephen takes a step toward transforming his grief over his mother's death into living words, acting on the artistic implications of the phrase from the Requiem Mass: "All flesh comes to thee."

As he begins to "scribble words," the constellation of Cassiopeia first appears as the symbol for artistic immortality. Seeing his "ending" shadow on the rocks as he writes, Stephen queries, "Why not endless till the farthest star? Darkly they are there behind this light, darkness shining in the brightness, delta of Cassiopeia" (*U* 3:406–10). Then he asks, "Endless, would it be mine, form of my form?" (*U* 3:413–14), which is the crucial question about personal immortality—"Will I be me?" Stephen's answer, though it is delayed until "Scylla and Charybdis," and though it applies only to Shakespeare, the extraordinary exemplar of the artist, is affirmative, so far as the personal immortality of artistic creation is concerned. Shakespeare "passes on towards eternity in undiminished personality," Stephen asserts, because "loss is his gain," that is, because from his mortal life Shakespeare "piled up" a creation in which his image became immortal (*U* 9:476–77), "the word that shall not pass away."

Yet the corollary of Stephen's pronouncement about the immortality of the artist's word is that "in woman's womb word is made flesh," a requirement that for Stephen and for Joyce involves both mother and wife.[25] The child is brought into the world by the mother, but he is made a man by the beloved woman. The fact facing Stephen in "Proteus" as he begins his poem about a "woman to her lover clinging" is that for him there is no woman. "What she?" he asks, and he has no answer. His poem thus springs from a love that is entirely hypothetical, completely unfleshed, in contrast to the love that Stephen presents as Shakespeare's in "Scylla and Charybdis," love that tied the artist to the life from which he fashioned his art. Stephen, whatever he may fantasize about creating a world in his own image, cannot reasonably give an affirmative answer to the question he asks himself early in "Proteus": "Am I walking into eternity along Sandymount strand?" (*U* 3:18–19). For with the death of his mother, he is radically disconnected from day-to-day living and most crucially from "the strandentwining cable of flesh" (*U* 3:37). And in "Oxen of the Sun," though he is nominally addressing "Erin," it is surely to his mother that he directs his accusation: "Thou hast left me alone for ever in the dark ways of bitterness: and with a kiss of ashes hast thou kissed my mouth" (*U* 14:379–80).

Stephen must have a stake in the "flesh that passes" before he can create "the word that shall not pass away." He must have a life before he can create from it the immortal artwork, the only escape he believes in from the death that is otherwise the inescapable end of life. For this escape, though, he must have love, which, to quote Bloom, "everybody knows . . . is really life" (*U* 12:1482–83). This is Stephen's problem on Bloomsday. Having lost his mother, he must establish a loving tie to the flesh so that he can become capable of immortalizing that flesh in art.

In "Scylla and Charybdis," Stephen's internal expressions of his need for a woman counterpoint his recital of Shakespeare's relationship with Ann Hathaway. Ann's seduction of Shakespeare prompts Stephen to ask himself, "And my turn? When? Come!" (*U* 9:261–62). As he offers the fabrication about Shakespeare's returning "from Shottery and from her arms," with the star still visible "over delta in Cassiopeia, the recumbent constellation which is the signature of his initial among the stars" (*U* 9:930–31),[26] he reflects, "Ay, meacock. Who will woo you?" (*U* 9:938). He then plays a word game with his initials, leading to "S. D.: *sua donna*" (his woman [*U* 9:940]). Since the woman appears to be *Gelindo* or "the icy one," who "resolves not to love S. D.," this is not a particularly encouraging reflection, but it emphasizes his need for a woman. *Sua donna* at any rate is the context for his answer to Lyster's question about the "celestial phenomenon," which Stephen further identifies as "A star by night . . . a pillar of the cloud by day" (*U* 9:942–44). Stephen here links the immortality associated with Cassiopeia to the escape from bondage promised by the pillar of the cloud and links both to his need for a woman.

At the end of "Scylla and Charybdis," standing outside the library, Stephen recalls that it was from this same portico that he had "watched the birds for augury" before his first flight to Paris, and he then remembers his dream of the night before. "Last night I flew. Easily flew" (*U* 9:1207), a dream happening that we may suppose is connected to Freud's observation in his psychobiography of Leonardo that in dreams "to fly or to be a bird" regularly disguises "a longing to be capable of sexual performance" (*SE* 11:126). Again the dream provides a kind of counterweight to the memories of the mother. For in *A Portrait*, Stephen had watched the birds outside the library to escape from the "sobs and reproaches" of his mother in the cool contemplation of the flight of birds, which, he had reminded himself, Emanuel Swedenborg links to "things of the intellect" (*P* 224). And in this earlier scene, Stephen turned from his contemplation of the birds back to the "calmly lit" library (*P* 226).

In *Ulysses*, however, the matching scene on the portico ends with Stephen's departure from the library, the home of "Coffined thoughts" with "an itch of death . . . in them" (*U* 9:352, 356–57), "things of the intellect" that contribute to his "mind's bondage." On Bloomsday there are "no birds" (*U* 9:1218), and Stephen's vision is dominated by his own flight in the context of his liberating dream of the "creamfruit melon", through which he has been promised the woman he needs. His advice to himself to "Cease to strive" signals an acceptance of the dream, which is heightened by the whole context of the "peace of the Druid priests of Cymbeline" (*U* 9:1221). For in *Cymbeline*, it was Cymbeline's soothsayer who interpreted the dream of Posthumus: "When as a lion's whelp shall, to himself unknown, without seeking find, and be embraced by a piece of tender air . . . then shall Posthumus end his miseries" (5.5.435–41). As the dream is interpreted, the miseries of Posthumus are at an end because he has found "without seeking" and been "embraced by" Imogen, who, by an etymological analysis that would surely delight Joyce, is "the piece of tender air, thy virtuous daughter, / Which we call 'mollis aer'; and 'mollis aer' / We term it 'mulier': which 'mulier' I divine / Is this most constant wife" (5.5.446–49).[27]

In the "kind air" outside the library (which we may call "tender air" with all that follows) Stephen remembers his own dream, which is a companion to the one interpreted by the "hierophantic" priest, since it promises that he, "without seeking," will be given a "creamfruit melon" by the great and magnanimous Haroun al Raschid, identified in the text (though this is not known to Stephen) with Leopold Bloom as the melon is identified with Molly. He can "cease to strive" because "she" will be given to him. He will fly, but the earth is his element rather than the sky and sea. The "crooked smokes" in the quotation from *Cymbeline* that closes the episode rise from a sacrifice on "wide earth an altar" (*U* 9:1222). These "crooked smokes" have appeared before. In "Aeolus," as the group in the newspaper office listen to MacHugh's recitation of John F. Taylor's speech, Stephen notes "their smokes ascending in frail stalks that flowered with his speech" and recalls the quotation from *Cymbeline*—"*And let our crooked smokes.*" He predicts, "Noble words coming," and asks himself, "Could you try your hand at it?" He hears MacHugh continue his recitation: "*I heard the voice of that Egyptian highpriest . . . I heard his words and their meaning was revealed to me*" (*U* 7:834–40), and the caption "FROM THE FATHERS" appears on the page, followed by a quotation that brings from Stephen the inner exclamation: "Ah, curse you! That's saint Augustine" (*U* 7:844).

For what comes into Stephen's mind is Augustine's great affirmation of the inherent goodness of everything that exists in this world, partially quoted in "Aeolus" but quoted more fully in the 1904 "Portrait of the Artist," where it undergirds the young artist's "conscious[ness] of the beauty of mortal conditions"—"It was manifested unto me that those things be good which yet are corrupted; which neither if they were supremely good, nor unless they were good could be corrupted: for had they been supremely good they would have been incorruptible but if they were not good there would be nothing in them which could be corrupted" (*FP* 65).[28] In the 1904 "Portrait," the sentence from Augustine, which the author identifies as "a philosophy of reconcilement," segues into the apostrophe to the "Dearest of mortals" who has "revealed him to himself," the first of Joyce's Anima figures (*FP* 66).

Thus, through a complex structure of allusion—to Shakespeare, to Augustine, and to Joyce himself—Stephen has been promised a reconcilement to the world of the flesh through a relationship with a woman, and as he follows Bloom out the gate, he is moving toward a realization of the freedom promised in the dream and associated with both the star and the pillar of the cloud. For it is recorded in "Ithaca" that Bloom has for a guide in all his wanderings, "At sea, septentrional [in the North] by night the polestar" and "On land, meridional [in the South], a bispherical moon, revealed in imperfect varying phases of lunation through the posterior interstice of the imperfectly occluded skirt of a carnose negligent perambulating female, a pillar of the cloud by day" (*U* 17:1992–99).

This complex "celestial phenomenon" at first appears to look backward to the "nextdoor girl" at Dlugacz's shop in "Calypso," whose "moving hams" Bloom was frustrated from following (*U* 4:146, 172–76). But the description also looks forward to Bloom's first act after entering the bed he shares with Molly. The last in the series of reflections that precede the act is Bloom's consideration of the fact that "posterior female hemispheres" are a source of satisfaction everywhere in the world, "in all habitable lands" (*U* 17:2229–32); and a reader is by this time aware that Bloom is *always* on the lookout for them. In "Ithaca," however, the "posterior female hemispheres" are available in his own bed, and Joyce presents an elaborate before-and-after activity ("antesatisfaction" and "postsatisfaction") for the "mellow yellow smellow" kiss that awakens Molly (*U* 17:2237–46).

The condensed Latinate diction that is characteristic of "Ithaca" makes this chiastic before-and-after structure difficult to paraphrase with certainty, but the following is roughly accurate. Bloom becomes aware of the beginnings of an erection ("approximate") as he observes Molly's bottom, which is apparently covered by her nightdress. He gradually lifts this covering, presumably the "imperfectly occluded" (or not quite closed) skirt referred to earlier, and reveals the "bispherical moon" of the earlier description. He then silently contemplates it. After the kiss, he reverses the order of the activities as he again silently contemplates Molly's bottom, "tentatively" veils it again by gradually lowering her nightdress, and then is aware of a "proximate" erection. Thus Bloom's "guide" in his wanderings may be seen to be Molly, who is certainly "carnose," as revealed in the "fleshy charms" of the "faded photo" shown to Stephen by Bloom in "Eumaeus" (*U* 16:1425–28), and whose "bispherical moon" is certainly a focus for Bloom's husbandly attentions when he enters the bed. And Molly is a guide Bloom is prepared to share with Stephen.

THE SHARED DREAM

The sharing begins in the text with Molly's appearance in "Circe," wearing the "scarlet trousers" (*U* 15:299) of Bloom's *Arabian Nights* dream, which is a companion to Stephen's. Bloom has dreamed of Molly with "red slippers on. Turkish. Wore the breeches" (13:1240–41), a dream later described as "a strange fancy of his dame Mrs Moll with red slippers on in a pair of Turkey trunks" (*U* 14:508–9). In "Circe," however, as her camel "ambles near with disgruntled hindquarters," she scolds him "in Moorish . . . Nebrakada! Femininum!" (*U* 15:315–17), which, though she is Bloom's apparition, repeats the "talisman" discovered by Stephen in an esoteric book under "How to win a woman's love" (*U* 10:847). Later, when Stephen struggles to remember his dream and says, "I dreamt of a watermelon," he is advised to "go abroad and love a foreign lady" (*U* 15:3922–24). He insists, however, that "it was here . . . I flew. My foes beneath me. . . . Free!" (*U* 15:3930–36).

In the brothel he acts out his freedom in his climactic rejection of the ghastly apparition of his mother, shouting "No! No! No!" and crashing down on the chandelier with his ashplant (*U* 15:4235–45). Whatever the "real" effect of Stephen's blow—which Bloom questions—it releases him from his entanglement with his mother, who at this point disappears from the brothel and from *Ulysses*. In Bloom's garden, following his descent into Bloom's kitchen and their colloquy, Stephen confirms his deliverance from bondage, intoning "*secreto*," the psalm that celebrates Israel's exodus from Egypt (*U* 17:1029–30). As he and Bloom stand together under the "heaventree of stars" (*U* 17:1039), among which is "the recumbent neversetting constellation of Cassiopeia" (*U* 17:1122–23), Bloom directs Stephen's gaze to the "visible luminous sign" of Molly's lamp, which reveals "the mystery of an invisible attractive person" by "a visible splendid sign" (*U* 17:1177–78). This mystery is suggestively similar to the one that accompanied the Israelites in the flight from Egypt as God went before them, a pillar of cloud by day and a pillar of fire by night. The "projected luminous and semi-luminous shadow" of Molly's lamp (*U* 17:1189–90), which adds a touch of the pillar of fire to the pillar of cloud, is the sign under which Stephen and Bloom can be united, as each contemplates the other "in both mirrors of the reciprocal flesh of theirhisnothis fellowfaces" (*U* 17:1183–84).

This picture of the two protagonists, mirroring each other and together bathed in the ambiguous shadowed light of Molly's lamp, figures the psychic situation as the narrative of *Ulysses* comes to a close in "Ithaca." The three-cornered relationship, as Stephen and Bloom take leave of one another, though only a potentiality, only a "suggestion" (*U* 17:1181), since Molly herself is not in view, significantly resembles Jung's theoretical Ego-Shadow-Anima configuration, in which the Anima, after the Ego's encounter with the Shadow, may become a mediator between consciousness and the unconscious. The Ego's acknowledgment of the Shadow has been accomplished, however tentative and incomplete Stephen's acceptance of Bloom may be, and, theoretically, the way is open to a new relationship with the Anima.

Of course, the relationship that joins Stephen, Bloom, and Molly is finally a purely Joycean construct, never neatly resolved, never surely determined, and the connections go all ways, so that it is both a triangle and a circle, like the mystery of the Trinity. In the Joycean trinity the gift of the Anima is offered but not accepted; Molly Bloom waits in the wings as a potential successor to the mother imago that Stephen has "sacrificed" in "Circe." In the extended and seemingly aimless conversation between Bloom and Stephen, Stephen has been offered access to Molly, who is a convincing image of the Anima proper. But Stephen never actually meets Molly; nor is there any clear promise at the novel's end that he will. He evades Bloom's offer and leaves, having come only to the threshold of the encounter with the Anima that is the "master-piece" of individuation.

Stephen Dedalus does, however, leave the novel as a free agent, with some kind of assurance of his identity as an artist, affirming "his significance as . . . a conscious rational reagent between a micro and a macrocosm ineluctably constructed upon the incertitude of the void" (*U* 17:1012–15). This is the mature statement of Joyce's earliest perceptions about the artistic endeavor: of the artist's "ineradicable egoism" as a "microcosm" in his first "Portrait" (*FP* 61); of the artist as "mediator between the world of his experience and the world of his dreams" in *Stephen Hero* (*SH* 77); and of the "syllogism of art" as "the only legitimate process from one world to another" (*SH* 78). As he leaves the scene of *Ulysses*, Stephen proclaims himself the mediator between the microcosm of the inner world and the macrocosm of the outer world. All this spells success for the artist. Then he takes on the identity of "the centrifugal departer," wandering off into the night and leaving Bloom, "the centripetal remainer," "alone" as the bells of the church of Saint George peal the hour (*U* 17:1214–42).

SEVEN

Promise and Prophecy in "Penelope"

Shadow and Anima in Relation

With the departure of Stephen, the stage of *Ulysses* is turned over to Leopold and Molly Bloom, two of the great characters in the history of the English novel, who by the end of *Ulysses* have become extraordinarily real to the reader and more appealing to many than Stephen, whose force as a character has been steadily diminished in the course of the novel. From a Jungian perspective, of course, Bloom and Molly are identified with largely unconscious psychic forces, personified by Jung as Shadow and Anima. Each of these "archetypal personalities" has a contribution to make to the conscious personality, who is paralleled in the fiction by Stephen, and they are also related to each other as Shadow and Anima. As the title indicates, I am dealing in this chapter with "Penelope," which is not really an "episode," though for convenience we call it that. It is rather a coda, outside the novel proper, whose function is just what Joyce said it was, to "countersign" what has come before and bring this novel to a close. From a Jungian perspective, this final segment illuminates the place of the Anima in *Ulysses*, which is, as it has been throughout the autobiographical fiction, outside the action. In this "last word" of *Ulysses*, Molly as Anima reveals herself as a promise for Stephen's future, and at the same time she reveals the nature of her relationship with Bloom, a relationship that in many ways foreshadows the direction of male-female relationships in the twentieth century.

THE NATURE OF THE BLOOMS

Here at the end of that century, we are perhaps too psychologically sophisticated to suppose that unconscious forces are less real than those admitted into consciousness, but Bloom and Molly make such an immediate impact on the reader that the "unconscious" identification seems somehow anomalous. We may remember, however, that Joyce described Bloom and Stephen in "Ithaca" as "heavenly bodies, wanderers like the stars at which they gaze," suggesting their existence in another dimension of reality. This description, to be sure, is contrasted in the same letter to Budgen with the "human, all-too-human" perspective of "Penelope" (*Letters* 1:160), but we may also remind ourselves of Jung's insistence that "the more personally [the Anima] is taken the better" (*CW* 7:199), which is echoed in his advice to a correspondent who had dreamed of an oversized Beatrice as an Anima figure: "Treat her as a person, . . . as a patient or a goddess, but above all treat her as something that does exist."[1]

Both Shadow and Anima "spontaneously" personify themselves in dreams, Jung says, which is the reason he has "taken over these personifications" and "formulated them as names" (*CW* 9.1:285). These psychic forces, however unconscious, have the effect of persons. Though they have "manifold and unmistakable connections with mythological ideas," they "form a species of singular beings whom one would like to endow with ego-consciousness; indeed," Jung says, "they almost seem capable of it," concluding, however, that "this idea is not borne out by the facts" (*CW* 9.1:286).

So it is with Bloom and Molly, both of whom carry immense conviction for a reader, which is not entirely borne out by the facts of the text, although it is only as we identify and analyze individual strands in the naturalistic web of fact with which Joyce has surrounded these characters that we are at all troubled about their credibility. In chapter 4, I examined the problem of Bloom's identity and concluded from the facts of the text that he truly lacks an ego-consciousness. James Maddox, who has noted Bloom's tendency toward an "ego-less identification with the world," has also pointed out that "it is a paradox of *Ulysses* that although no character has ever been subjected to such intense scrutiny as Mr. Bloom, neither has any character ever so triumphantly escaped final definition."[2]

The case is similar for Molly, whose dossier over the years of her critical history has accumulated a catalogue of textual facts that quarrel with each other and cast doubt not only on what Hayman has called the "empirical" Molly but also on earlier interpretations of Bloom's wife as an easily recognizable and relatively uncomplicated symbolic figure—Woman as Flesh, Joyce's hyperbolic Wife of Bath. For Joyce has artfully woven into his portrait of her such radical contradictions that she does not quite make sense as an actual character. Almost twenty-five years ago James Van Dyck Card pointed out that in Molly "contraries are deliberately embodied,"[3] and this consciously assembled contradictory evidence about Molly extends beyond "Penelope" to the most significant contradiction of all: the textual fact that, despite Bloom's famous list of her twenty-four lovers before Blazes Boylan, despite the mildly salacious tone of the allusions to Molly in the episodes preceding "Penelope," and despite the sexual focus of Molly's meditations in "Penelope," Molly has been steadfastly faithful to Bloom up to Bloomsday, even though Bloom has not had "complete carnal intercourse" with her for over ten years (*U* 17:2278–80).[4] For Adams, the idea that the woman who reveals herself in "Penelope" "would be content with one sexual contact in ten years is simply grotesque,"[5] a judgment that Marilyn French echoes, though in more measured terms, in her observation that "this contradiction makes Molly a little unbelievable."[6]

Believable or not in detail, both Bloom and Molly are believed as characters, and the conviction that they carry for the reader—as opposed to an exegete—may well be grounded in Joyce's conception of them as in some way mythological or archetypal.[7] Thus if we consider them as psychic forces, this does not really deny their validity as fictional characters; it may even add a dimension to this validity. In the interior drama of individuation, each of these psychic forces has a separate contribution to make to the conscious personality, the nature of which is revealed in the fiction in quite different ways. The Shadow inhabits the *personal* unconscious and is thus directly accessible to the Ego, as the Anima, whose domain is the collective unconscious, is not. In harmony with this psychological pattern, Bloom's contribution to Stephen is realized through their relationship, as is the Shadow's contribution to the Ego in the individuation process, whereas Molly's contribution is revealed entirely apart from the action of the novel.

At the point of Stephen's departure from *Ulysses*, Bloom as the Shadow has done his part in the resolution of the Ego's crisis: he has revealed himself to the Ego and has received in return some acknowledgment of his own reality. Theoretically this meeting and accommodation with the Shadow should result in a significant expansion of consciousness for the Ego and even a new humility as he senses the existence of a larger personality than that bounded by consciousness. And however partial Stephen's accommodation with Bloom has been, the manner of his "exodus from the house of bondage to the wilderness of inhabitation" suggests a positive result of the meeting. Having retrieved his ashplant and his hat from Bloom, Stephen inwardly affirms his artistic vocation as mediator between the two worlds of experience and, also inwardly, recites Psalm 113, the psalm that commemorates Israel's deliverance from Egyptian slavery (*U* 17:1011–31).[8]

Bloom has, of course, offered Stephen a "proposal of asylum," which includes suggestions of Italian lessons for Molly and singing lessons for Stephen, as well as further meetings between himself and Stephen (*U* 17:954–72). It is worth noting that Bloom acknowledges that the "realisation" of these meetings is "problematic" because of "the irreparability of the past" and the "imprevidibility of the future," while the text offers two miniparables, each exemplifying one of these barriers. The first example is the story of the clown at Albert Hengler's circus who claimed that Bloom "was his (the clown's) papa," followed eventually by the question, "Was the clown Bloom's son?" and the answer, "No." The second parable relates Bloom's experiment with marking a florin for possible return to him, with the catechistic exchange: "Had Bloom's coin returned? Never" (*U* 17:973–88). The past cannot be changed, and whatever Bloom's sorrow over the loss of his own son, he cannot father Stephen.[9]

The future likewise cannot be foreseen or predetermined, and whatever Bloom's desires for a continuing relationship with Stephen, as well as for a possible relationship between Molly and Stephen, there is no way to guarantee these associations. Stephen, at any rate, declines the offer of asylum, with all the potential ramifications that Bloom visualizes. He thus does not actually experience a new Anima relationship in the confines of the novel. Still, what such a relationship could mean for the artist is suggested in "Penelope," in which Molly, an Anima figure that is never in a direct relationship to the Ego, promises that in her way she can take over from the mother the function of relationship that is the province of the Anima.

PROMISE OF THE ANIMA

Molly promises, like the Anima, a relationship with the physical world and with the eternal. "*The archetype of life itself*," Jung wrote, the Anima is "on the one hand an allurement to an intensification of life, but on the other she opens our eyes to its religious aspect" (*CW* 9.1:32, Jung's emphasis).[10] "Penelope" demonstrates both these effects through Molly. The Gilbert schema designates "Flesh" as the "organ" associated with "Penelope," and it is a critical commonplace that the episode is suffused with Molly's affirmation of the life of the flesh. Joyce, after all, appended to his list of adjectives describing the essential *Weib* of this episode the female affirmation, "*Ich bin das Fleisch das stets bejaht*" (*Letters*, 1:170). Molly's yea-saying, to be sure, focuses primarily on sexuality and her own sexual experience, although she has something to say about the goodness of food as well. She recalls the "fine salty taste" of the "port and potted meat" she and Boylan had shared that afternoon (*U* 18:132) and remembers wishing that she could have "picked every morsel" of the chicken at the Glencree dinner "out of my fingers it was so tasty and browned and as tender as anything" (*U* 18:430–32). As she considers going to the market in the morning, she exults in the thought of the "vegetables and cabbages and tomatoes and carrots and all kinds of splendid fruits all coming in lovely and fresh . . . Id love a big juicy pear now to melt in your mouth" (*U* 18:1499–1504).

In addition she demonstrates a curiosity and concern about the feelings and experiences of others, most prominently her husband's, about which, as John Henry Raleigh remarks, she pours out a "torrent of explicit information, speculation, exasperation, desperation, and even admiration" in "Penelope."[11] She also considers Stephen's situation, with his mother gone, "running wild now out at night away from his books and studies and not living at home on account of the usual rowy house" (*U* 18:1442–44). She ponders about Milly's feelings and activities (*U* 18:1004–39), assuring herself that "if there was anything wrong with her its me shed tell not him" (*U* 18:1021). And she expresses sympathy for the grief of Bloom's father after his wife's death: "poor old man I suppose he felt lost" (*U* 18:1062). Her thoughts about Rudolph Bloom connect in turn with her rather wistful and certainly ungrammatical definition of *love* as "two people . . . full up of each other that would feel the same way as you do" (*U* 18:1059–60).

This interest in the life around her, somewhat anomalous in light of her apparent isolation, is accompanied by her straightforward view of "the religious aspects of life." She acknowledges God as "the real father" to whom she confesses (*U* 18:112–13) and also as the Creator, "the first person in the universe before there was anybody that made it all" (*U* 18:1569–70). And whether the subject is the sexuality that so dominates her ramblings or the "nature" with which she feels so akin, she refers to this Creator as a capitalized *He*. "I suppose thats what a woman is supposed to be there for," she muses, "or He wouldnt have made us the way He did so attractive to men" (*U* 18:1518–20). This is followed, to be sure, by her calculated vision of using God's plan to her own advantage to extract money from her husband (*U* 18:1520–39), an angry calculation that gives way in turn to her concluding hymn to nature, beginning with "God of heaven" (*U* 18:1558). Twice in her soliloquy, at the beginning and at the end, she denies what "they" say, that "theres no God" (*U* 18:137, 1564), echoing the psalmist, who observes, also twice, in Psalms 14 and 53, that "The fool hath said in his heart, 'There is no God,' " following this with his assertion about such fools: "There is none that doeth good" (Psalms 14:1; 53:1). Molly herself concludes that "I wouldnt give a snap of my two fingers for all their learning" and then asks the question that goes to the heart of *Ulysses* and involves both protagonists: "Why dont they go and create something" (*U* 18:1564–65).

Both Bloom and Stephen are preoccupied throughout the day with the "why not?" and "how?" of creation, on the separate levels of biological and artistic creation. Bloom has "of his body no manchild" (*U* 14:271–72) and yearns for one, even as Stephen yearns for a "son of his soul" (*U* 9:171), the artistic creation "consubstantial with the father" (*U* 9:481). Both protagonists, however, remain sentimentalists in the sense of George Meredith's epigram, misquoted by Stephen in his telegram to Mulligan: "*The sentimentalist is he who would enjoy without incurring the immense debtorship for a thing done*" (*U* 9:550–51).[12] The final phrase is then reprised throughout the novel. Both Bloom and Stephen are evading "the thing done." Bloom wants to reproduce himself in a son but will not have sexual intercourse with his wife; Stephen wants to recreate the world in art but is as yet incapable of sustaining a viable relationship with the created world. Molly does not merely ask the question about creation and suggest that the answer lies in an acceptance of the natural order of the created world; she also embodies the solution for both men.

The Anima's ultimate role as a "function of relationship between the Ego and the unconscious" (*CW* 7:225) is realized through Molly, for Molly mediates between Stephen and Bloom. The exchange of identity between the two protagonists, to which Joyce referred in his notesheets, is curiously accomplished in their shared relationship with Molly. They have been accompanied in their journey together by memories of parallel *Arabian Nights* dreams involving Molly, and as the novel moves toward its close, the actualization of each protagonist's dream is promised to the other. Although in Stephen's dream he has been offered access to Molly, he departs, leaving her to Bloom, who thus enjoys the "land of promise" represented by the "adipose anterior and posterior female hemispheres, redolent of milk and honey and of excretory sanguine and seminal warmth" (*U* 17:2231–

33),[13] Molly's breasts and the "plump mellow yellow smellow melons of her rump" (*U* 17:2241). Bloom thus realizes Stephen's melon dream, which throughout the day has competed for dominance with Stephen's dream of the "ghostwoman" and has won out, freeing Stephen from the paralyzing relationship with his mother. Stephen's dream, then, becomes an actuality for Bloom.

On the other hand, Bloom's companion *Arabian Nights* dream of "his dame Mrs Moll with red slippers on in a pair of Turkey trunks" (*U* 14:509)—who has materialized in "Circe" quoting Stephen's talisman about winning a woman's love (*U* 15:315–17)—is in effect appropriated by Stephen, textually at least. For although Molly's soliloquy begins with her consideration of Bloom's request to "get his breakfast in bed with a couple of eggs" (*U* 18:1–2), it is of Stephen she is thinking when she muses, "I could have brought him his breakfast in bed" (*U* 18:1478–79), and decides that she would buy for the occasion "a nice pair of red slippers like those Turks with the fez used to sell" (*U* 18:1494–95). Thus Bloom's dream of "Mrs Moll with red slippers on" is textually transferred to Stephen by Molly.

The fruit of this circular relationship will apparently be Stephen's production of the son Bloom has been mooning about during the day—not a physical heir but the "son consubstantial with the father" represented by a work of art. Stephen, that is, will create *Ulysses*, the crowning expression of the spirit of the creative artist, which is at the same time dominated by Bloom, whose world, like Molly's, is the world of the flesh. Bloom is supremely comfortable in "the land of Phenomenon" (*U* 14:439); indeed, of the twenty-one uses of the word *phenomenon* in *Ulysses*, eighteen are associated with Bloom. The other three are attached to Stephen, all of them connected with his hope of escaping the rules of the land of Phenomenon through art. In the library, when Lyster asks about a "celestial phenomenon," Stephen's answer—"A star by night . . . a pillar of the cloud by day"—names the symbols that promise the personal immortality of the work of art and the escape from bondage to the flesh and death. Then, at the maternity hospital, Stephen rejects the general law of Phenomenon that all men must die, as well as the biblical law of achieving immortality through propagation, claiming instead his power to call "the past and its phantoms" into "life" through his art (*U* 14:438–43, 1112–14).[14]

Stephen in his artwork can offer Bloom the immortality that Bloom cannot achieve on his own, a deficit that is underlined by his inability to produce a son "of his body." Thus, despite Bloom's "tacit" dissent from Stephen's views on "the eternal affirmation of the spirit of man in literature" (*U* 17:29–30), he is made a part of that affirmation through the artistic immortality symbolized by Cassiopeia. In "Ithaca" it is promised that whatever his "selfcompelled" wanderings, Bloom will "somehow appear reborn above delta in the constellation of Cassiopeia" (*U* 17:2013–20).

Cassiopeia, the mother of Andromeda, is a minor character in the Perseus legend; the constellation that bears her name is sometimes called "the lady in the chair." Her position, however, is somewhat less genteel than this title would indicate: according to at least one account, when Poseidon placed her among the stars in a chair, he tied her on her back with her feet in the air as a punishment for her vanity. This would appear to explain Joyce's adjective "recumbent" and may well be a part of one of his involved jokes, especially since it is Bloom's memory of Molly "in Citron's basketchair" (*U* 4:206–7) that identifies her with the "creamfruit melon" of Stephen's dream. The constellation does indeed present the lopsided *W* Stephen claims for Shakespeare's "signature" among the stars. Yet the *W* may stand not only for the *William* of Shakespeare's name and hence for the immortality of the artist but also for *Woman*—who as the mother Eve has given the artist his mortal life and sustained him through childhood and who in the person of Molly, Joyce's comic Helen figure, can release him to manhood.

But if we turn the *W* upside down, it becomes an *M*, which is Molly's "signature." Presented by the narrator in "Ithaca" as "recumbent" (*U* 17:2314), Molly also participates in the immortalization associated with "neversetting" Cassiopeia, since she is the one who, in "Penelope," confirms Stephen as a poet and declares her faith in his ability to immortalize her, linking this confirmation to her own relationship with him. Remembering Stephen as a "darling little fellow" of five or six, she moves from that memory to a speculation about his development into a university student and a poet, slipping easily into a vision of his writing about her: "they all write about some woman in their poetry well I suppose he wont find many like me" (*U* 18:1311, 1333–34). She winds up her fantasy, then, with her prediction that he will "write about me lover and mistress publicly too with our 2 photographs in all the papers when he becomes famous" (*U* 18:1364–66), an outcome that has been substantially realized for Stephen's creator. In addition, Molly concludes the novel by reaffirming her original "yes" on the physical level to Bloom: "yes I said yes I will Yes" (*U* 18:1608–9). In sum, she countersigns not only "Bloom's passport to eternity," as Joyce promised (*Letters* 1:160), but Stephen's as well—and through Stephen's her own.

The promise of the Anima figure represented by Molly is thus a textual reality, affirmed and detailed in Molly's soliloquy, even though no conscious relationship between Ego and Anima is presented through the narrative of *Ulysses*. The promise of "Penelope" is instead attached in the text to the integrated artist of the future, who encompasses the psychic realities embodied in both Stephen and Bloom.[15]

SHADOW AND ANIMA IN RELATION: A GENDER EXCHANGE

Both Bloom and Molly are thus presented as potentially facilitating forces in Stephen's life. But they are also related to each other, a fact that is concretized in the text for the first time as "Ithaca" concludes with the picture of the two in bed together. And their fictional relationship shares in a complication that is a part of Jung's vision of Shadow and Anima in relation. For the Shadow stands between the Ego and the Anima, producing "an isolating layer of personal unconscious" (*CW* 12:177, note 118), a literal shadow that hides the Anima (*CW* 9.2:166). This shadow is permeable, though to what degree it may be dissipated depends on how successfully the Ego assimilates the contents that have formed the Shadow. If the Ego has not adequately taken in the reality of the Shadow, the Anima may be indistinguishable from the Shadow (*CW* 9.1:244), or, since both are largely unconscious, they may become "contaminated with each other," appearing in dreams as married (*CW* 12:177, note 118), like the Blooms in *Ulysses*. In this psychic situation, the masculine Shadow takes on feminine characteristics, while the feminine Anima takes on masculine characteristics. Such an assimilation of characteristics "natural" to the opposite sex is evident in the relationship between Leopold and Molly Bloom.

Jung characteristically insists that the forces at work in the individual psyche are intimately connected with psychic movements in society at large, so that psychic facts "are *not* just private concerns, but *social* phenomena" (*CW* 9.1:47). Thus, in a 1927 essay, "Woman in Europe" (*CW* 10:113–33), he extends to the social arena this psychic phenomenon of "mutual assimilation" (*CW* 10:127), identifying a confusion of masculine and feminine principles as characteristic of the "modern" relationship between the sexes. He makes clear that, when he refers to the "modern European woman" and her relationship to men, he is "necessarily writing about a minority," and an urban minority at that, since most men and women living outside the cities do not "really live in the Europe of today" (*CW* 10:114–15). In this essay he offers insights that are related to what Joyce intuitively expresses through Bloom and Molly in *Ulysses*.

Appropriating names from tradition, as is his habit, Jung has called the feminine principle of relatedness *Eros* and the masculine principle of intellectual discrimination *Logos*, insisting that these "empirical" concepts formulate "certain observable psychological facts."[16] In "Woman in Europe," Jung redefines *Eros* and *Logos* in modern terms as "psychic relatedness" and "objective interest" (*CW* 10:123), equating the feminine principle with insight into one's own psyche and masculinity with "knowing what one wants and doing what is necessary to achieve it." Both sexes, Jung points out, have been forced by changes in their society to take on qualities of the other: woman has acquired the "independence and critical judgment" (*CW* 10:126) associated with *Logos* because it has been necessary in order that she might "take her place as an independent factor in the social world" (*CW* 10:124), and man has won a "needful feminine insight into his own psyche," acquisitions so valuable, Jung says, that neither sex will ever part with them again (*CW* 10:126). Nor have they in the seventy years since this essay was published.[17]

In *Ulysses* we are given a fictional picture of this kind of "mutual assimilation" and the exchange of gender roles and attitudes that Jung prophesies, at least in embryo; for a considerable degree of confusion of masculine and feminine attributes underlies the portraits of Leopold and Molly Bloom. Bloom's feminine qualities are evident and remarked on from various perspectives throughout the novel, and they are explicitly dramatized in "Circe," where, as Stanley Sultan pointed out in his *Argument of* Ulysses, Bloom's hallucinatory progress duplicates a pattern identified in Richard von Krafft-Ebing's *Psychopathia Sexualis* as the "classic development of male perversion." Bloom moves, that is, "from passivity to masochism to feminization" in his successive psychic encounters with Molly, Bella, and Bello, during the last of which he is finally transformed into a woman.[18] Molly's assumption of masculine attitudes and roles remains a much less obvious aspect of her presence in the novel, which, of course, is mediated through most of the day by Bloom. Her apparently domineering role in "Calypso," for example, may be considered an aspect of Poldy's subservience or possibly a compensatory shift in the traditional feminine attitude, triggered by Poldy's abandonment of the traditionally masculine attitude of dominance. This role also surfaces in "Circe" when Molly, in her *Arabian Nights* persona, directs her "poor little hubby" to call her "Mrs Marion from this out" (*U* 15:306–7). At any rate, the gender confusion that is visually represented in "Circe" is confirmed in "Penelope." Both Bloom and Molly invade the sphere of the other sex.

Bloom's feminine characteristics have received considerable critical attention ever since the publication of *Ulysses*.[19] The text, of course, insists on these qualities in "Circe," most obviously in Dr. Dixon's caricature of Bloom as "a finished example of the new womanly man" (*U* 15:1798–99), a designation that is quoted in most discussions of this aspect of Bloom's character. This designation is almost immediately followed in the text by Bloom's cry: "O, I so want to be a mother" (*U* 15:1817). Indeed, in the last couple of decades, Bloom's feminine qualities, as well as his assumption of feminine roles, have received substantial critical approval as evidence of a wholesome androgyny. This is especially the case among feminist critics, for whom, as Bonnie Kime Scott has pointed out, the "androgynous individual was the most widely discussed model in the mid-1970s," noting further that Bloom offers "a model of androgyny and male nurturing."[20]

Marilyn French, whose deservedly influential *Book as World* was first published in 1976, defends Bloom's androgyny as more or less natural and asserts that Joyce "saw feminacy in men somewhat positively despite the narrator's scorn,"[21] referring to possibly the most vivid picture of Bloom's feminization outside "Circe," that is, the "Cyclops" narrator's description of Bloom as "one of those mixed middlings . . . lying up in the hotel . . . once a month with a headache like a totty with her courses" (*U* 12:1658–60). Asserting that with Bloom Joyce was challenging "profoundly Western sexual mores, the attitudes of an entire culture" toward sexuality and gender, French chides critics like Stanley Sultan and Darcy O'Brien with their tendency to see Bloom's "problem as a 'failure to be unequivocally masculine.' " These critics, and Hugh Kenner as well, she points out, had seen Bloom's sexuality as "a sickness that must be cured."[22]

To be sure, attitudes toward sexuality and gender have changed in the generations following Bloom's appearance on the scene of the novel, and evaluations of Bloom's feminine qualities have changed as well. Indeed, Diane Henderson identifies "heterosexual male readers . . . who perceive themselves as 'womanly,' sensitive, post-Dedalian," for whom "Leopold Bloom can stand as Everyman."[23] Not long ago John Bormanis claimed for Bloom, in addition to his traditionally designated role as "spiritual father," the status of "surrogate mother for Stephen Dedalus," since "the functions and attributes of mothering belong to Bloom,"[24] while Suzette Henke has also recently asserted that "Bloom has become more of a *mother* to Stephen than a substitute father."[25] When Henke lists the "prominent signifiers" of Bloom's "psychological androgyny" as "sympathy, gentleness, vulnerability, and solicitude," however, she points out that, when Bloom actually "becomes" a woman in "Circe," all these admirable qualities "are radically transformed in the context of cultural interpretation" into "masochistic subservience."[26]

In Henke's discussion of Bloom's androgyny, as in most such discussions, Dr. Dixon's label of "the new womanly man" is prominent. But this designation, as Robert Byrnes has forcefully asserted, brings into the discussion Otto Weininger, who originated the phrase in his 1906 *Sex and Character*, where he claimed that Jewish men were by nature womanly, a "pet theory" also of James Joyce, according to Ellmann (*JJ* 463). In his essay on "Bloom's Sexual Tropes," Byrnes, acknowledging that by the time Joyce wrote "Circe" his sophistication about psychoanalytic theory had long since gone beyond the "inspired quackery" of Weininger's "passé pop psychology," nevertheless makes a convincing case for Joyce's use of Weininger plus Krafft-Ebing as a "template" for his portrait of Bloom. Byrnes's answer to the question of why Joyce attached "these anachronistic theories" to Bloom is simple and for me convincing: "In the interests of high comedy."[27] We should perhaps remember Frank Budgen's contention that sexual perversity was an aspect of life that was to Joyce "comic."[28]

Bloom, Byrnes contends, is a great character "because of his perversities, not in spite of them,"[29] a contention that recalls the responses of earlier nonscholar critics. In the late twenties, Rebecca West saw Bloom as a "serious representation of the court jester," embodying "the liberation of a suppressed human tendency" and thus accounting for the "tremendous force behind *Ulysses*."[30] "Nothing is suggested in the course of the book," West asserted, "which would reconcile him to the nobility of life"; at the same time, however, she asserted, "most solemnly," that "Leopold Bloom is one of the greatest creations of all time."[31] In a review of the first American edition of *Ulysses* in the thirties, Horace Gregory pronounced Bloom "one of the great comic characters of all literature."[32] And a generation later Marshall McLuhan characterized Bloom as Charlie Chaplin's "literary twin."[33]

Certainly Bloom's feminine qualities contribute to this comic effect, and they are a fact of the text that is confirmed by a number of Molly's memories of Poldy in "Penelope." Remembering him during an illness, she comments that he "looked more a man with his beard a bit grown" (*U* 18:30), which may be paired with her wish that he would "even smoke a pipe like father to get the smell of a man" (*U* 18:508). As for his housewifely ways, she is pleased that he "always wipes his feet on the mat when he comes in wet or shine" (*U* 18:226) but irritated that "he prefers plottering about the house so you cant stir with him any side whats your program today" (*U* 18:506–7). Cooking, Molly says, is something Poldy "thinks he knows a great lot about . . . mathering everything he can scour off the shelves into it" (*U* 18:519–20), and she has nothing good to say about his obsessive interest in women's clothes, especially the "black closed breeches he made me buy takes you half an hour to let them down . . . always with some brandnew fad every other week" (*U* 18:251–53). Although she remembers nostalgically an earlier time when "I liked the way he made love . . . he knew the way to take a woman" (*U* 18:328–29), even if he "never knew how to embrace well like Gardner" (*U* 18:332), she concludes that "hes not natural like the rest of the world" (*U* 18:268). And she has given reasons for her conclusion.

Molly herself, however, as she reveals herself in her soliloquy, participates in the interchange, characteristic of modern male-female relations, Jung says, of traditionally gender-specific attitudes and roles. On a purely practical level, she appears to have turned to employment outside the home, "selling the clothes and strumming in the coffee palace" (*U* 18:561–62), when Poldy lost his job with Hely's, and Scott surmises that in another culture "Molly might have been the better breadwinner."[34] Scott also points to Molly's downgrading of the authority of priests and their secular counterparts, doctors,[35] in contrast to the traditional feminine awe of these authority figures. But it is in her expressions of sexual desires and attitudes that Molly reveals how far she is from the "purely feminine sexual pattern of unconsciousness and passivity," which Jung sees as "natural" for women (*CW* 10:117) but a pattern that the modern woman has to a degree renounced.

Indeed, the modern woman's "mental masculinization," Jung says, may well result in her replacing the "receptive sexuality of woman" with "an aggressive, urgent form of sexuality that is more characteristic of a man" (*CW* 10:119), a tendency that has been regularly perceived in "Penelope" and is underlined by Molly's desire, expressed twice, to *be* a man, "to get up on a lovely woman" (*U* 18:1146–47) "just to try with that thing they have swelling up on you so hard and at the same time so soft when you touch it" (*U* 18:1382–83). Mary Colum's observation that for "normal people" the revelation of Molly's mind in "Penelope" would seem "an exhibition of the mind of a female gorilla who has been corrupted by contact with humans"[36] has often been quoted. This assessment suggests that even reasonably liberated contemporaries considered Molly far from "purely feminine," and Harriet Shaw Weaver's "pre-human" label for "Penelope" (*Letters* 1:180, note 1) points in the same direction.

Darcy O'Brien early on identified the origins of Molly's powerful sexuality in traditional Irish ideas about woman as "an eternally recurring version of Sheela-na-gig," corresponding to "the usual Irish portrayal of women as randy birds of prey."[37] This view of Molly as conforming to a recurring archetype, in one form or another, to one degree or another, has been a constant of the *Ulysses* critical tradition since its beginnings.[38] Even Jung, in the course of his debate with himself about whether *Ulysses* could be categorized as "symbolic," suggested that

"Mrs. Bloom perhaps conceals an anima entangled in worldliness" (*CW* 15:123). And French's more recent reminder that to discuss Molly "as if she were a discrete and autonomous character is to mistake her function in the novel"[39] assumes the same kind of archetypal role for Molly.

But the longevity of the archetypal perspective does not necessarily make this view a meaningless cliché. John H. Lammers has recently examined closely a favorite analog for Molly in Chaucer's Wife of Bath, another "strong woman," who is "powerfully and obsessively sexual," and has suggested an archetypal basis for similarities between these characters.[40] Both these fictional women, Lammers points out, "continually attempt to dominate men and life"[41] under cultural conditions that are similarly discouraging for such an attempt. We may remember that in addition to the revelations of the Wife of Bath's Prologue, her concern with domination is reflected in the central question of her tale and the unchallenged answer. The question is the one that has also been attributed to Freud in somewhat different form: What do women most desire?" And the answer, which the loathly lady of the Wife's tale provides to the young knight, is "Wommen desiren to have sovereyntee / As wel over hir housbond as hir love" (lines 1038–39).

Certainly Molly demonstrates this desire for sovereignty and domination. When she lays out her campaign for seducing Stephen (*U* 18:1363–64)[42] or for managing Bloom (*U* 18:1521–39), she reveals her determination to be in control, despite the inhibitions of the culture in which she finds herself, one very similar to Chaucer's society: "male-dominated, decadent, Roman Catholic."[43] It is furthermore obvious that Molly has planned the Bloomsday rendezvous with Boylan with considerable care and initiative, an element of control that extends to the afternoon's activity as well: "I made him . . . " "I let him . . . " (*U* 18:154–56). This kind of control at least hints at Molly's appropriation of the primary masculine characteristic, as Jung defines it in modern terms: "knowing what one wants and doing what is necessary to achieve it" (*CW* 10:126).

Lammers notes that "both Chaucer and Joyce seem to deal with the same type of society" and theorizes that "two great artists might create the same artistic archetype."[44] His linkage of the societal matrix with the appearance of archetypal characters could hardly be more Jungian, even though his terminology quarrels with Jung's insistence that an archetype is itself "a hypothetical and irrepresentable model." Thus neither the Wife of Bath nor Molly Bloom could be called an archetype by Jung's definition, but both are archetypal images, each "tak[ing] its colour from the individual consciousness in which it happens to appear" (*CW* 9.1:5). In Jung's view such images are the gift of the poet to his culture, for in the same way that "one-sidedness" in an individual's conscious attitude is balanced and corrected by "reactions from the unconscious," art represents "a process of self-regulation in the life of nations and epochs" (*CW* 15:83), serving as a societal unconscious. Jung envisions archetypal images, produced spontaneously by the artist, as a kind of collective remedy for the psychic imbalance of an era. If indeed Chaucer and Joyce were both dealing with a society that overstressed nobility and piety and Christian virtue, the Wife of Bath and Molly Bloom may be seen as confirming Jung's theory of the archetype as a remedy, for each presents a corrective for such one-sidedness.

Admittedly there is much in Joyce's fiction and in his biography to suggest that he did not much like women, especially, to quote once again his much-quoted remark to Mary Colum, "women who know anything." This remark is in fact included by Ellmann in his account of Joyce's Paris years, along with a cluster of other notably misogynist comments (*JJ* 631). Frank Budgen, too, remembering those Paris years, has remarked on Joyce's bitterness about "woman's . . . perpetual urge to usurp all the functions of the male" and especially "to rivalize with menfolk in the things of the mind."[45] Together, these reports suggest that Joyce accepted the traditional, gender-bound assumption that "things of the mind" represent a male province essentially alien to women, an assumption that is also basic to Jung's definitions of masculine and feminine principles as *Logos* and *Eros*: the principle of intellectual discrimination *versus* the principle of relationship.[46]

Joyce is intuitively a truth teller, whatever the quality of his misogyny, about which there is continuing debate,[47] and the bitterness of his reported remarks about women's invasion of masculine domains may well testify to his awareness that the old assumptions about the nature of an accepted masculine-feminine opposition, which he had shared, were threatened, if not crumbling. Indeed, when he spoke with Arthur Power about the relationship between men and women, it was in terms of a revolution. In *The Doll's House*, he told Power, Ibsen's purpose was "the emancipation of women, which has caused the greatest revolution in our time in the most important relationship there is—that between men and women; the revolt of women against the idea that they are the mere instruments of men." Joyce gave no assent to Power's assertion that the relationship between the sexes had been "ruined" by the revolution, and he had no opinion to offer on whether men and women were "happier or unhappier than they were before." He simply said that "the relationship between the sexes is now on a different basis."[48] This difference is foreshadowed in the marriage of the Blooms as it is revealed in "Penelope," where Molly "countersigns" Bloom's intermittent revelations of this relationship through the day of *Ulysses* and also confirms much that is dramatized in "Circe."

In "Penelope" the archetypal Molly Bloom, who has already appeared as Gea-Tellus in Joyce's text (*U* 17:2313),[49] may also be seen as a comic Helen of Troy, Jung's personification of the Anima proper. In this identification she offers to Stephen, the conscious artist, the promise of an authentic relationship with the physical world and mediates between him and the world of the unconscious—Bloom's world and beyond. Through Molly as Anima, Stephen is also promised the possibility of artistic immortality, for through a relationship with her he will truly experience life and can thus legitimately recreate that life in his art. All this, though not realized in the narrative of *Ulysses*, may be drawn from the text of "Penelope."

In addition, Molly reveals herself as an aggressively sexual figure, foreshadowing a feminine insistence on sexual autonomy in the twentieth century that has perhaps reached its height with the contemporary phenomenon of the single mother by choice. She is complemented by her husband, Bloom, the womanly man, whose passive life strategies offer a striking contrast to the traditional hero. Thus, Molly and Leopold Bloom, individually and in relation to each other, reveal and foreshadow the tendency toward cultural androgyny that has been increasingly characteristic of male-female relationships in the twentieth century.

PART THREE

Epilogue

EIGHT

Beyond Integration
The Artist as Prophet

Ulysses has more than one ending, as might be expected of a novel with more than one protagonist.[1] The narrative comes to a close in "Ithaca," the episode that brings Bloom and Stephen back to Number 7 Eccles Street and, at its close, introduces Molly in relation to Bloom for the first time in the novel, thus providing a lead-in for Molly's concluding monologue. We see Bloom with Stephen at the beginning of "Ithaca" and with Molly at the end, and in between there is a long stretch of time when Bloom is alone. Although Bloom appears to be the sustaining character in "Ithaca," all three of the major characters in the novel, who in this Jungian reading parallel the major characters in Jung's interior drama of individuation, are successively in focus, with no subsidiary characters in evidence. The novel then ends for each separately, in "Ithaca" for Stephen and then for Bloom, in "Penelope" for Molly. Stephen's exit from Bloom's garden, almost exactly halfway through "Ithaca," marks the ending to his story. Bloom exits into sleep as "Ithaca" closes, and, of course, we have a third ending in Molly's final reiterated "Yes" at the conclusion of "Penelope."

INTIMATIONS OF INTEGRATION IN *ULYSSES*

All these endings are clearly positive, an affirmative judgment that is not necessarily supported by narrative incident but instead depends upon evidence in the text—*as* text. For by the time the novel closes, the text has taken on an autonomy that enables the reader to identify what Karen Lawrence in her *Odyssey of Style in* Ulysses calls "possibilities of meaning," or "possibilities of plot," although these multiple possibilities make it difficult for a critic to "force [the novel] into a statement of meaning" or a "single pattern."[2] The Jungian reading I have been tracing is thus a possibility of meaning that does not obviate other possible meanings. It is, I believe, supported by the text, which, as I stated earlier, may support other meanings as well. As Lawrence has demonstrated, by the close of the novel, we no longer have a narrator, reliable or otherwise, and *Ulysses* has moved from "the psychology of characters" to what she calls "the consciousness of the book."[3] As I read this "consciousness," *Ulysses* closes on an affirmative note.

Taking the optimistic endings in order, when Stephen walks through Bloom's garden gate, under the "heaventree of stars," it is with a textual promise of a new relationship to the world and to himself, indeed, a rebirth in a new dimension. In the light from Molly's window, he and Bloom have seen each other "in both mirrors of the reciprocal flesh of theirhisnothis fellowfaces" (*U* 17:1183–84), and Stephen is thereafter reborn into the world as an artist capable of recreating that world in art. As the narrative concludes at the end of "Ithaca," the text also promises a rebirth for Bloom, "the childman weary, the manchild in the womb" (*U* 17:2317–18). And the episode closes with a vision of "Darkinbad the Brightdayler" (*U* 17:2329–30), an image that may be seen as combining Bloom and Stephen, the darkness of the unconscious dimension of the artist's personality with the daylight of consciousness, both essential parts of the "larger and greater personality within" (*CW* 9.1:131). This final image, in fact, clearly harmonizes with Jung's description of the superordinate personality that he names the Self, "bright and dark and yet neither" (*CW* 14:107, note 66). Finally, Molly's "Yes," which is the last word of the novel, argues against Joyce's claim that "Penelope" has "no beginning, middle, or end" (*Letters* 1:172), for this final consent has always been seized upon as a conclusion to the novel that is affirmative in letter and in spirit.

Thus, at the close of *Ulysses* Joyce's autobiographical fiction reaches a resolution, tentative though it may be, which significantly resembles the successful outcome of Jung's individuation process, remembering always that success in individuation tends to be a somewhat unstable compound. As the Ego confronts the Shadow and assimilates previously unconscious contents, the process of individuation, Jung says, gradually ceases to be linear and evolves into what he calls "a circumambulation of the self" (*MDR* 196). An analogous shift in structuring may be seen in Joyce's autobiographical fiction. *A Portrait of the Artist as a Young Man*, that is, follows the social/psychic development of the artist-hero, who is the absolute center of the novel, in a comparatively straight line. In *Ulysses*, however, the subject is split into Stephen and Bloom, who together embody the psychic situation of the developing artist as he confronts the unconscious dimension of his personality and accommodates to it. Joyce first emphasizes the split in his artist-subject by providing parallel narratives for the morning hours, one for Stephen, one for Bloom, at the same time introducing a circular movement through verbal and situational correspondences in the text of the first six episodes that point to a larger unity that embraces both protagonists. The circular movement around an unspecified center continues as these connections multiply in later episodes, subordinating linear progression in the narrative to a web of correspondences that, from a Jungian perspective, point toward the Self.

In his autobiography, Jung says that his realization that "everything points toward the center" gave him "stability" and an "inner peace" (*MDR* 197). And

Ulysses closes with a promise of this kind of stability, the integration of the personality of the artist. It is true that Stephen stops short of an authentic encounter with the Anima, but he has freed himself from the crippling relationship with his mother, and the text presents the promise that Molly holds for Stephen's future. There is thus at least a tentative balance achieved in the text of the novel between male and female and between consciousness and the unconscious, with the conscious personality in control—somewhat humbled perhaps by his awareness that he is only part of a greater personality but still in charge of his destiny as an artist. The text gives us reason to assume that, with the expanded awareness of the dimensions of the unconscious, revealed through Bloom, Stephen has experienced a beneficial humbling of the Ego and a "shifting of the centre of the personality from the ego to the self" (*CW* 9.1:181).

Even though much of the last half of *Ulysses* leaves the beaten track of the conscious world for excursions into the trackless domain of the unconscious, so that the connections between Joyce's text and outer reality become difficult to assess, the balance in *Ulysses* holds. "A critical line of demarcation" has been drawn, as Jung says it must be, between the Ego and "the unconscious figures" at the same time that these figures have been granted "relative autonomy and reality (of a psychic nature)" (*CW* 9.2:23–24). The Ego, having won some apprehension of the nature of the Self, maintains his position as mediator between the outer and inner worlds. It has been, of course, the thesis of this study that *Ulysses* exhibits patterns of psychic development that parallel stages in Jung's hypothetical individuation process, and my conclusion is that the outcome of the novel parallels the productive expansion of consciousness that leads theoretically to an integrated personality. This wholeness is the sine qua non for the artist of the future.

PSYCHIC INFLATION IN *FINNEGANS WAKE*: A SCHIZOPHRENIC TEXT

Ulysses, of course, is not the end of Joyce's autobiographical fiction. *Finnegans Wake* continues the portrait of the artist, and with *Finnegans Wake* the fiction moves beyond the integration that is tenuously promised at the close of *Ulysses*. The *Wake* indeed presents a fictional situation that parallels another possible outcome of the assimilation of unconscious contents, a situation in which the Ego becomes "dissolved in identification with the self." This overreaching of the Ego—which is sometimes temporary but may be permanent—gives rise, Jung says, to "a sort of nebulous superman" (*CW* 8:225). The Ego, Jung points out, "lives in space and time and must adapt itself to their laws if it is to exist at all" (*CW* 16:291), so that for the living subject this disintegrating outcome of the assimilation of unconscious materials is extremely unfortunate. A similar judgment may be made—and has been made from time to time—about *Finnegans Wake*, in which time disappears, linear historicity disappears, and personality disappears,[4] dissolving into its paired opposites, as the fiction attempts to make the *whole* of the unconscious conscious, to absorb the Self into the Ego.[5]

But the Self cannot be completely comprehended by the Ego, Jung says, without a paradoxical loss of conscious identity, an unmitigated psychic disaster that Jung equates symbolically with being "devoured by the monster" (*CW* 7:281).[6] An analogous situation presents itself to readers of *Finnegans Wake*, who find themselves in what Margot Norris has so aptly labeled a "decentered universe," in which there are no "characters as such, but ciphers in formal relation to each other."[7] Even the sleeping hero, as John Bishop points out in his 1986 study of the *Wake*, "has no consciousness of himself as an 'ego' or an 'identity' at all."[8] Thus Joyce's autobiographical fiction, which has progressed from the Ego-centered subject of *A Portrait* as a child and a young man to the split subject—a diminished Ego and a dominant non-Ego—in *Ulysses*, finally arrives at an Ego-deprived landscape in *Finnegans Wake*.

Throughout Jung's writings on the relations between the Ego and the unconscious, he cautions repeatedly that the assimilation of unconscious contents, necessary though it is for mature individuation, carries with it a very real danger: it may go too far. For "the rediscovered unconscious," Jung points out, "often has a really dangerous effect on the ego" (*CW* 8:87): "a liberated unconscious can thrust the ego aside and overwhelm it" (*CW* 8:88). Thus "the great psychic danger which is always connected with individuation, or the development of the self," Jung reminds his reader, "lies in the identification of ego-consciousness with the self. This produces an inflation which threatens consciousness with dissolution" (*CW* 9.1:145). "Psychic inflation," or the "state of being puffed up" (*CW* 7:140), appears over and over in Jung's discussions of individuation, in which he sees this inflation as an "illegitimate" extension of the personality (*CW* 7:270) or even "a psychic catastrophe" (*CW* 9.2:24).

Jung pictures the state he calls "inflation" as an almost literal blowing up, the personality likened to an overinflated balloon that bursts. The personality comes apart, breaks into pieces, when the conscious personality "takes too many unconscious contents upon itself." The "distortion of the personality" that results, Jung says, "is almost impossible to deal with" (*CW* 7:274). Almost any of Jung's numerous descriptions of psychic inflation may also be used to describe the character of *Finnegans Wake*, which has proved, if not impossible, certainly extremely difficult for critics to deal with in any of the ways to which they have become accustomed. Margaret Schlauch, the eminent medieval scholar, writing immediately after the publication of the *Wake*, warned of "the danger of charging language with so many counterpointed meanings that in the end it signifies nothing at all—except in the creator's imagination."[9] Recognizing that the effects that Joyce apparently wanted to achieve in the *Wake* would be "perceptible only to the most sophisticated and literate of readers,"[10] Schlauch also cautioned that "the better (i.e., more creative) a reader is, the farther he may get away from the author's intent." And whatever the virtues of the "participating reader," "the book as a whole has been so carefully and consciously planned . . . that it would obviously be a serious thing to diverge from the main scheme . . . by way of some tangent of personal interest or prejudice. One might never get back again."[11]

In 1965, a generation after its publication, Bernard Benstock, a most flexible and perceptive critic, recorded the "cold, logical realization that *Finnegans Wake* as an enigma may well go unsolved," predicting that "*Finnegans Wake* will never be fully read by any reader."[12] Thirty years later, Thomas Jackson Rice, in the 1995 *Joyce Studies Annual*, resurrecting Joyce's own tunneling metaphor for the composition of the *Wake*, points out that "those who have 'tunneled into the mountain' from the top-down, analyzing its grand themes and meaning, have yet to meet those who have tunneled into the novel from the bottom-up, examining the book's allusions, motifs, microstructure, and origins and development."[13] Rice suggests that a consideration of the *Wake* in the light of the "emergent sciences of complexity" may lead to a better grasp of this "literary model of complexity," but it is fair to note that his essay concludes with a pair of conditional sentences, beginning "If we can . . . "[14] The fairly standard critical approach to *Finnegans Wake* as a dream is seemingly supported by Joyce's comment to Ole Vindig that "what I write simply cannot be expressed in any other way than like dream talk,"[15] but as Jung points out about dreams in general, "Without a knowledge of the conscious situation, the meaning of the dream [must remain] in doubt" (*CW* 16:155), a psychic fact that Norris echoes in her observation about *Finnegans Wake* that, "without the waking events and conscious thoughts of the subject, it is difficult to make sense of Wakean events."[16]

In a 1916 essay, "The Structure of the Unconscious," Jung pointed out that schizophrenia, "the most common form of madness," is "characterized precisely by the fact that the unconscious almost entirely suppresses the function of the conscious mind and supplants it" (*CW* 7:277). However consciously constructed, the text of *Finnegans Wake* exhibits this usurpation of consciousness and may thus in a very literal sense be called a schizophrenic text. Margaret McBride, in fact, has suggested in a presentation to the Eighth Miami J'yce Conference in 1994 that Joyce consciously employed language patterns associated with schizophrenia in the *Wake*.[17] And Dr. N. J. C. Andreasen, a professor of psychiatry in the School of Medicine at the University of Iowa, has "diagnosed" *Finnegans Wake* as "psychotic" in her 1973 "Portrait of the Artist as a Schizoid." In her diagnosis, however, she distinguishes between the artist and the artwork: "Although eccentric, the man never became psychotic. But his art did."[18] This diagnosis brought an immediate protest from J. B. Lyons, a Dublin physician and author of *James Joyce and Medicine* (1973). "If such a thing as psychotic art can exist," queried Dr. Lyons, "must it not be the creation of a psychotic artist?"[19] Andreasen, in response, pointed out that "a fundamental assumption of my article and of much modern criticism" is that, "in the case of a creative writer," we can indeed "separate a man from his work and judge the value of each independently."[20]

In this she agrees with Jung, who has asserted that "the work of art has its own psychology, which is sometimes notably different from the psychology of the artist."[21] Indeed, Jung has more than once registered his objection to "the way [psychoanalysis] meddles with art" (*CW* 7:138), treating the work of art as "nothing but a symptom." "A work of art," Jung insists, "is clearly not a symptom but a genuine creation," which "can only be understood on its own merits" and not "in the same terms as a neurosis" (*CW* 8:365). He has given considerable thought to the distinction between the psychology of the artist and the independent psychology of the work of art, whether literary or plastic. Joyce, Jung points out, is a "literary brother" of Pablo Picasso (*CW* 15:135), whose work also exhibits schizophrenic elements, though Jung states unequivocally that "I regard neither Picasso nor Joyce as psychotics" (*CW* 15:137, note 3).[22] In his essay, " 'Ulysses': A Monologue" (*CW* 15:109–34), Jung acknowledges that the analogy between the language of *Ulysses* and schizophrenic writing is "startling" but asserts that any notion of its being written by a schizophrenic is contradicted by that fact that "the whole book is borne along on a subterranean current of life that shows singleness of aim and rigorous selectivity, both these being unmistakable proof of the existence of a unified personal will and directed intention" (*CW* 15:116).

Hans Prinzhorn makes the same kind of distinction between the character of the artwork and the mental state of the artist in his *Artistry of the Mentally Ill*, published in German in 1922, the same year, of course, that *Ulysses* was first published. Prinzhorn found traits in the art of schizophrenics that were clearly related to "the most serious recent art," especially "a renunciation of the outside world" and "a decisive turn inward upon the self." He countered "the astonishing fact that the schizophrenic outlook and that displayed in recent art can be described only by the same words" with the reminder that the artist's alienation from reality, unlike the schizophrenic's, "involves conscious and rational decisions."[23] Indeed the fragmentation and the retreat from representation that characterize much of the last half of *Ulysses* and all of *Finnegans Wake* are also characteristic of art as a whole in the first half of the century, appearing first in the plastic arts but evidenced in literature and music as well. At the time Joyce was producing his "Work in Progress," Arthur Power recalls that "everybody was experimenting wildly" in all the arts, determined "to create a new art to express modern life."[24]

"What is wrong with our art, that most delicate of all instruments for reflecting the national psyche?" Jung asked. "How are we to explain the blatantly pathological element in modern paintings? Atonal music? The far-reaching influence of Joyce's fathomless *Ulysses*?" (*CW* 10:210). A possible answer, he suggested to one of his correspondents, is that "the unconscious comes to the surface in modern art and . . . destroys the orderliness that is characteristic of consciousness."[25] Painters, who regularly "give visible shape to the dominant trends of the age," had been for some time taking as their subject "the disintegration of forms," producing pictures that were "distinguished by their 'meaninglessness' as much as by their deliberate aloofness from the spectator" (*CW* 10:383). Thus, if Stanislaus Joyce could declare that *Finnegans Wake* was "not only unreadable but unprintable,"[26] so also could his brother James, the author of this "unreadable" book, complain that Igor Stravinsky was writing music that "not even a canary could sing" (*JJ* 669).

Jung quotes Carola Giedion-Welcker's characterization of "Work in Progress" as "projected into a sphere of absolute irreality" (*CW* 15:111, note 6), an assessment that echoes Joyce's own judgment that his final work was "completely above reality," to which he added that it "transcend[s] humans, things, senses, and enter[s] the realm of complete abstraction." Joyce's identification of Anna Livia and HCE as "at the same time the city and its founder, the river and the mountain, as well as both sexual organs," added to his reminder that there is no "chronological ordering of the action,"[27] supports his location of the *Wake* in "the realm of complete abstraction."

It is, of course, significant that *Finnegans Wake*, "an acknowledged but unread masterpiece," in David Hayman's phrase, continues to engage the intellectual energies of an impressive group of Joyceans. And even though Hayman, one of the leading figures in that group, may characterize the *Wake* as "a cult item conned by footnote hounds and citation grubbers,"[28] the fascination exercised by this magnificent oddity is clearly genuine and testifies to the power of the work. Jung, no admirer of modern art, has observed that "the more deeply the vision of the creative mind penetrates [into the collective unconscious], the stranger it becomes to mankind in the mass," until it reaches a depth where "it is difficult to decide whether it is a morbid product or whether it is incomprehensible because of its extraordinary profundity" (*CW* 6:192). Eric Neumann, noting that in modern art the "devastation of all that was held to be real" was a response to "an overwhelming force from within," saw Joyce among the great artists who made "conscious use of the situation, dissolving configured outward reality into a stream of feeling and action that, though coming from within, is nevertheless directed."[29]

After more than half a century we have not yet discovered with any certainty toward what end the "stream of feeling and action" that is *Finnegans Wake* is directed, nor has any consensus been reached about whether the *Wake* is morbid or extraordinarily profound. To be sure, early hopes that the work would become comprehensible have in the main dissipated. Nevertheless, whether as a continuation of the autobiographical fiction or as a gloss on its earlier stages, the *Wake* represents the last stage in a fictional voyage of self-discovery, self-definition, and self-revelation, a voyage that, like the self-analyses of Joyce's great contemporaries, Freud and Jung, turned inward and engaged the world beyond consciousness. The Self that is being discovered, defined, and revealed in Joyce's fiction is not, of course, identical with that of James Joyce;[30] rather, the successive fictions, moving ever inward, continue the development of the portrait of the artist-hero that Joyce began in 1904 with the slight, not quite comprehensible essay that he named "A Portrait of the Artist." Even as he insisted in his interview with Adolf Hoffmeister that his work "goes in a straight line of development," indeed is "almost indivisible," Joyce responded to Hoffmeister's question about the similarity or difference between *Ulysses* and "Work in Progress" with "I believe that there is no difference."[31]

But there is a difference between the two, and the difference is crucial: *Ulysses* is comprehensible and *Finnegans Wake* is not. To be sure, in its later episodes, where the unconscious is given considerable latitude in the text, *Ulysses* exhibits much of the same kind of abstraction that led Joyce to locate the *Wake* in a realm "completely above reality." But this abstraction is balanced by the exhaustive concreteness of the initial presentation of characters and scene. Even though the Bloom and Stephen we see in "Ithaca" are visualized by their creator as "heavenly bodies, wanderers like the stars at which they gaze" (*Letters* 1:160), both men have been solidly established as characters in the earlier episodes. In addition, they have been placed in an almost compulsively *real* setting, on a specific historical date, during which their movements, for the most part, may be not only traced but timed.[32] And this grounding, so generously and convincingly done, cannot be undone. Both men retain their proper names and their individual fictional histories through any side trips in the domain of the unconscious, and for the reader they retain their authenticity as fictional characters to the end. "Penelope," then, which returns, as Joyce said, to the "human," not only presents the living Molly to the reader but restores Bloom and Stephen to human dimensions in relation to Molly. The balance between consciousness and the unconscious holds, and *Ulysses* endures as an integrated whole, "the most finished," Joyce said, of all his works.[33] In contrast to the fragmented portraits in *Finnegans Wake*, Picasso-like in their distortions, *Ulysses* completes a recognizable portrait of The Artist in the twentieth century, a combination of autobiography and modern myth.

ARTIST AS PROPHET

Despite the use of timeless myth as an ordering device, attributed to Joyce by T. S. Eliot in his early essay and accepted by generations of critics, *Ulysses* is also solidly placed in time, in history. Jung saw it as "a *document humain* of our time" (*CW* 15:123), and Rebecca West concluded that, even though it was not particularly pleasant for her to read *Ulysses*, it was something she had to do because in this novel Joyce had analyzed and synthesized in art the experience of his time and her own.[34]

Joyce himself claimed even more for his novel in his "conversations" with Arthur Power.[35] Power's *Conversations with James Joyce* is a unique account, virtually the only record we have of extended comments by Joyce on his published work, especially *Ulysses*.[36] Reconstructed by Power from notes he had made after returning home from various talks with Joyce in Paris after the publication of *Ulysses*, these approximated transcriptions of Joyce's words were compiled and published more than thirty years after Joyce's death. Although Power acknowledges a certain inadequacy in his method of recording Joyce's comments,[37] there is an authenticity and a consistency in his reconstructions that is reminiscent of Frank Budgen's reports of his conversations with Joyce in *James Joyce and the Making of* Ulysses, to which Power's account provides a kind of companion piece in miniature. In this chapter I refer to the comments Power reports as a reasonably reliable measure of Joyce's attitudes toward *Ulysses* and its place in history.

Asserting that "you must be caught up in the spirit of your time," Joyce reminded Power that "the best authors of any period have always been the prophets,"[38] echoing the dictum in *Stephen Hero* that "the poet is the intense centre of the life of his age to which he stands in a relation than which none can be more vital" (*SH* 78). Jung too assigns a prophetic role to the artist, who, because of his "relative lack of adaptation," "takes to the back streets and alleys because he cannot endure the broad highway" and is thus "the first to discover what it is that would meet the unconscious needs of his age" (*CW* 15:83). Therein lies the "social significance" of the artist, who, by giving shape to the archetypal image, "educat[es] the spirit of the age, conjuring up the forms in which the age is most lacking" and thus "compensat[ing] the inadequacy and one-sidedness of the present" (*CW* 15:82–83).

Among the artist-prophets, "those who brought something new into literature,"[39] Joyce naturally included himself, as did Jung, for that matter, although Jung left it to history to decide whether Joyce was a major or a minor prophet. "Like every true prophet," Jung says, "the artist is the unwitting mouthpiece of the psychic secrets of his time and is often as unconscious as a sleep-walker" (*CW* 15:122), a judgment that is supported by Joyce's response to Power about his intentions in *Ulysses*: "What do we know about what we put into anything? Though people may read more into *Ulysses* than I ever intended, who is to say that they are wrong: do any of us know what we are creating?"[40] Nevertheless, in the comments that Power reports it is clear that Joyce was in fundamental agreement with Jung's judgment that the "prompter" of the creation of *Ulysses* was "the spirit of the age" (*CW* 15:122–23), which was such that, according to Jung, "we must expect 'prophets' like James Joyce" (*CW* 14:324). In *Ulysses*, Jung concludes, Joyce was "rub[bing] the noses of our contemporaries in the shadow-side of reality" (*CW* 15:119–20), a necessary corrective since "whole sections of the population are so bound to their spiritual environment that nothing less than Joycean explosives are required to break through their hermetic isolation." "Joyce's contemporaries," Jung concluded, "are so riddled with medieval prejudices that such prophets of negation as he and Freud are needed to reveal to them the other side of reality" (*CW* 15:121). Indeed, Jung linked Joyce—Freud's "literary counterpart"—with Nietzsche, with the Great War, and with Freud himself as the "answer to the sickness of the nineteenth century" (*CW* 15:37).

Ulysses, after all, was planned and written during the years of World War I and published in its entirety almost immediately after its close.[41] In an afterword to *The Proud Tower: A Portrait of the World Before the War, 1890–1914*, Barbara W. Tuchman points out that this war represented "four years of the most intense and heroic effort the human race has ever made," and "when the effort was over, illusions and enthusiasms possible up to 1914 slowly sank beneath a sea of massive disillusionment," to be replaced by humanity's "painful view of its own limitations."[42] Her summary description of that prewar world gives a clue to what Jung means by "the sickness of the nineteenth century":

> The proud tower built up through the great ages of European civilization was an edifice of grandeur and passion, of riches and beauty and dark cellars. Its inhabitants lived, as compared to a later time, with more self-reliance, more confidence, more

> hope; greater magnificence, extravagance and elegance; more careless ease, more gaiety, more pleasure in each other's company and conversation, more injustice and hypocrisy, more misery and want, more sentiment including false sentiment, less sufferance of mediocrity, more dignity in work, more delight in nature, more zest.[43]

Tuchman's descriptive list includes some stark contrasts, epitomized in her "riches and beauty and dark cellars." And she points out that, although the nineteenth century was "a century of the most accelerated rate of change in man's record," a century in which "the industrial and scientific revolutions had transformed the world," it was also an era of "new pressures in prosperity and poverty . . . in antagonisms of classes and groups." It was a time when science, which offered so many new possibilities for man, also "took away [modern man's] belief in God and [his] certainty in a scheme of things he knew."[44] Indeed, Tuchman concludes, at the turn of the century, European man "had as much new unease as ease." And society was "bursting with new tensions and accumulated energies," a "surplus force" that, Tuchman relates, Stefan Zweig connected causally with the outbreak of World War I: "a tragic consequence of the internal dynamism that had accumulated in forty years of peace and now sought violent release."[45]

As the twentieth century draws to a close, it is difficult for us to empathize with the privileged world's boundless optimism or to understand the depth of its disillusion and despair at the onset of World War I. Jung comments in "Wotan" that before 1914 Europeans had begun "to regard war between civilized nations as a fable, thinking that such an absurdity would become less and less possible in our rational, internationally organized world" (*CW* 10:179).[46] Robert Spoo, in his recent *James Joyce and the Language of History*, identifies "dominant nineteenth-century conceptions of history as progress, development, teleology, the self-realization of Spirit, the revelation of God's will in time."[47] These "received notions of progress and civilization"[48] found a popular slogan in Émile Coué's formula, "Every day, and in every way, I am becoming better and better,"[49] but as sophisticated an observer as Henry James, faced with the fact of the war, saw in this "tragedy" the "wreck of our belief that through the long years we had seen civilization grow and the worst become impossible." "I'm sick beyond cure to have lived on to see it," he wrote to Rhoda Broughton in August 1914, while to Edith Wharton he communicated his conviction of the "utter extinction of everything" by the reality of the war. "Life goes on after a fashion," he wrote, "but I find it a nightmare from which there is no waking save by sleep."[50] James's sentence resonates for any Joycean, since, as Spoo notes, it "uncannily anticipate[s]" Stephen's much-quoted comment about history as "a nightmare from which I am trying to awake" (*U* 2:377), though with no reasonable possibility of James's figure being a source for Stephen's.[51] The First World War thus revealed "the shadow-side of reality," the "dark cellars" beneath the "richness and beauty," to a culture that had for too long repressed the acknowledgment of what was *not* bright and orderly and progressive in man.

So too did *Ulysses*, a work that Jung claimed had sprung "more from the spirit of the age than from the perverse inventive gifts of the author" (*CW* 14:324).

Even as Jung recognized that "the psychologist cannot avoid coming to grips with contemporary history" (*CW* 10:177),[52] so Joyce saw the artist's need to understand the nature of the world in which he lives and its demands, an insight that gives his work a measure of prophecy. Joyce knew intuitively what his world was and, Morton P. Levitt asserts, "could tell us with a shock of recognition that the orderly world of the Victorians had disintegrated forever."[53] To be sure, the base of *Ulysses*, like all Joyce's fiction, is autobiographical: "In *Ulysses*," Joyce told Power, "I have tried to forge literature out of my own experience, and not out of a conceived idea, or a temporary emotion."[54] But in all his musings about his intentions in *Ulysses*, scattered as they are through the conversations with Power, Joyce stresses also his felt obligation—which he had met in *Ulysses*—to deal with "the modern theme," which he identifies as "the subterranean forces, those hidden tides which govern everything and run humanity counter to the apparent flood."[55]

Jung's confrontation, during the "critical years" from 1913 to 1918, of these "subterranean forces" in himself enabled him to formulate his psychology, "a rich and complex system of sophisticated psychological ideas," Homans asserts, which "continues to be very explicitly and openly a theory of how to live in the contemporary world."[56] His theory, like Joyce's fiction, is autobiographically based, but "in the very act of naming his own personal experiences," Homans says, "Jung created a unique system of psychological ideas," and he emerged from his "journey" into the unconscious with "enough material for the rest of a life's work."[57] Jung begins his autobiography—or "automythology," to use Homan's descriptor—with the summary sentence: "My life is a story of the self-realization of the unconscious" (*MDR* 3), a sentence that describes Joyce's lifework as well. Beginning with the 1904 "Portrait of the Artist," Joyce was resolved, according to Ellmann, "to gather the stages of his spiritual experience together in a connected pattern," and "at the age of twenty-one . . . found he could become an artist by writing about the process of becoming an artist" (*JJ* 144). The stages of this "process of becoming an artist," as they move steadily inward, paralleling the stages of Jung's individuation process, also become "a story of the self-realization of the unconscious."

Thus both Jung and Joyce, contemporaries in an age that discovered and validated the role of unconscious motivations in human behavior, and both great innovators in their separate fields of endeavor, were engaged in a lifelong investigation of what goes into the making of a personality. It should not be surprising that their separate investigations eventuated in similar end products or that both of these products were of great significance to the culture of the twentieth century. Each had an unusually acute interest in his own psyche and an unusually acute observation of himself, and both of them moved from the primary, observed facts of their lives toward some kind of depiction of the substrata of this conscious material in the unconscious, an inward direction that has characterized psychology and fiction in the twentieth century.[58]

The social outcome of this observation, analysis, and synthesis was for Jung a theory of psychic development that prophetically looked toward the future. Though rejected by Freud and his circle at the time, Jung's psychology of the Self was the forerunner—though unacknowledged—of the most recent development in Freudian psychoanalysis: Heinz Kohut's self-psychology.[59] Individuation, the core process in Jung's system, has for its goal the realization of the Self, a goal that is quite different from the original aim of therapeutic Freudian psychoanalysis, which has striven to enable the individual to adapt himself to the demands of civilized society through bringing into consciousness previously unconscious inhibitions and repressions that make this adaptation painful.[60] Jung's psychology, "younger by twenty years" than Freud's,[61] was formulated during the years surrounding World War I and reflects a shift in focus from adaptation to an outer reality in society to accommodation with the discovery of an inner reality.[62]

Psychoanalysis, like literature, is not completely ahistorical; its "truths" may change with changing conditions. Indeed, the nature of the unconscious itself—what is "in" the unconscious—may be "culture specific,"[63] a conclusion that is implicitly supported by Jung's notions of the complementarity of conscious and unconscious, the tendency of the unconscious to compensate for one-sidedness in the conscious personality, an imbalance that changes with historical change. Jung, Homans stresses, having internalized Freud's psychological theory, "sincerely and persistently applied it to his own personal life as well as to the lives of his patients for a considerable time." But when Jung tried to use Freud's theory "to interpret his own crisis experience," he found that it did not work for him, even as it did not work for his patients. "For," says Homans, "like that of his patients, Jung's personal organization was narcissistic and preoedipal."[64] He thus had to move beyond Freud.

Narcissism, of course, is a label that still carries the pejorative connotations of immaturity at the least and pathology at the worst that were attached to it in the early years of psychoanalysis. This bias continues, and even today, in a society Christopher Lasch has labeled *The Culture of Narcissism* (1978),[65] there is a reluctance to accept narcissism as "a healthy and approvable psychological constellation."[66] Indeed, "the hypocrisy toward narcissism that pervades life today," Homans points out, "resembles the hypocrisy toward sexuality in Victorian times."[67] One of the most recent and most controversial developments in the Freudian line of psychoanalysis is Heinz Kohut's psychology of narcissism, a psychology of the Self that, according to Mario Jacoby, signals "a convergence with the Jungian position," though with no indication by Kohut of any acquaintance with Jung.[68] Homans points out that Kohut builds on Freud's perception of narcissism as a stage in early psychosexual development, but, responding to "new clinical problems and new cultural conditions,"[69] Kohut goes beyond Freud to suggest that "narcissism follows an independent line of development." Rather than representing an immature fixation, "the narcissistic organization persists into adult life and fuels it with energy." In fact, Homans cites Kohut's observation that "when a man enters a phase of creativity . . . he reenters the stage of narcissism" to support his assertion that the psychology of the Self is "crucial to understanding such introspective, like-minded, and creative men as Freud and Jung,"[70] a shortlist that may be expanded to include Joyce.[71]

We may assume, I think, that Joyce, whose entire lifework represents, in Ralph W. Rader's words, an "imaginative reconstruction of his own unique history and the inner integrity of his unique artistic mission,"[72] shares in the narcissistic personal organization that became characteristic of a post-Freudian era and is reflected in his fiction. For Joyce the outcome of his self-observation and analysis was a body of fiction that poses a goal of self-realization for the hero, in contrast to the happy ending of the traditional nineteenth-century *Bildungsroman*, which required the hero's successful adaptation to his society, his taking up a suitable position in that society. There is no such happy ending in Joyce's *Ulysses*. Instead, the artist-hero splits into two heroes, both of whom are essential to the artist's self-realization; and in *Ulysses*, Joyce explores, through his antihero Bloom, an inner or underworld that the society of his birth and nurturing had studiously ignored, a world, however, that is vitally connected to external reality.

Convinced, he told Power, that the "modern mind" is "interested above all in . . . the subterranean complexities which dominate the average man," Joyce nevertheless insisted on the writer's obligation "to create a new fusion between the exterior world and our contemporary selves,"[73] and this new fusion is accomplished in *Ulysses*. Already in possession of the artist figure represented by Stephen Dedalus, Joyce created from within the prophetic figure of Leopold Bloom, a character who represents the "twilight of the human personality" that Joyce identifies as the modern writer's subject.[74] Bloom, an archetypal corrective for the one-sidedness of Victorian culture, edges into the compulsively factual exterior world of *Ulysses*, complementing Stephen and completing the "new fusion" Joyce perceives as the goal of the modern author. The "subterranean complexities" revealed in Bloom are set off not only against the intellectual/spiritual posture of Stephen but also against an environment that is filled with verifiable events and artifacts, while his interior ramblings are interwoven with everyday physical activities ignored in the great novels of the nineteenth century, in which, for example, no major character defecates, masturbates, urinates, or menstruates, all activities that are not only mentioned but highlighted in *Ulysses*.[75]

With justice Joyce could boast to Power that, in *Ulysses*, "I have opened the new way, and you will find that it will be followed more and more. In fact, from it you may date a new orientation in literature—the new realism."[76] What he had done, he assured Power, was "to liberate literature from its age-old shackles," comparing himself to Pushkin and Tolstoy, who, great as they were, "thought only on one plane." But the modern writer, Joyce continued, "must take both worlds into consideration."[77] Like the Shakespeare of Stephen's theory, Joyce "found in the world without as actual what was in his world within as possible" (*U* 9:1041–42) and re-created both worlds in his fiction.

THE SPLIT SUBJECT UNITED

To be sure, Joyce identified "the hidden or subconscious world" as the "most exciting," and this "unexplored and hallucinatory" world[78] is developed in *Fin-*

negans Wake to the near exclusion of the world of experience. In *Ulysses*, however, by common critical consent, Joyce has consistently engaged both worlds. And to an extraordinary degree these worlds can be identified separately with his two protagonists, fashioned, Bertram Higgins pointed out in a 1925 essay, "in an antithetical form inherited from great writers of the past." In this essay, which Joyce recommended to Harriet Shaw Weaver as "a good article on me" (*Letters* 3:120), Higgins points to "matter and mind, intellect and feeling, subject and object" as "radical opposing concepts" that "have become flesh" in works of art, and he identifies the protagonists of *Ulysses* as "perhaps the most logically opposed pair that ever issued from this convention."[79] Certainly the view of Stephen and Bloom as opposites has become firmly established in the critical tradition of *Ulysses*, though the meaning of the opposition shifts with differing perspectives.

For the purposes of my study, the immediately relevant opposition in Higgins's list is matter versus mind, an opposition that in the Christian tradition is variously stated as flesh and spirit or body and soul. In Joyce's view, these opposites are united in one person, as is true in the doctrinal view of Christ and, by analogy, of all men. The body, Joyce reminded Budgen, "is the home of a full human personality," and when Budgen started to object that "the minds, the thoughts of the characters" were also significant, Joyce cut him off with "If they had no body they would have no mind. . . . It's all one."[80]

In *Ulysses*, as I have argued, Joyce split the one into two, incarnated separately in Stephen and Bloom, but at the same time he constructed a web of connections that asserted subliminally that the two belonged together and were really one: mind and matter, spirit and flesh, soul and body. Mary Colum maintained in her review of *Ulysses* that, "in the quality of pure intellect . . . Joyce is probably unsurpassed by any living writer," and Joyce gives this quality to Stephen, his bioenergetic surrogate, "Joyce in his skin" in Scholes's conception. That Colum saw this quality as a "peculiar fault" in the writing of "lesser men" of Joyce's time[81] appears to link Stephen's mastery of the intellectual sphere to an overemphasis in Joyce's culture on the mind, spirit, and soul. Bloom, on the other hand, is as strongly tied in the text to the material facts of existence as Stephen is to mind and spirit. As has been noted in chapter 7, Bloom, the cybernetic self-portrait, lives wholly in the "Land of Phenomenon," inclining toward a view of the soul as "convolutions of the grey matter" (*U* 16:752) and dissenting "tacitly from Stephen's views on the eternal affirmation of the spirit of man in literature" (*U* 17:29–30).

The symbolic identification of Stephen with mind/spirit and Bloom with matter/flesh is something of a critical commonplace, but like many clichés it is nevertheless true and important. In the twenties, Rebecca West equated Bloom with "the dark force of matter" and Stephen with "the spirit of light,"[82] striking the same note as Jung's somewhat later identification of the two protagonists with "the eternal figures of spiritual and carnal man" (*CW* 15:123). And this widely accepted opposition is most relevant to Bloom's significance as a prophetic archetypal figure who enters literary history in *Ulysses* as a corrective for the one-sidedness of the Victorian culture from which he arose. This was a culture that, on the surface at least, was overinvested in mind, spirit, and soul and in something of a state of denial about matter, the flesh and the body. Bloom, a misfit in this Victorian culture, prophesies a culture to come, the culture, in fact, in which the critical tradition about *Ulysses* has developed.

Half a century after the publication of *Ulysses*, Morton Levitt hailed Leopold Bloom as "A Hero for Our Time," the "first of our anti-heroes." Bloom is "a schlemiel, to be sure," but a schlemiel with impressive "fictional successors," among whom Levitt lists Bernard Malamud's Fixer, Saul Bellow's Mr. Sammler, and John Updike's Rabbit,[83] a list to which we may surely add Arthur Miller's Willy Loman. Theodore Holmes, however, writing at almost the same time as Levitt, objected to Bloom *because* he was a hero for our time. "The trouble with Bloom, as he represents a latter-day Everyman, is . . . in the very grain of his mind and innermost texture of his being," which is "radically, unalterably, and unselfconsciously [*sic*] practical, physical, and material." In Bloom's "very limited" vision of "the good," Holmes sees "a distillation and exemplar of our own." His conclusion that, "like the age he represents," Bloom "has forgotten his humanity"[84] contrasts sharply with S. L. Goldberg's conviction of a decade before that Bloom is the protagonist of *Ulysses* "simply because he is so thoroughly representative of humanity," indeed "an image of what is still alive in the human spirit."[85]

Differences in individual reactions of readers to fictional characters are, of course, much of what criticism is about. But it is noteworthy that both Levitt and Holmes, however differently they react to Bloom, see him as an exemplar of their own time, half a century after his appearance on the scene. In the years since 1922, there has been a general trend in the critical assessments of Bloom—and of Stephen too as his opposite—that has resulted in the enhancement of Bloom and the denigration of Stephen. This shifting evaluation of the protagonists of *Ulysses* is not entirely the result of our greater sophistication as readers or our better understanding of Joyce's intentions. It has cultural roots as well. For our society has moved a long way from the Victorians, and Bloom, an alien in his 1904 world, as well as in the world of the twenties when *Ulysses* was published, has gradually become an acceptable Everyman, much more comfortable for an audience of the last half of the century than that of the first half. He is at home in his future, whereas Stephen has gradually come to seem embarrassingly out of tune with the spirit of the age. It is not simply that we have learned better what Joyce was about in his portrait of Bloom; we have also come to recognize Bloom as one of us. Bloom, though always acknowledged as a great creative achievement, has not always been what a critic called "the sentimental favorite" of recent years.[86] Nor has Stephen always seemed the "insufferable prig" that Leslie Fiedler has rejected.[87]

Indeed, as late as 1934, William Troy saw Stephen as "not only one of the most perfectly realized characters in modern fiction, but also the character with whom the modern reader can most easily identify himself," adding that Joyce's influence on other writers "has been almost exclusively the influence of the character of

Stephen, and not of the characters of Leopold and Molly Bloom."[88] Fiedler, of course, associated his own move from identification with Stephen to an identification with Bloom with "the simple process of growing old," suggesting that Joyce might have called *Ulysses* "The Portrait of Everyone as a No-Longer-Young Man,"[89] and no one can rule out this explanation entirely. But Bloom's archetypal function as a social corrective is also surely operative.

Dr. Joseph Collins, the psychiatrist who reviewed *Ulysses* for the *New York Times* in 1922, though full of praise for the novel and for the authenticity of Joyce's portrait of Bloom, nevertheless predicted the unacceptability to "ninety-nine men out of a hundred" of the "vile contents" of the mind of this "moral monster, a pervert and an invert, an apostate to his race and his religion, the simulacrum of a man who has neither cultural background nor personal self-respect, who can neither be taught by experience nor lessoned by example."[90] A few years later, Rebecca West, though declaring Bloom "one of the greatest creations of all time," saw in him all the "gross characteristics" and "dark meaning" of the father figure.[91] "Simply he stands before us, convincing us that man wishes to fall back from humanity into the earth."[92]

Thirty years later, however, Fiedler claimed that "it was not Joyce-Stephen who wrote *Ulysses*, it was Joyce-Bloom," elevating Bloom from the "bit of the artist" attributed to him in the text of *Ulysses* to the full-fledged creator of the novel.[93] Bloom's status continued to improve, and a decade after Fiedler's pronouncement, Marilyn French, an admirably perceptive and convincing interpreter of *Ulysses*, conferred a kind of sainthood on Bloom as "a walking exemplar of *caritas*."[94] In support of this characterization she quotes Saint Augustine's definition of *caritas*: "the motion of the soul toward enjoyment of God for His own sake, and the enjoyment of one's self and of one's neighbor for the sake of God." She then interprets this to mean that "charity consists in the enjoyment of things" not "for the sake of God" as Augustine prescribed but "in their selfhood,"[95] which may indeed be characteristic of Bloom but is antithetical to Augustine's definition. But then her view of Bloom as the embodiment of *caritas* is in the context of a world—Joyce's world—"without God,"[96] which excludes Bloom entirely from the possibility of Saint Augustine's *caritas* because the very concept of *caritas* depends on a relationship to God.

Accepting Bloom with all his oddities is doubtless in the spirit of *Ulysses*, but canonizing him as French does is much more dubious. Holmes, I think, is on solid textual ground when he points out that, though Bloom is "the picture of the kind, considerate, respectable family man: soft-toned, circumspect, polite, prudent," a closer examination of the text reveals that his "kindness is self-interest, his respectability is sham, his innocuousness a cover for corruption, his politeness expedience, his business fraud, his prudence fear."[97] French may insist that we as readers "find ourselves defending or at least countenancing" Bloom's acts, however "outrageous," because of his "decency and honesty and his approach to sex as natural and human,"[98] but Molly herself contradicts the accuracy of the "natural" label (*U* 18:268). Granted, it is much harder to be outraged by Bloom's polymorphous perverse sexual impulses in a time when these are so much a part of the exploitable conscious phenomena of our world, indeed a significant commercial reality. Still, Vladimir Nabokov, no stranger to the comic possibilities of perversion in our own time, points out that "Bloom is, if not on the verge of insanity, at least a good clinical example of extreme sexual preoccupation and perversity with all kinds of curious complications," which include "acts and dreams that are definitely subnormal in the zoological, evolutionary sense."[99]

Bloom is a uniquely great comic character, an archetypal figure that has served his culture as a corrective to the psychic imbalance of the era out of which he arose, but he is not a saint and he cannot bear the whole weight as *the* hero of *Ulysses*. He is a "part-hero," in Higgins's phrase;[100] in him, as West asserts, "something true is said about man,"[101] but it is not the whole truth. Here at the end of the twentieth century, our culture has come to accept what Bloom embodies with few reservations. In contrast to the Victorians, our culture is probably "overbought" on matter, the flesh, and the body and quite possibly in something of a state of denial about mind, spirit, and soul. The kinds of things our society represses, the kinds of impulses that are buried in the personal unconscious are undoubtedly quite different from those of the society Joyce knew. These repressed contents may well have to do with notions of spirituality as a legitimate and attainable goal and obligation for men. Although Stephen comes nowhere near representing this value satisfactorily in himself, it is through him, most especially through his learning and the analogical power of his mind, that the values of mind and spirit and soul are incorporated in *Ulysses*. Bloom and Stephen are presented in "Eumaeus" as "poles apart" on the question of belief in the soul, "as they were both in schooling and in everything else" (*U* 16:774–75), but it is a mark of the greatness of *Ulysses* that Joyce has incorporated in the novel both poles of the traditional oppositions in The Artist's personality.

In the past decade or so there have been signs that we are ready for a reawakening to Stephen's validity and a more rational recognition of Bloom's limitations. A panel at the 1984 Joyce Symposium in Frankfurt, titled "Dedalus Redux," aimed at a reevaluation of Stephen's place in *Ulysses*. Margot Norris's 1992 *Joyce's Web*, whose "critical procedure" Norris describes as "a teasing apart and reknitting of writing intertexted with itself," necessarily focuses in large part on the work of the artist: "the Stephens in *Stephen Hero*, *Portrait*, and *Ulysses*" as well as Shem in the *Wake*.[102] Most recently, Robert Spoo recognizes that his 1994 study of the historiographic concerns of *Ulysses* "rehabilitates Stephen as the novel's hero" because such concerns "are ultimately *his* concerns," and Stephen's "intellectual attitudes . . . continue to shape the text's contestatory stance toward history long after he has receded as a character."[103] Spoo notes that recent studies focusing on "popular discourses that shaped Joyce's Dublin and his fictional representations of it, tend to emphasize those aspects of his texts that are dominated by the world of Leopold Bloom," noting also, however, that because his own study stresses "the intellectual, 'high culture' sources of Joyce's historiographic art," he hopes to "restore the balance by foregrounding the mind of Stephen Dedalus."[104]

Similarly, it is Stephen's odyssey that is in focus as I trace the stages in the development of the Self of The Artist. His interaction with Bloom, who comes into Stephen's world from the world of the repressed unconscious, dramatizes a crucial stage in this development. For, Jung has pointed out, "our European ego-consciousness is inclined to swallow up the unconscious . . . [or] try to suppress it"—a "dangerous" course, "because the unconscious is life and this life turns against us if suppressed." And Jung follows this warning with a recipe for wholeness that is realized, I believe, in *Ulysses*:

> Conscious and unconscious do not make a whole when one of them is suppressed and injured by the other. If they must contend, let it at least be a fair fight with equal rights on both sides. Both are aspects of life. Consciousness should defend its reason, and the chaotic life of the unconscious should be given the chance of having its way too—as much of it as we can stand. (*CW* 9.1:288)

Stephen's role in *Ulysses*, in this reading, parallels the role of the Ego in Jung's drama of individuation, and Stephen discovers in the course of the novel what Jung says the Ego discovers during the realization of the Shadow: that he cannot "settle everything and do everything by the force of [his] will" (*CW* 14:371). But what Stephen is conscious of has much to do with the power—the *staying* power—of *Ulysses*. For with all of Joyce's acknowledgment and representation of disorder, even chaos, in this prophetic work, much of which is realized through Bloom, *Ulysses* remains connected, through layers upon layers of allusion, to the bedrock of a traditional order, in literature, in classical philosophy, and in the patristic writings of the church. Indeed, as Richard Kain recognized over forty years ago, the "final grandeur" of *Ulysses* lies in its "referentiality."[105] And all this referentiality comes into *Ulysses* through Stephen. Joyce, through Stephen, has tapped into the main arteries of Western thought in his extreme application of the allusive method; and in an odd way, like the monasteries of the Dark Ages, Joyce's work preserves the great monuments of his culture, to which he has added his own: *Ulysses*.

Neither of the protagonists of this novel can stand alone as a complete person, or even perhaps as a completely comprehensible character, but Joyce has provided in Stephen and Bloom convincing embodiments of opposing forces in the Self of The Artist. "The life of Bloom and Stephen," Joyce told Hoffmeister, "is not the life of real people," but, he added, "it is tied in with human life."[106] Whether we see the opposites represented in *Ulysses* by Bloom and Stephen in Jungian terms as Shadow and Ego or in Christian terms as flesh and spirit, body and soul—or in more general terms as matter and mind, feeling and intellect, maturity and youth—this tie to humanity seems destined to endure.

NOTES

BIBLIOGRAPHY

INDEX

NOTES

I. INTRODUCTION: THE SPLIT SUBJECT OF *ULYSSES*

1. See Fredric Jameson's discussion of the "antiinterpretive current" in contemporary criticism, in which he credits Gilles Deleuze and Felix Guattari with "a whole new method for the reading of texts," which no longer asks " 'What does it mean?' but rather '*How does it work?*' " *The Political Unconscious: Narrative as a Socially Symbolic Act* (Ithaca: Cornell University Press, 1981), 23, 22.

2. Valéry Larbaud, "The 'Ulysses' of James Joyce," *Criterion* 1 (October 1922): 97–98. This early essay was excerpted from Larbaud's 7 December 1921 lecture.

3. Larbaud, " 'Ulysses,' " 103. Stuart Gilbert, *James Joyce's* Ulysses*: A Study* (New York: Vintage Books, 1955), 58.

4. John Francis Byrne, *Silent Years: An Autobiography with Memoirs of James Joyce and Our Ireland* (New York: Farrar, Strauss, & Young, 1953), 164–65. Note that William Empson claims that "Joyce would have laughed" at the notion of a "spiritual father; it could only mean to him a priest, and he was cross with priests" ("The Theme of *Ulysses*," in *A James Joyce Miscellany*, 3d ser., ed. Marvin Magalaner. [Carbondale: Southern Illinois University Press, 1962], 134). See also Fredric Jameson's dismissal of "the fetishisation of the text in terms of 'archetypal' patterns of father-son relationships, the quest for the ideal father or the lost son, and so forth," " 'Ulysses' in History," in *James Joyce and Modern Literature*, ed. W. J. McCormack and Alistair Stead (London: Routledge & Kegan Paul, 1982), 131.

5. Edmund Epstein, *The Ordeal of Stephen Dedalus: The Conflict of the Generations in James Joyce's* A Portrait of the Artist as a Young Man (Carbondale: Southern Illinois University Press, 1971), 28, 173.

6. Sheldon Brivic, *Joyce Between Freud and Jung* (Port Washington, N.Y.: Kennikat Press, 1980), 175, 194.

7. Richard Kain elaborates briefly on each of these labels in "The Significance of Stephen's Meeting Bloom," *James Joyce Quarterly* 10 (fall 1972): 159.

8. Empson, "Theme of *Ulysses*," 142.

9. Jameson, *Political Unconscious*, 61.

10. See Mary Colum, *Life and the Dream*, rev. ed. (Chester Springs, Pa.: Dufour Editions, 1966), 20–22, on her convent education, and 81, on her university education in Ireland.

11. Mary Colum, "The Confessions of James Joyce," in *The Freeman Book, 1920–1924* (New York: B. W. Huebsch, 1924), 328. See also Colum's statement, "I have never known a mind so fundamentally Catholic in structure as Joyce's own," Padraic Colum and Mary Colum, *Our Friend James Joyce* (Garden City: Doubleday, 1958), 207.

12. William Noon, "A Delayed Review," *James Joyce Quarterly* 2 (fall 1964): 9.

13. Frank Budgen, "Further Recollections of James Joyce," *Partisan Review* 23 (fall 1956): 533.

14. Thomas S. Eliot, "*Ulysses*, Order and Myth," in *James Joyce: Two Decades of Criticism*, 2d ed., ed. Seon Givens (New York: Vanguard, 1963), 202.

15. See John Kerr, *A Most Dangerous Method: The Story of Jung, Freud, and Sabina Spielrein* (New York: Knopf, 1993), 443–44, on the question of whether the early Freudian psychoanalysis was an art, a science, or a craft.

16. See Weldon Thornton, *Allusions in* Ulysses*: A Line-by-Line Reference to Joyce's Complex Symbolism* (New York: Simon & Schuster, Touchstone, 1973), 199, for the allusion to the "new Viennese school." See Chester Anderson, "Leopold Bloom as Dr. Sigmund Freud," *Mosaic* 6 (fall 1972): 23–43, for Joyce's use of Freud's *Psychopathology of Everyday Life* in *Ulysses*. See also Jean Kimball, "Freud, Leonardo, and Joyce: The Dimensions of a Childhood Memory," *James Joyce Quarterly* 17 (winter 1980): 165–82, on traces of Freud's psychobiography of Leonardo as well as Jung's "Significance of the Father." For traces of Otto Rank's work, see Kimball, "James Joyce and Otto Rank: The Incest Motif in *Ulysses*," *James Joyce Quarterly* 13 (spring 1976): 366–82; "Family Romance and Hero Myth: A Psychoanalytic Context for the Paternity Theme in *Ulysses*," *James Joyce Quarterly* 20 (winter 1983): 161–73; and "An Ambiguous Faithlessness: Molly Bloom and the Widow of Ephesus," *James Joyce Quarterly* 31 (summer 1994): 455–72. And see Kimball, "Jung's 'Dual Mother' in Joyce's *Ulysses*: An Illustrated Psychoanalytic Intertext," *Journal of Modern Literature* 17 (spring 1991): 477–89, for traces of Jung's 1912 *Wandlungen und Symbole der Libido*.

17. Frank Budgen, "Joyce's Chapters of Going Forth by Day," in *James Joyce: Two Decades of Criticism*, 2d ed., ed. Seon Givens (New York: Vanguard, 1963), 344. Note Budgen's further comment that psychoanalysis "was like the foehn wind: you couldn't escape it." On the importance of the Zurich group to Freud's plans for the development of psychoanalysis, see Sigmund Freud, *On the History of the Psycho-Analytic Movement* (in *SE* 14:26–30). Compare Kerr's assertion that "It was Jung and [Eugen] Bleuler [of the Zurich School] who put Freud on the scientific map, not the other way around" *Dangerous Method*, 9.

18. The city and canton libraries in Zurich were consolidated into the present Zentralbibliothek during Joyce's residence in Zurich. See H. Escher, "*Die Errichtung der Zentralbibliothek in Zurich*," *Zentralblatt für Bibliothekswesen* 32 (1915): 86–104. Accession records at the Zentralbibliothek Zurich indicate that the library subscribed to three of the four journals established by the psychoanalytic movement between 1909 and 1913 and had acquired an impressive number of books by Freud, Jung, and Otto Rank before 1919 (when Joyce left Zurich).

19. Wyndham Lewis, "An Analysis of the Mind of James Joyce," in *Time and Western Man*, by Wyndham Lewis (New York: Harcourt, 1928), 103.

20. Quoted in Rosa M. B. Bollettieri, "The Importance of Trieste in Joyce's Work, with Reference to His Knowledge of Psycho-Analysis," *James Joyce Quarterly* 7 (spring 1970): 181. See also William Carlos Williams' attack on Rebecca West for her "descent to Freudian expedients of classification" in her remarks on *Ulysses*, "A Point for American Criticism," *transition* 15–17 (winter 1929): 161–62. And see Frederick J. Hoffman, *Freudianism and the Literary Mind*, 2d ed. (New York: Vanguard, 1963), 119–25.

21. Mark Shechner, *Joyce in Nighttown: A Psychoanalytic Inquiry into* Ulysses (Berkeley: University of California Press, 1974), 15–16.

22. Richard Kain, ed., "An Interview with Carola Giedion-Welcker and Maria Jolas," *James Joyce Quarterly* 11 (winter 1974), 120.

23. Freud's *Psychopathology of Everyday Life*, the fourth psychoanalytic work listed, was purchased after the move to Zurich. See Richard Ellmann, *The Consciousness of Joyce* (New York: Oxford University Press, 1977), 97–134, for the listing, and 54, for the probable date of Joyce's purchase of the texts. See Michael Patrick Gillespie, with Erik Bradford Stocker,

James Joyce's Trieste Library: A Catalogue of Materials at the Harry Ransom Humanities Research Center, The University of Texas at Austin (Austin: The Harry Ransom Humanities Research Center, 1986), for bibliographical information on these texts: Freud's *Eine Kindheitserinnerung des Leonardo da Vinci* and *Zur Psychopathologie des Alltaglebens*, Jones's *Das Problem des Hamlet und der Ödipus-Komplex*, and Jung's *Die Bedeutung des Vater für das Schicksal des Einzelnen*. Hereafter I refer to these, as well as other German titles in the text, in English.

24. Bollettieri, "Importance of Trieste," 179.

25. Étienne Gilson, *The Spirit of Mediaeval Philosophy*, trans. A. H. C. Downes (New York: Scribner, 1936), 218.

26. Gilson, *Spirit*, 96.

27. Edmund Wilson, *Axel's Castle* (New York: Charles Scribner's Sons, 1931), 204.

28. Saint Augustine, *The City of God*, trans. Marcus Dods (New York: Modern Library, 1950), book 13, chapter 21.

29. Saint Augustine, *On Christian Doctrine*, trans. D. W. Robertson, Jr. (New York: Bobbs-Merrill, Library of the Liberal Arts, 1958), 2, 28, 44.

30. Quoted in Jessie Taft, *Otto Rank: A Biographical Study Based on Notebooks, Letters, Collected Writings, Therapeutic Achievements, and Personal Associations* (New York: Julian, 1958), 49.

31. See Didier Anzieu, *Freud's Self-Analysis*, trans. Peter Graham (Madison, Conn.: International Universities Press, 1986), x, on Freud's oscillation between the need to "[*tell*] himself to others" and a "conscious glee" at his own "hide-and-seek ploy" during his lifetime, as well as with posterity, and see Freud's own admission that "in scarcely any instance have I brought forward the *complete* interpretation of one of my own dreams, as it is known to me. I have probably been wise in not putting too much faith in my readers' discretion" (*SE* 4:105n).

32. See especially Alexander Grinstein, *Sigmund Freud's Dreams*, 2d ed. (New York: International Universities Press, 1980).

33. Henri Ellenberger, *The Discovery of the Unconscious: The History and Evolution of Dynamic Psychiatry* (New York: Basic Books, 1970), 450–51.

34. Ronald R. Thomas, *Dreams of Authority: Freud and the Fictions of the Unconscious* (Ithaca: Cornell University Press, 1990), 19.

35. George Hogenson, *Jung's Struggle with Freud* (Notre Dame, Ind.: University of Notre Dame Press, 1983) 22–23.

36. More than one commentator has questioned how consciously directed Jung's inner journey actually was. See, e.g., Paul J. Stern's assertion that "Jung's own descent into the psychic netherworld was less self-propelled than he liked to think," *C. G. Jung: The Haunted Prophet* (New York: Braziller, 1976), 9. Compare Kerr's suggestion that Jung's account of his struggle as "self-willed" "romanticizes" it and makes it "psychologically false" (*Dangerous Method*, 446). See Ellenberger, *Discovery*, 39, on the concept of "initiatory illness" or "creative illness"; see 672, for his identification of the period in Jung's life from 1913 to 1919 as that of a creative illness; and see 450, for his assertion that Freud's self-analysis, which produced the material for his *Interpretation of Dreams*, also represented a creative illness.

37. The distinguishing label was required because of the bitterness of the break between Jung and Freud, but see James Hillman's assertion that "all forms of depth psychology . . . any of these movements that takes the soul deeper . . . might be called psychoanalysis." *Healing Fiction* (Barrytown, N.Y.: Station Hill, 1983), 45.

38. Peter Homans, *Jung in Context: Modernity and the Making of a Psychology* (Chicago: University of Chicago Press, 1979), 109.

39. Quoted in Ellenberger, *Discovery*, 276.

40. See, for example, Otto Rank's discussion of the myth of the birth of Jesus, in which "the birth from the virgin is the most abrupt repudiation of the father, the consummation of the entire myth," in *The Myth of the Birth of the Hero and Other Writings*, ed. Philip Freund, trans. F. Robbins and Smith Ely Jelliffe (New York: Vintage Books, 1964), 80–82.

41. Budgen, "Further Recollections," 533.

42. Hugo Rahner, *Greek Myths and Christian Mystery*, trans. Brian Battershaw (New York: Harper & Row, 1963), 26. Note Rahner's reminder that Paul and the church fathers of the third and fourth centuries took over materials from the mystery religions "not as seekers after treasure, but as possessors thereof" (11), and compare Gilson, *Spirit*, 27, "All truth is by definition Christian."

43. Quoted in Rahner, *Greek Myths*, 96.

44. See Rahner's chapter on "Odysseus at the Mast," *Greek Myths*, 328–86. On scriptural bases for Christian appropriation of pagan learning, see E. R. Curtius, *European Literature and the Latin Middle Ages*, trans. Willard R. Trask (Princeton: Princeton University Press, 1953), 40; Gilson, *Spirit*, 26–28; and D. W. Robertson, Jr., *A Preface to Chaucer: Studies in Medieval Perspectives* (Princeton: Princeton University Press, 1962), 355–57.

45. It is also important to note that Joyce was introduced to his "Favorite Hero" (*JJ* 46) through Charles Lamb's *Adventures of Ulysses*, written as a supplement to François Fénelon's immensely popular *Adventures of Telemachus*, in which the son's adventures parallel the father's, suggesting a father-son configuration somewhat different from the Homeric model and closer in fact to Joyce's *Ulysses*. See W. B. Stanford, "Joyce's First Meeting with Ulysses," *The Listener* 46 (19 July 1951): 99 and 105.

46. See W. B. Stanford, *Ireland and the Classical Tradition* (Totowa, N.J.: Rowman & Littlefield, 1976), on the "extraordinary readiness" of medieval Irish translators and adapters of classical works, whom he compares to "Irish raiders in Britain or Gaul" (73), to "alter the canonical versions of the Greek and Roman writers," resulting in "a new literary fusion which is both scholarly and creative, derivative and inventive, classical and Celtic, which cannot be fitted into any of the orthodox genres" (87).

47. See Kristeva, *Desire in Language: A Semiotic Approach to Literature and Art*, ed. Leon S. Roudiez, trans. Thomas Gora, Alice Jardine, and Leon S. Roudiez (New York: Columbia University Press, 1980), 64–66, on the connection between Bakhtin and her own notion of intertextuality, and 15, for the translators' definition of *intertextuality*.

48. M. M. Bakhtin, *The Dialogic Imagination: Four Essays*, ed. Michael Holquist, trans. Caryl Emerson and Michael Holquist (Austin: University of Texas Press, 1981), 299–300.

49. On Joyce's selective memory regarding his reading, see Stanislaus Joyce, *BK* 79; see also Michael Gillespie's assertion that "any reading which did not yield data for his own work seems to have had little effect on him," in *Inverted Volumes Improperly Arranged: James Joyce and His Trieste Library* (Ann Arbor: UMI Research Press, 1983), 64.

50. John Livingston Lowes, *The Road to Xanadu: A Study in the Ways of the Imagination* (Boston: Houghton Mifflin, 1927), 40, 32.

51. Compare Ellmann's speculation about the nature of Joyce's identification with great figures who appealed to his imagination as a desire for "an interplay among their images and his own" (*JJ* 47), as well as Robert E. Scholes and Richard M. Kain, *The Workshop of Daedalus: James Joyce and the Raw Materials for* A Portrait of the Artist as a Young Man

(Evanston, Ill.: Northwestern University Press, 1965), xiii, on Joyce's interweaving of material relating to famous artists with events of his own life in *A Portrait.*

52. Compare Thomas, *Dreams of Authority*, 8–10, on the "interdependence" of psychoanalysis and literature and "the dialogical relationship" between them, especially the influence of nineteenth-century novelists on Freud's "scientific theory of how we conceive of ourselves as human subjects."

53. J. P. Hodin, *Modern Art and the Modern Mind* (Cleveland: The Press of Case Western Reserve University, 1972), 69.

54. Theoharis Constantine Theoharis, *Joyce's* Ulysses*: An Anatomy of the Soul* (Chapel Hill: University of North Carolina Press, 1988), 27–28.

55. Robert Martin Adams, *Surface and Symbol: The Consistency of James Joyce's* Ulysses (New York: Oxford University Press, 1962), 84–85. Compare Philip Toynbee's suggestion a generation earlier that such limitation is "an artificial necessity" for any critic of *Ulysses*, "A Study of *Ulysses*," in *James Joyce: Two Decades of Criticism*, ed. Seon Givens (New York: Vanguard, 1963), 258.

56. John Paul Riquelme, *Teller and Tale in Joyce's Fiction: Oscillating Perspectives* (Baltimore: Johns Hopkins University Press, 1983), 40–41; Brook Thomas, *James Joyce's* Ulysses*: A Book of Many Happy Returns* (Baton Rouge: Louisiana State University Press, 1982), 19.

57. See Maurice Beebe, *Ivory Towers and Sacred Founts: The Artist as Hero from Goethe to Joyce* (New York: New York University Press, 1964), especially his chapter on "The Divided Self: The Artist as Archetype," 21–64, for a survey of the literary history of this concept.

58. Gilbert Seldes, quoted in Robert Deming, ed., *James Joyce: The Critical Heritage* (New York: Barnes & Noble, 1970), 1:238. Compare Aubrey F. G. Bell, *Cervantes* (Norman: University of Oklahoma Press, 1947), 186, on Don Quixote and Sancho Panza as "the two voices" of "Cervantes talking to Cervantes."

59. R. P. Blackmur, "The Jew in Search of a Son," *Virginia Quarterly Review* 24 (1948): 113.

60. H. E. Rogers, "Irish Myth and the Plot of *Ulysses*," *ELH* 15 (1948), 325–26.

61. Robert Scholes, "*Ulysses*: A Structuralist Perspective," *James Joyce Quarterly* 10 (fall 1972): 164–65.

62. James H. Maddox, Jr., *Joyce's* Ulysses *and the Assault upon Character* (New Brunswick, N.J.: Rutgers University Press, 1978), 194–95. Maddox's notion of complementarity, like several of his conclusions, harmonizes with my own view of the relationship in a frame of Jungian individuation, though clearly with no intention of making the connection with Jung's thinking.

63. For Brivic's discussion of the contrasting attitudes of the two protagonists, which he extends to the contrasting dominant functions, see Brivic, *Joyce Between Freud and Jung*, chapter 9, "Joyce's System and Jung's Types," 140–167, especially 143–52.

64. See Adams, *Surface and Symbol*, 95–99, on "Blephen/Stoom." See also Brivic, *Joyce Between Freud and Jung*, 170–73; and Jean Kimball, "The Hypostasis in *Ulysses*," *James Joyce Quarterly* 10 (summer 1973): 429–30; and Kimball, " '*Lui, C'est Moi*': The Brother Relationship in *Ulysses*," *James Joyce Quarterly* 25 (winter 1988): 230–32.

65. Adams, *Surface and Symbol*, 95–99.

66. See Kimball, "Hypostasis," 426–36.

67. Saint Augustine, *The Trinity*, trans. Stephen McKenna, (Washington, D.C.: Catholic University of America Press, 1963), 4, 6.

68. Rebecca West, *The Strange Necessity* (Garden City: Doubleday, 1928), 19.

69. Adams, *Surface and Symbol*, 250, 249.

70. Richard Ellmann, *Ulysses on the Liffey* (New York: Oxford University Press, 1972), 73.

71. Homans, *Jung in Context*, 79, 153–54. See also Kerr, *Dangerous Method*, 384, on the possibility of Jung's "secretly experimenting with a Christianized version of psychoanalysis" as a threat to Freud.

72. Homans, *Jung in Context*, 184, 140, 56, 184, 185.

73. See Saint Thomas Aquinas, *Summa Theologiae* (New York: McGraw-Hill, 1964–72), vol. 11, *Man*, trans. Timothy Sutter, appendix 4, for the comment that the Christian fathers, in their insistence on the "integral soul-body completeness of Christ," had "outlined a philosophy of man almost without noticing it" (259).

74. Ellenberger, *Discovery*, 670.

75. See Jung's comment: "In every treatment of neurosis the discovery of the shadow is indispensable, otherwise nothing changes" (*CW* 10:216).

76. Arthur Power, *Conversations with James Joyce*, ed. Clive Hart (New York: Barnes & Noble, 1974), 54.

77. See Jung's 1952 monograph, "Synchronicity: An Acausal Connecting Principle" (*CW* 8:417–519), in which he gives "a consistent account of everything I have to say on this subject," a subject to which he had been "alluding," however, for twenty years (419). See also Jung's "On Synchronicity," a short lecture drawn from his monograph (*CW* 8:520–31).

78. See Ira Progoff, *Jung, Synchronicity, and Human Destiny* (New York: Julian, 1973), 98–99.

79. Edward Glover, *Freud or Jung* (London: George Allen & Unwin, 1950), 5.

80. See Fritjof Capra, *The Tao of Physics: An Exploration of the Parallels Between Modern Physics and Eastern Mysticism*, 2d ed. (Boulder, Colo.: Shambala Publications, 1983), 309–21. See also Jameson, *Political Unconscious*, 25, on the "loose contemporary consensus on the 'outmoded' character of causality as such" and the assumption that "mechanical causality" has been replaced by the "indeterminacy principle of modern physics."

2. THE AUTOBIOGRAPHICAL BASE: SOME SYNCHRONICITIES

1. William O. Walcott, "The Paternity of James Joyce's Stephen Dedalus," *Journal of Analytical Psychology* 10 (1965): 86. See also Walcott's "Notes by a Jungian Analyst on the Dreams in *Ulysses*," *James Joyce Quarterly* 9 (fall 1971): 37–48.

2. William York Tindall, *A Reader's Guide to James Joyce* (New York: Noonday, 1959), 131.

3. Sheldon Brivic, *Joyce the Creator* (Madison: University of Wisconsin Press, 1985), 145–53. See also his discussion of the synchronicities exhibited by Stephen and Bloom in *Joyce Between Freud and Jung*, 168–73.

4. Brivic, *Joyce the Creator*, 68. With this broadened definition, Brivic sees "all events in a text," as well as all allusions to other texts as synchronicities, since "they do not follow physical causes, but psychic ones" (145).

5. See Progoff, *Jung*, 141, on the "ambiguity and unclearness" in Jung's writings on synchronicity in human life.

6. Barbara diBernard, *Alchemy and* Finnegans Wake (Albany: State University of New York Press, 1980), 8. See 9–10, for DiBernard's discussion of the alchemical allusions added

"virtually all . . . at one time" to "the most important section of the *Wake* in which alchemy and writing are connected (182.30–186.18)."

7. See Ellmann's account of Joyce's first "Portrait" (*JJ* 144–47), which was rejected by Fred Ryan and John Eglinton, the editors of *Dana*, Eglinton remarking, "I can't print what I can't understand." See *FP* (56–74) for the description and text of the manuscript.

8. See Ellmann's account of what he calls "one of the strangest ideas in literary history" (*JJ* 591–93).

9. Lewis, "Analysis," 92.

10. Nino Frank, "The Shadow That Had Lost Its Man," in *Portraits of the Artist in Exile: Recollections of James Joyce by Europeans*, ed. Willard Potts (Seattle: University of Washington Press, 1979), 78, 86; and in the same edited volume, see also Jacques Mercanton, "The Hours of James Joyce" (226, note 27), on Joyce's own awareness of "his prolonged juvenility."

11. See "General Index" (*CW* 20:372–73).

12. See the appendix to "Ulysses" (*CW* 15:132–34) on the three published explanations of the genesis of the paper.

13. The original, C. G. Jung, *Wandlungen und Symbole der Libido: Beiträge zur Entwicklungsgeschichte des Denkens* (Leipzig and Vienna: Franz Deuticke, 1912), was first published in the *Yearbook*, part 1, vol. 3 (1911): 120–227; part 2, vol. 4 (1912): 162–464. The English translation (*PU*) is the first version of *Symbols of Transformation: An Analysis of the Prelude to a Case of Schizophrenia* (*CW* 5), which was an extensively rewritten version.

14. See also Stern, *Haunted Prophet*, 150, for speculation that Jung himself advised Mrs. McCormick to withdraw her support.

15. Frank Budgen, *Myselves When Young* (New York: Oxford University Press, 1970), 200.

16. Homans, *Jung in Context*, 27.

17. John Kerr, "Beyond the Pleasure Principle and Back Again: Freud, Jung, and Sabina Spielrein," in *Freud: Appraisals and Reappraisals*, ed. Paul E. Stepansky, vol. 3 of *Contributions to Freud Studies* (Hillsdale, N.J.: Analytic, 1988), 48.

18. C. G. Jung, *Analytical Psychology: Notes of the Seminar Given in 1925 by C. G. Jung*, ed. William McGuire, Bollingen Series, no. 99 (Princeton: Princeton University Press, 1989), 27. See also Kerr, *Dangerous Method*, 329–32.

19. See Jung's comment in his foreword to the second edition of his "Significance of the Father" essay: "While I was working on the mother-complex in my book *Wandlungen und Symbole der Libido*, it became clear to me . . . why not only the father, but the mother as well, is such an important factor in the child's fate" (*CW* 4:301).

20. See Kimball, "Jung's 'Dual Mother,' " 482–83, on the progress of "Circe" at the time of Joyce's letter to Budgen.

21. See also D. W. Winnicott's review of Jung's *Memories, Dreams, Reflections* for the opinion that Jung's picture of himself in the opening chapter of his autobiography is that of "childhood schizophrenia" (*International Journal of Psycho-Analysis* 45 [1964]: 450).

22. See *JJ* (662–81) for Joyce's attempts to deal with Lucia's problem at this time.

23. Ellenberger, *Discovery*, 658.

24. See Duane P. Schultz, *Intimate Friends, Dangerous Rivals: The Turbulent Relationship between Freud and Jung* (Los Angeles: Jeremy P. Tarcher, 1990), 45, on the "emotional ambivalence" of Jung's relationship with his father, who, Schultz concludes, actually "behaved in a more traditionally maternal fashion" than Jung's mother.

25. Ellenberger, *Discovery*, 662.

26. See also Jean Kimball, "James and Stanislaus Joyce: A Jungian Speculation," in *Blood Brothers: Siblings as Writers*, ed. Norman Kiell (New York: International Universities Press, 1983), 93–98, on the nature of the brothers' relationship to their father.

27. Constantine Curran, *James Joyce Remembered* (New York: Oxford University Press, 1968), 35.

28. Carola Giedion-Welcker, "Meetings with Joyce," in *Portraits of the Artist in Exile: Recollections of James Joyce by Europeans*, ed. Willard Potts (Seattle: University of Washington Press, 1979), 268.

29. The facts about Spielrein's biography are taken from Kerr, *Dangerous Method*, 19–38. Kerr's exhaustive investigation of the whole complex of Jung, Freud, and Spielrein has been invaluable to me in this study.

30. For references, see *F-J* and its index s.v. *Spielrein.*

31. Kerr, *Dangerous Method*, 12.

32. Aldo Carotenuto, *A Secret Symmetry: Sabina Spielrein Between Jung and Freud*, trans. Arno Pomerans, John Shepley, and Krishna Winston (New York: Pantheon Books, 1982).

33. Originally Jung's heirs would not give permission to publish Jung's letters; but, while they are not yet available in English, they can be found, according to Kerr's "Bibliographical Essay," in the German edition of Carotenuto's book. See Kerr, *Dangerous Method*, xliii, and see 571, for bibliographical information.

34. Carotenuto, *Secret Symmetry*, xlvi.

35. These additional finds, however, do nothing to change the basic story. See Adeline Van Waning, "The Works of Pioneering Psychoanalyst Sabina Spielrein: 'Destruction as a Cause of Coming into Being,' " *International Review of Psycho-Analysis* 19 (1992), 399. See also Kerr, *Dangerous Method*, 12–13.

36. See chapters in, for example, Lisa Appignanesi and John Forrester, *Freud's Women* (New York: Basic Books, 1992), 204–27; David James Fisher, *Cultural Theory and Psychoanalytic Tradition* (New Brunswick, N.J.: Transaction Publishers, 1991), 79–90; and Andre Haynal, *Psychoanalysis and the Sciences: Epistemology—History*, trans. Elizabeth Holder (Berkeley: University of California Press, 1993): 174–88. René Major, in "Love for Transference and Passion for Signifiers: Between Sabina S. and Anna G.," *Psychoanalytic Inquiry* 4 (1984): 171–91, presents a comparison between Spielrein's case and the fictional case history in D. W. Thomas's *The White Hotel*, a comparison that Thomas, in his review of *Secret Symmetry* also suggests, though claiming that "the details of [Spielrein's] life were unknown to me when I wrote the novel." See D. W. Thomas, "A Fine Romance," *New York Review of Books*, 13 May 1982: 6.

37. See Eva M. Schepeler, "Jean Piaget's Experiences on the Couch: Some Clues to a Mystery," *International Journal of Psycho-Analysis* 74 (April 1993): 258–64, on Piaget's analysis with Spielrein.

38. Peter Homans asserts that Carotenuto's claims for "the significance of Spielrein's life and ideas for the Freud-Jung relationship and for the history of the psychoanalytic movement" represent an "overestimation" but also acknowledges the hazard of underestimating that significance. See Peter Homans, Review of *A Secret Symmetry*, by Aldo Carotenuto, *Journal of the History of the Behavioral Sciences* 19 (1983): 243. But see Appignanesi and Forrester, *Freud's Women*, 204–5, on the significance of Spielrein's "theoretical impact"; and see Van Waning, "Works," 402–11, for an extended discussion of Spielrein's work.

39. Kerr, *Dangerous Method*, 13.

40. Kerr, *Dangerous Method*, 34.

41. Kerr, *Dangerous Method*, 38.

42. Kerr, *Dangerous Method*, 308. After the love relationship with Sabina was thrust out of Jung's life, he turned to another "dark Jewish girl," Toni Wolff, who was first his patient and then his mistress for thirty years. See Stern, *Haunted Prophet*, 129–42 (his chapter, "Toni Wolff—Eros-Winged Muse").

43. Kerr, *Dangerous Method*, 36, 68; and see 68–69, for Kerr's rationalization of the surprising fact that Jung's analysis "utterly missed" this significant fact.

44. Kerr, *Dangerous Method*, 154. See Kerr's note that what Jung "did not find [was] a sexual assault in childhood," an issue that "was very much up for discussion at this time" (67).

45. Bruno Bettelheim, "Commentary by Bruno Bettelheim," in *A Secret Symmetry: Sabina Spielrein Between Jung and Freud*, by Aldo Carotenuto, trans. Arno Pomerans, John Shepley, and Krishna Winston (New York: Pantheon Books, 1984, augmented edition), xxxviii. See also Carotenuto's speculative assessment of the degree and permanence of the cure, 144–46.

46. See Kerr, *Dangerous Method*, 66–72.

47. Kerr, *Dangerous Method*, 72–73.

48. Carotenuto, *Secret Symmetry*, 167.

49. Paraphrased and quoted in Kerr, *Dangerous Method*, 205.

50. Kerr, *Dangerous Method*, 224; Fisher, *Cultural Theory*, 83; Haynal, *Psychoanalysis*, 181.

51. Thomas, "Fine Romance," 3; Appignanesi and Forrester, *Freud's Women*, 211.

52. Carotenuto, *Secret Symmetry*, 11.

53. Carotenuto, *Secret Symmetry*, 12–13. Spielrein also notes Jung's desire to introduce her into his household and make her his wife's friend, the pattern he followed later with Toni Wolff, but finds it "understandable" that Emma "wanted no part of this business" (12).

54. Carotenuto, *Secret Symmetry*, 13.

55. See Carotenuto, *Secret Symmetry*, 160–72, on "psychotic transference and countertransference" and his speculative reconstruction of "the emotional atmosphere" that determined the course of the affair between Spielrein and Jung.

56. See the entry on *Counter-Transference* in Jean LaPlanche and J.-B. Pontalis, *The Language of Psycho-Analysis*, trans. Donald Nicholson-Smith (New York: Norton, 1973), 92–93, and note that increasing attention to the concept has coincided with the growing tendency to view psychoanalytic treatment "as a *relationship*." Freud alluded to the concept "only on very rare occasions."

57. Carotenuto, *Secret Symmetry*, 94. All we have of Sabina Spielrein's two letters to Freud are draft copies that were found with her papers, which may not be exactly what she sent. But from Freud's reaction, conveyed to Jung (*F-J* 149F), the second letter, which traced something of the history of the relationship with Jung, came close to the confusion of the draft. All quotations from the correspondence between Jung and Mrs. Spielrein, which are quoted by Sabina in her second letter to Freud, are taken from this draft, written over a period of ten days, Carotenuto, *Secret Symmetry*, 92–107. Kerr covers what he titles "The End of the Affair" in *Dangerous Method*, 205–9.

58. Carotenuto, *Secret Symmetry*, 94, 95. According to Spielrein's account, there were five letters to Mrs. Spielrein from Jung, all of which "deeply offended" her mother (98–99).

59. Carotenuto, *Secret Symmetry*, 96.

60. Kerr, *Dangerous Method*, 208.

61. See Saul Rosenzweig, *Freud, Jung, and Hall the King-Maker: The Historic Expedition*

to America (1909), with G. Stanley Hall as Host and William James as Guest (St. Louis: Rana House, 1992), 38–39, on the lasting importance of this meeting for Jung.

62. Here Jung is pairing Spielrein's case with his treatment of Otto Gross (see *F-J*, 33J, note 7).

63. See also Freud's letter of 8 June 1909 to Spielrein, Carotenuto, *Secret Symmetry*, 113–14.

64. Carotenuto, *Secret Symmetry*, 114.

65. Carotenuto, *Secret Symmetry*, 92–93.

66. Kerr, *Dangerous Method*, 222; see 223–27, for Kerr's analysis of Spielrein's letter, especially the "code word, 'poetry.' "

67. Carotenuto, *Secret Symmetry*, 104.

68. Carotenuto, *Secret Symmetry*, 102, 104.

69. See Kerr, *Dangerous Method*, 227–28, for a discussion of the effect of the Spielrein affair on the personal relationship between Freud and Jung.

70. See Bettelheim's speculation in "Commentary," xviii–xix, that "possibly all of the central Jungian concepts might be owed directly or indirectly to Spielrein," but especially the concept of the Anima and the Shadow, which "either comes from Spielrein or was developed around Jung's relation to her."

71. See Kerr, "Beyond the Pleasure Principle," 48–50, on the "almost miraculous" clarification of Jung's thinking in the Fordham lectures.

72. See Kerr, *Dangerous Method*, 9–11, for his summary of the importance of Jung and the Zurich complex to Freud and the psychoanalytic movement, and see also 442, on the effects of the split on the three principles: Jung, Freud, and Spielrein.

73. Carotenuto, *Secret Symmetry*, 8.

74. See *F-J* (144J, note 2), for a brief summary of Spielrein's career; and see the final three chapters of Carotenuto, *Secret Symmetry*, for more extended coverage.

75. Carotenuto, *Secret Symmetry*, 190.

76. Letter of 9 November 1955 to Theodor Bovet, C. G. Jung, *Letters of C. G. Jung*, 2 vols., ed. Gerhard Adler, with Aniela Jaffe, trans. R. F. C. Hull (Princeton: Princeton University Press, 1973–75), 2:276–77.

77. Kerr, *Dangerous Method*, 418–19.

78. Rodney Wilson Owen, *James Joyce and the Beginnings of* Ulysses (Ann Arbor: UMI Research Press, 1983), 9–11. Pointing out that 16 June "was neither their first date nor the physical consummation of their relationship," Owen calls Ellmann's speculation "romantic but mythical" (9).

79. Brenda Maddox, *Nora: The Real Life of Molly Bloom* (Boston: Houghton Mifflin, 1988), 12, 22.

80. Curran, *James Joyce*, 66.

81. Alice Curtayne, "Portrait of the Artist as a Brother: An Interview with James Joyce's Sister," *Critic* 21 (1963), 43.

82. Curtayne, "Portrait," 44.

83. Ellmann had access to Stanislaus's "Book of Days," a copy of which—for the period from January 1907 to early 1909—is among the Ellmann papers at Tulsa. This is an astonishingly detailed record in its unretouched form, and it is augmented by an unfinished letter that Stanislaus wrote to his father in 1910, which outlines the "heartless and thankless sweating of me that has been Jim and his wife's chief profit" since Stanislaus's arrival in Trieste. Ellmann's copy of this draft is also in the Ellmann papers.

84. This indignity, particularly galling because the original plan called for Stanislaus to take Giorgio back to Dublin, is recorded in the unsent letter from Stanislaus to his father.

85. Byrne, *Silent Years*, 155–56.

86. Byrne, *Silent Years*, 156.

87. Byrne, *Silent Years*, 156.

88. In addition to Frank, "Shadow," 74–105, note Louis Gillet's description of Joyce as "not of this world. He was a stranger, a phantom whose shadow only was among us," "Farewell to Joyce," in *Portraits of the Artist in Exile: Recollections of James Joyce by Europeans*, ed. Willard Potts (Seattle: University of Washington Press, 1979), 168.

89. Byrne, *Silent Years*, 156, 157. And see letters to Stanislaus of 10 August and 16 August (*Letters* 2:234–35), and note that Eva is to "sleep with Georgie in the room you occupy."

90. See Maddox, *Nora*, 95–107, for a useful paraphrase of the letters, and see her appendix (385–401), for a history of the letters up to their final publication.

91. Maddox, *Nora*, 103.

92. Maddox, *Nora*, 106.

93. See Jean Kimball, "Autobiography as Epic: Freud's Three-Time Scheme in Joyce's *Ulysses*," *Texas Studies in Literature and Language* 31 (winter 1989): 490–91, on the composition of *Exiles* as it follows the time scheme outlined by Freud for the imaginative writer's translation of his life into his work.

94. See, for example, William Empson's comments on the "contorted attitude to sexual jealousy" in this "disgusting play," as well as his characterization of the notes for *Exiles* as "the public sweat of monks" ("Theme of *Ulysses*," 144–46).

95. Power, *Conversations*, 54.

96. See Ellmann's attempts to find models for Boylan (*JJ* 378).

97. Colum, "Confessions," 332.

3. FROM *BILDUNGSROMAN* TO INDIVIDUATION: *A PORTRAIT* AS PRELUDE

1. Adams, *Surface and Symbol*, 252, note 1.

2. Blackmur, "Jew in Search," 113.

3. Joseph Prescott, *Exploring James Joyce* (Carbondale: Southern Illinois University Press, 1964), 66.

4. Prescott, *Exploring*, 25.

5. Beebe, *Ivory Towers*, 266.

6. Adolf Hoffmeister, "Portrait of Joyce," in *Portraits of the Artist in Exile: Recollections of James Joyce by Europeans*, ed. Willard Potts (Seattle: University of Washington Press, 1970), 128, note 14.

7. Hoffmeister, "Portrait," 131, 132.

8. Richard Ellmann, *Wilde, Yeats, Joyce, and Beckett: Four Dubliners* (New York: Braziller, 1987), 85.

9. See Kimball, "Autobiography as Epic," 479–84, on the implications of this fusion of times in the creative process. And see William A. Gordon, "Submission and Autonomy: Identity Patterns in Joyce's *Portrait*," *Psychoanalytic Review* 61 (1974–75), 535–36, on Joyce's direct appropriation of his own day-to-day experience for "a literary end other than the telling of his own life history."

10. Morris Beja, *James Joyce: A Literary Life* (Columbus: Ohio State University Press,

1992), 65. Compare Ruth Von Phul's early analysis of Joyce's work after *Dubliners* as a "long autobiography that depicts faithfully enough the actualities of his world and treats its spiritual and emotional realities with the utmost veracity," "Circling the Square: A Study of Structure," in *A James Joyce Miscellany*, 3d ser., ed. Marvin Magalaner (Carbondale: Southern Illinois University Press, 1962), 241.

11. Jung's descriptions and definitions of individuation are scattered throughout his work, though concentrated in "The Relations Between the Ego and the Unconscious" (*CW* 7:121–239). See also Marie-Louise von Franz, "The Process of Individuation," in *Man and His Symbols*, ed. C. G. Jung (Garden City: Doubleday, 1964), 160–229; and Jolande Jacobi, *The Way of Individuation*, trans. R. F. C. Hull (New York: Harcourt, 1967).

12. See Jameson, *Political Unconscious*, 60, for his claim that the "dominant form taken by ethics in our own situation" is "psychologizing," in which "notions of personal identity, myths of reunification of the psyche, and the mirage of some Jungian 'self' or 'ego' stand in for the older themes of moral sensibility and ethical awareness."

13. Power, *Conversations*, 36.

14. Note that Jerome Hamilton Buckley's *Season of Youth: The Bildungsroman from Dickens to Golding* (Cambridge, Mass.: Harvard University Press, 1974) includes a chapter titled "Portrait of James Joyce as a Young Aesthete" (225–47). And see A. M. Abrams, *A Glossary of Literary Terms*, 5th ed. (New York: Holt, Rinehart & Winston, 1988), 120, s.v. *Bildungsroman*, where he lists *A Portrait* as an example of the *Künstlerroman* "an important subtype of the *Bildungsroman*" in which the young artist is the subject. See also Maurice Beebe, "Joyce and Stephen Dedalus: The Problem of Autobiography," *A James Joyce Miscellany*, 2d ser., ed. Marvin Magalaner (Carbondale: Southern Illinois University Press, 1958), 74, on Joyce's *Portrait* as "the apotheosis of a movement [the portrait-of-the-artist novels] rather than the beginning of one."

15. See Elizabeth Abel, Marianne Hirsch, and Elizabeth Langland, eds. *The Voyage In: Fictions of Female Development* (Hanover: University Press of New England, 1983), 5, for the quotation from *Wilhelm Meister*, as well as the "historical and intellectual circumstances" out of which the *Bildungsroman* emerged.

16. Wilhelm Dilthey, quoted in Abel et al., *Voyage*, 5. Gregory Castle, "The Book of Youth: Reading Joyce's Bildungsroman," *Genre* 22 (1989), 25, gives the same criteria with slight variations in the translation.

17. Castle, "Book of Youth," 22.

18. Castle, "Book of Youth," 29.

19. Homans, *Jung in Context*, 21.

20. See Homans, *Jung in Context*, 102, on the "breakdown of the persona" as constituting "the typically Jungian moment both in therapy and in development," that is, the stage at which Jung's theory and therapy significantly diverge from Freud's.

21. See Jung's 1916 essay, "The Structure of the Unconscious," on the "more or less voluntary repression of tendencies and elements which could just as well be conscious, a repression whose purpose is precisely to establish that portion of the collective unconscious which we call the persona" (*CW* 7:276).

22. See Jung on the "inferior function" (attached to the Shadow), which, "on being made conscious, drags the whole of the unconscious with it" (*CW* 12:152–53).

23. Jung, *Letters*, 2:481.

24. See Polly Young-Eisendrath and James Hall, *Jung's Self-Psychology: A Constructivist Perspective* (New York: Guilford, 1991), 100, on "Freud's lack of a specific construct of self,"

but note Jung's comment that "so long as the self is unconscious, it corresponds to Freud's superego and is a source of perpetual moral conflict" (*CW* 11:261). For a useful summary of the uses of *Ego* and *Self* by various schools, see J. W. T. Redfearn, "Ego and Self: Terminology," *Journal of Analytical Psychology* 28 (1983): 91–106. Note his suggestion that "the use of the word Self with a capital 'S' " for the Jungian sense of the word would help clear up the present "muddle," a usage that was "suggested, but apparently abandoned, for the English version of Jung's works" (102).

25. See Mario Jacoby, *Individuation and Narcissism: The Psychology of the Self in Jung and Kohut*, trans. Myron Gubitz and Francoise O'Kane (London: Routledge, 1990), 58, citing Jung's repeated emphasis, "it is the very nature of the self that it cannot be clearly defined by consciousness." Note Jacoby's own definition of the Self as "an irrepresentable central ordering factor that is the basis of psychic balance and ultimately of psychic development and evolution."

26. See Jung on "inflation," which he emphasizes repeatedly is the "great psychic danger" of the assimilation of unconscious contents, when the individual tries to attach "the collective psyche," and thus "extends the domain of his personality in an illegitimate way" (*CW* 7:270). In his numerous explanations of "inflation," Jung pictures this state as almost a literal blowing-up, so that the personality comes apart and consciousness is threatened with "dissolution" (*CW* 9.1:145). (See also, e.g., *CW* 7:136–40, 273–77; 8:225.)

27. Compare Jean Piaget and Barbel Inhelder on personality as "the decentered ego. . . . the submission of the ego to an ideal which it embodies but which goes beyond it and subordinates it," in "The Adolescent as a Total Personality," in *A Piaget Sampler: An Introduction to Jean Piaget Through His Own Words*, ed. Sarah F. Campbell (New York: John Wiley & Sons, 1976), 70.

28. See Andrew Samuels, *Jung and the Post-Jungians* (London: Routledge & Kegan Paul, 1985), 102, on the distinction between individuation, which can never be completed and remains "an ideal concept," and "individuality or the attainment of an individual ego-identity," which is achievable.

29. See Hans Walter Gabler, "The Seven Lost Years of *A Portrait of the Artist As a Young Man*," in *Approaches to Joyce's* Portrait*: Ten Essays*, ed. Thomas F. Staley and Bernard Benstock (Pittsburgh: University of Pittsburgh Press, 1976), 35, on the probable late date of the completion of the opening section.

30. See Hugh Kenner, "The *Portrait* in Perspective," in *James Joyce: Two Decades of Criticism*, ed. Seon Givens (New York: Vanguard, 1948) on these first two pages as a "microcosm" of the entire novel (137) and even a statement of "the entire lifework of James Joyce" (142).

31. See Stanislaus's account of this real-life event: "He must have been thrown heavily against barbed wire, for my mother had to mend the rips in his clothes, so that he could go to school the following morning" (*BK* 55).

32. Note that in *Stephen Hero* Stephen says to Lynch, "I can't say I consider harlots as human beings. *Scortum* and *moechus* are both neuter nouns" (*SH* 192).

33. Note that Stephen's later definitions of the artist's function continue to stress the earthiness of life—"lumps of earth," "the gross earth" (*P* 189, 207)—as the essential raw material of the artist's creation of beauty.

34. See Kimball, "Freud," 174–76, for a tracing of the homosexual threat through *A Portrait* and *Ulysses*. See also Kimball, "Joyce and Rank," 376–77. Compare Joseph Valente, "Thrilled by His Touch: Homosexual Panic and the Will to Artistry in *A Portrait of the*

Artist as a Young Man," *James Joyce Quarterly* 31 (spring 1994): 169, on "Joyce's phobic denial or denegation of his own homoerotic energies" as a "*fundamental determinant*" of the narrative structure of *A Portrait*, and see 185–86, for his interpretation of the scene with Cranly.

35. For a convenient summary of such responses, see Michael Levenson, "Stephen's Diary in Joyce's *Portrait*—The Shape of Life," *ELH* 52 (winter 1985): 1017–18.

36. Don Gifford, *Joyce Annotated: Notes for* Dubliners *and* A Portrait of the Artist as a Young Man. 2d ed. (Berkeley: University of California Press, 1982), 287. Even so perceptive a critic as Bernard Benstock ("Text, Sub-Text, Non-Text: Literary and Narrational In/Validities," *James Joyce Quarterly* 22 [summer 1985]: 355) accepts this source in his evaluation of the effectiveness of the allusion: "Will Dante's heroic effort to sublimate Eros in favor of Agape in his appreciation of the pre-nubile Beatrice Portinari suffice to substantiate a similar transition in Stephen's attitude toward Emma . . . ?" Mary Reynolds, in her listing of Joyce's allusions to Dante in *A Portrait*, lists the passage but gives no specific identification of a source in Dante; see her *Joyce and Dante: The Shaping Imagination* (Princeton: Princeton University Press, 1981), 265.

37. Dante Alighieri, *The Inferno*, trans. John Ciardi (New York: New American Library, Mentor Books, 1954), canto 34, lines 1–54.

38. It is also oddly reminiscent of Joyce's assurance to Nora that it was not only her body that he wanted, but "I want also your company" (*Letters* 2:273).

39. See Timothy Martin's discussion of Stephen's identification with Siegfried in *A Portrait* (*Joyce and Wagner: A Study of Influence* [New York: Cambridge University Press, 1991], 41).

4. REALIZATION OF THE SHADOW

1. See Rogers, "Irish Myth," 310–13, on the context of the "tower of death which is at the same time the tower of birth" in Irish myth.

2. Gilbert, *James Joyce's* Ulysses, 30.

3. See Kimball, "Hypostasis," 429–31, and "'*Lui, C'est Moi*,'" 230–31, on these correspondences; and compare Brivic, *Joyce the Creator*, 145–53.

4. Compare Jung (*CW* 14:253): "The sight of [the shadow's] darkness is itself an illumination, a widening of consciousness through the integration of hitherto unconscious components of the personality."

5. See Beryl Smalley, *The Study of the Bible in the Middle Ages* (Oxford: Clarendon, 1941), 13, on the medieval opposition between synagogue and church as darkness and light, as well as its transference to the individual Jew.

6. See Jung, "Christ, a Symbol of the Self" (*CW* 9.2:42–43), on the psychological need for a shadow side to balance the perfection of the Christ, a need that is in practice provided by Lucifer, or Satan.

7. On the self-regulating nature of the psyche and the compensatory function of the unconscious, see, e.g., *CW* 7:194; 8:208; 9.1:261; 14:497.

8. Oliver St. John Gogarty, *As I Was Going Down Sackville Street* (New York: Reynal & Hitchcock, 1937), 293. Gogarty's estimate of the awe and goodwill of the Dubliner toward "Medicine" as having "something of the mysterious and magical about it," is, of course, confirmed by the scene with the old milkwoman in this episode (*U* 1:415–23).

9. Gogarty, *As I Was Going*, 293.

10. Gogarty, *As I Was Going*, 295. Note that Stephen identifies himself as "a jester at the

court of his master" in connection with his contributions to "Haines's chapbook" (*U* 2:42–44).

11. Oliver St. John Gogarty, *Mourning Became Mrs. Spendlove and Other Portraits, Grave and Gay* (New York: Creative Age, 1948), 43. Joyce's description of the Martello Tower is, like most of his descriptions of places and people, allusive rather than explicit, and Gogarty's descriptions of the living arrangements in the tower, both here (43–45) and in *It Isn't This Time of Year at All!: An Unpremeditated Autobiography* (Garden City: Doubleday, 1954), 85–87, are really very helpful.

12. This picture also suggests that Mulligan is another kind of "dogsbody," one of his epithets for Stephen (e.g., *U* 1:112).

13. See Gifford, *Joyce Annotated*, 205, on "gall his kibe" (*Hamlet* 5.1.151–54), which he translates into modern English and interprets as "the peasant walks so close to the courtier that he 'rubs a blister on the courtier's heel.' "

14. See Thornton, *Allusions*, 213–14, 217.

15. See *Odyssey*, book 12, where Circe advises Odysseus to sacrifice six of his men to Scylla to escape the whirlpool of Charybdis.

16. Thornton, *Allusions*, 90.

17. See Stanislaus's opinion, expressed in his diary, that Gogarty was "treacherous in his friendship towards Jim" (*CDD* 25). "Jealous of Jim" and wishing "to put himself before him by any means he can" (*CDD* 26), Gogarty, in Stanislaus's estimation, was "a dangerous companion" and "a most demoralizing friend intellectually" (*CDD* 32).

18. Lenehan goes on to say that "there's a touch of the artist about old Bloom" (*U* 10:582–83), an observation that again applies to Mulligan, who, like his real-world model, Gogarty, does write poetry.

19. See Fredric Jameson, *Fables of Aggression: Wyndham Lewis, The Modern Fascist* (Berkeley: University of California Press, 1979), 103, on the "eclipse of the subject or ego" in Lewis's *Tarr*, published in 1918. It is suggestive that Jameson sees Tarr, the nominal hero of the novel, as "the artist as detached as possible from life and sex, the rational mind attempting to confine itself to the pure, atemporal realm of art." Jameson further sees this artist as opposed in the fiction to the "instinctual Kreisler" (96), a view that is remarkably similar to the accepted view of the opposition between Stephen and Bloom. I should perhaps make clear that my reading of *Ulysses* was solidified long before I became aware of Jameson's work, and I tend to see this parallel in the fictional agendas of Joyce and Lewis as synchronistic. And see Jameson's commentary on Lewis's postwar fiction, which "explicitly raises questions about the nature of the personality," as well as staging "something like a search for the ego, for the unifying principle of some autonomous, central subject" (106).

20. Frank Budgen, *James Joyce and the Making of* Ulysses (New York: H. Smith and R. Haas, 1934), 116.

21. See Maddox, *Joyce's* Ulysses, on Joyce's use of "soul" to express the "irreducible identity a human being possesses" and his conviction that "it is the task of the artist to mold his words around that mysterious central identity" (9, 11).

22. See Jameson, *Fables*, 8, on "the mirage of the continuity of personal identity, the organizing unity of the psyche or the personality." *Mirage* is a favorite label for Jameson in this connection; but note that in *Political Unconscious*, 153, Jameson points out that the "mythic conquest of personal identity," though it may be a "mirage," is "also evidently in some fashion an objective reality," as I believe it is for Joyce. See Hillman, *Healing Fiction*, 82, on "the unity fantasy"; and Thomas, *Dreams of Authority*, 282, on the "neurotic cultural obsession with the conception of a unified self."

23. Budgen, *James Joyce*, 52; note that Budgen quotes Joyce's explanation of the strange idiom of this paragraph: "My Sir Lout has rocks in his mouth instead of teeth. He articulates badly" (52). "Sir Lout's toys," provides a suggestive near echo of a phrase Jung uses in *Transformations*—"the 'toys of giants' "—in connection with a discussion of Hiawatha's successful effort to take the place of his parents (*PU* 363–64).

24. As Thornton, *Allusions*, 177, points out, this figure apparently alludes to Walter Pater's conclusion to *The Renaissance*.

25. See Kimball, "Autobiography as Epic," for a fuller discussion of the fusion of times in *Ulysses*.

26. Gogarty, *As I Was Going*, 84. See also the similar opinion of Wyndham Lewis, also a contemporary, whose comment in "Analysis," 101, is limited to Bloom as a Jew: "Such a Jew as Bloom, taken altogether, has never been seen outside the pages of Mr. Joyce's book. . . . Usually the author . . . is alone performing before us."

27. Scholes, "*Ulysses*," 165.

28. Erwin Steinberg in his "Reading Leopold Bloom/1904 in 1989," *James Joyce Quarterly* 26 (spring 1989), 404, quotes Jean-Paul Sartre's statement that "The Jew is one whom other men consider a Jew" and claims that "that is the only criterion by which Bloom can be considered a Jew." Steinberg's conclusion remains what it was in his earlier "James Joyce and the Critics Notwithstanding, Leopold Bloom Is Not Jewish," *Journal of Modern Literature* 9 (winter 1981–82):27–49.

29. Colum, "Confessions," 330–31.

30. See Adams, *Surface and Symbol*, 99–106, on Bloom as Irishman and Jew, and note his association of Bloom's Jewishness with Joyce's "anti-semitism" and "masochistic self-loathing" (104, note 5). See Steinberg, "Reading," for a comprehensive review, as of 1989, of the critical literature on the question of Bloom's Jewishness.

31. See also Steinberg, "Reading," on Bloom's "outsiderhood" (409–10).

32. Adams, *Surface and Symbol*, 186, 187, 188–89.

33. Clive Hart and Leo Knuth, *A Topographical Guide to James Joyce's "Ulysses"* (Colchester, U.K. Wake Newsletter, 1976), 16.

34. Hart and Knuth, *Topographical Guide*, 29.

35. Hart and Knuth, *Topographical Guide*, 34, 16.

36. Adams, *Surface and Symbol*, 61.

37. Adams, *Surface and Symbol*, 184.

38. Clive Hart, *James Joyce's* Ulysses (Sydney, Australia: Sydney University Press, 1968), 96.

39. Hugh Kenner, "Bloom's Chest," *James Joyce Quarterly* 16 (summer 1979), 508.

40. Adams, *Surface and Symbol*, 184.

41. Byrne, *Silent Years*, 157.

42. Adams, *Surface and Symbol*, 184.

43. Scholes, "*Ulysses*," 164.

44. Budgen, *James Joyce*, 105.

45. See Owen, *James Joyce*, 50.

46. William Noon, "James Joyce: Unfacts, Fiction, and Facts," *PMLA* 76 (June 1961), 274. See also Hugh Kenner, *Joyce's Voices* (Berkeley: University of California Press, 1978), 47: "We are always in 1904."

47. Danis Rose, "The Source of Mr. Bloom's Wealth," *James Joyce Quarterly* 25 (fall 1987): 129.

48. Jung's essay first appeared in English translation in Paul Radin, *The Trickster: A*

Study in American Indian Mythology (London: Routledge & Kegan Paul, 1956), which presents a cycle of legends about the trickster in the mythology of the Winnebago Indians.

49. But see Leslie Fiedler, who has claimed that "it was not Joyce-Stephen who wrote *Ulysses*, it was Joyce-Bloom," "Bloom on Joyce; or Jokey for Jacob," *Journal of Modern Literature* 1 (fall 1970): 29.

50. Compare Joyce's comment to Frank Budgen: "Why all this fuss and bother about the mystery of the unconscious? . . . What about the mystery of the conscious? What do they know about that?" ("Further Recollections," 536).

51. See Jung's definition of the inferior function in *Psychological Types* (*CW* 6:450–51). See also chapter 2, "Schiller's Ideas on the Type Problem" (*CW* 6:67–135), for a discussion of the "introverted thinking type," which is particularly applicable to Stephen and to Joyce. See Marie-Louise von Franz, "The Inferior Function," in *Lectures on Jung's Typology*, by Marie-Louise von Franz and James Hillman (Dallas: Spring Publications, 1979), 1–72. And see Brivic, *Joyce Between Freud and Jung*, 150–51, on the complementary relationship between Stephen and Bloom.

52. See Patricia Berry on Jung's view that "the shadow may be a superior part of the personality . . . a figure more moral than the ego" (*Echo's Subtle Body: Contributions to Archetypal Psychology* [Dallas: Spring Publications, 1982], 189).

53. See W. R. Rodgers, ed., *Irish Literary Portraits* (New York: Toplinger Publishing, 1973), 34, for Gogarty's description of the Joyce home in Cabra: "The banisters were broken, the grass in the back-yard was all blackened out. There was laundry there and a few chickens, and it was a very, very miserable house." And see Stanislaus's bitter complaint in his diary, a significant resource for Joyce in writing *Ulysses*: "I hate the commonplace. I was born amongst it; I belong to it, body and blood. Therefore I hate it. When I think of the commonplace I feel like a scientist who is watching an evil-smelling gas. It repeats in me like a gastric juice" (*CDD* 110).

54. See *PU* 40. This 1916 translation of Jung's 1912 *Wandlungen und Symbole der Libido* was extensively revised in 1956, when this reference, as well as a great many other references to the sexual nature of unconscious contents, was deleted. Compare *CW* 5:32 (*Symbols of Transformation*).

55. Adams, *Surface and Symbol*, 252–53.

56. Maddox, *Joyce's* Ulysses, 42; and see Jung on the "primitive" nature of the Shadow, who "is not only the passive victim of his affects but also singularly incapable of moral judgment" (*CW* 9.2:9).

57. Michael Seidel, *Epic Geography: James Joyce's* Ulysses (Princeton: Princeton University Press, 1976), 132–33.

58. Mulligan's insinuations give voice to Stephen's own concern about his relationship with Mulligan. See Kimball, "Freud," 175–76, on the homosexual threat represented by Mulligan, to whom Bloom is, of course, the alternative. I also address this threat in chapter 5 of this study.

59. See Morton P. Levitt, "The Radical Consistency of Point of View in 'Ulysses': A Traditional Reading," *James Joyce Quarterly* 26 (fall 1988): 81, for further examples of this sharing of consciousness, which Levitt sees as the narrowing of the "narrative community of Dubliners" to "a community of two," with "powerful archetypal echoes of Jung."

60. Matthew Arnold, *Culture and Anarchy*, ed. J. Dover Wilson (Cambridge: Cambridge University Press, 1950), 44. See also the "deaf gardener . . . masked with Matthew Arnold's face" (*U* 1:173), and note the context of Mulligan's suggestion that he and Stephen could "Hellenise" Ireland (*U* 1:158).

61. See A. Walton Litz, *The Art of James Joyce: Method and Design in* Ulysses *and* Finnegans Wake (London: Oxford University Press, 1961), 22, for Joyce's note on the union of Bloom and Stephen in "Eumaeus": "Ul & Tel exchange unity."

62. Note that Freud uses this scene from the *Odyssey* as a "simile" for the indestructibility of unconscious wishes—"ghosts who awoke to new life as soon as they tasted blood" (*SE* 5:553, note 1).

63. W. B. Stanford, *The Ulysses Theme: A Study in the Adaptability of a Traditional Hero*, 2d ed. (Ann Arbor: University of Michigan Press, 1968), 215.

64. Samuel Taylor Coleridge, *Biographia Literaria*, vol. 1, ed. J. Shawcross (1907; reprint, London: Oxford University Press, 1958), 189. Note the context of Coleridge's discussion (173–89) of the contrarieties of "SUBJECTIVE" and "OBJECTIVE" (or "INTELLIGENCE" and "NATURE") as they are united in the "I AM," the principle that embraces both.

65. See Jung's description of the compromise necessary in the assimilation of unconscious contents:

> Consciousness should defend its reason and protect itself, and the chaotic life of the unconscious should be given the chance of having its own way too—as much of it as we can stand. This means open conflict and open collaboration at once. That, evidently, is the way human life should be. It is the old game of hammer and anvil: between them the patient iron is forged into an indestructible whole, an "individual." (*CW* 9.1:288)

66. See Jung, "Concerning Mandala Symbolism" (*CW* 9.1:355–84). See also Marie-Louise von Franz, *C. G. Jung: His Myth in Our Time*, trans. William H. Kennedy (New York: C. G. Jung Foundation for Analytical Psychology, 1975), 139–57.

67. In *Ulysses*, the squared circle is identified with Bloom (e.g., *U* 15:2401, 17:1072, 17:1696).

68. Dante, *The Paradiso*, trans. John Ciardi (New York: New American Library, 1970), canto 33, lines 121–46.

69. Note that in the *Paradiso* Dante, metaphorically at least, is, like Ulysses, a mariner, in a "great ship that sails and sings" (canto 2, lines 1–18), and note that the nautical reference is picked up again in the final lines through the repeated allusion to the Argonauts (canto 2, lines 16–18, and canto 33, lines 94–96). I have no doubt that Joyce is conscious of parallels between Dante's conclusion and his own in "Ithaca."

70. See Jung's observation that, with the assimilation of unconscious contents, "linear evolution" in psychic development is replaced by "a circumambulation of the self" (*MDR* 196), and note that this kind of circumambulation starts with "Penelope," continuing, of course, in *Finnegans Wake*. On the circular structure in "Penelope," see Diane Tolomeo, "The Final Octagon of *Ulysses*," *James Joyce Quarterly* 10 (summer 1973): 439–54.

5. FLIGHT FROM THE MOTHER

1. Joyce also sent to Linati a schema for the novel for him to use as a guide for a possible Italian translation of *Ulysses*. See the comparison of the Linati and Gorman-Gilbert schemas in Ellmann, *Ulysses on the Liffey*, 186–87 ff.

2. See Thornton, *Allusions*, 177. Note also that Margot Norris identifies her critical approach as a "metaphor" of "weaving and raveling," *Joyce's Web: The Social Unraveling of Modernism* (Austin: University of Texas Press, 1992), 20.

3. Note Joyce's comparison of his work to the "intricate illuminations" of the *Book of*

Kells (*JJ* 545), which have something of the effect of a tapestry; and see Toynbee's judgment that Joyce "aimed at a *total* impression in a way which no novelist had done before," "A Study" (272).

4. Jung finds the series—"the heterosexual Eros- or anima-figure in four stages"—in Goethe's *Faust* (*CW* 16:174).

5. Empson, "Theme of *Ulysses*," 134.

6. See Owen, *James Joyce*, 87, 89, for Joyce's translating jobs in Zurich. See *JJ* 413–15, 457, for Harriet Shaw Weaver's patronage in Zurich; *JJ* 422–23, 467, for Edith Rockefeller McCormick's subsidy. Much of the time Joyce lived in Zurich, he was within walking distance of the Zentralbibliothek.

7. See Kimball, "Family Romance," 164 and note 11, on the mix of allusions in this discussion. Other echoes of Jung's *Transformations* include Joyce's parodic inner recital of a Hermetic ritual (*U* 9:61–64), which duplicates the rhythms of a quoted ritual in Jung's discussion of the "sexual symbolism of fire production" (*PU* 165), and Stephen's thought about Mulligan at the close of "Scylla and Charybdis"—"My will: his will that fronts me" (*U* 9:1202)—which echoes Jung's discussion of "an internal resistance" against sexuality: "will opposes will; libido opposes libido" (*PU* 171).

8. Curtayne, "Portrait," 43. See also Mark Shechner's analysis of Joyce's dependence on his mother in "The Song of Wandering Aengus: James Joyce and His Mother," *James Joyce Quarterly* 10 (fall 1972): 72–89, especially 73–75.

9. See Stanislaus Joyce, "James Joyce: A Memoir (1941)," trans. Felix Giovanelli, *Hudson Review* 2 (winter 1950): 491, 513.

10. Curran, *James Joyce*, 66. For a fuller discussion of Joyce's relationship with his mother and the effect of her death on his life, see Kimball, "James and Stanislaus," 101–3.

11. Gogarty, *It Isn't This Time*, 92.

12. See Jung's statement equating incest with this desexualized regression: "Just as libido is the onward driving force, so incest is in some manner the backward urge into childhood. For the child, it cannot be spoken of as incest. Only for the adult who possesses a completely formed sexuality does the backward urge become incest" (*PU* 266, note 45).

13. Budgen, *James Joyce*, 240–41. See also *JJ* (456–57) for details of this visit.

14. Phillip Herring, *Joyce's Notes and Early Drafts for* Ulysses: *Selections from the Buffalo Collection* (Charlottesville: University Press of Virginia, 1976), 194. See 211–49, for the first draft, 244–46, for the encounter with The Mother.

15. In the English translation, "terrible mother" always appears in quotation marks.

16. Note the English translations listed for these two adjectives: *frightful*, *terrible*, *awful*, *dreadful*, *horrible*, *hideous*.

17. The English reads "love and life-giving," whereas in the German it is clear that the mother is designated as giving both love and life.

18. See, for example, my discussion, in connection with Stephen's Shakespeare lecture, of Otto Rank's speculations about the son's inevitable failure in the oedipal triangle as a source of disillusion with the mother, which he connects with homosexual tendencies in the son. Rank also connects this line of argument to Shakespeare and his marriage to a woman older than himself. Kimball, "Joyce and Rank," 376.

19. See Jung's letter of 17 June 1910 to Freud (*F-J* 198J).

20. Note that this grip on Stephen's arm in *A Portrait* is kept in focus through much of the conversation, as Cranly "presse[s] Stephen's arm," takes it again (*P* 239), and "tighten[s] his grip on Stephen's arm" (*P* 241).

21. See Thornton, *Allusions*, 64, on this final phrase as a possible allusion to Wilde's

Picture of Dorian Gray. See also the juxtaposition of Cranly and Mulligan in "Scylla and Charybdis" where Stephen's reference to Cranly—"My soul's youth I gave him, night by night"—is followed by his reminder to himself of the telegram he has sent to Mulligan refusing to meet him for lunch (*U* 9:39, 41).

22. See Thornton, *Allusions*, 14, and references to Wilde in his index.

23. See, for example, Joyce's letter of 7 August 1909 to Nora, "the girl I loved, who . . . took me so easily into her arms and made me a man" (*Letters* 2:233), and Bertha's claim in *Exiles*: "I made him a man" (*E* 100). Compare Jung on the hero's birth as "a rebirth from the mother-wife," *CW* 5:321.

24. Shechner, *Joyce in Nighttown*, 27.

25. *Joyce and Shakespeare: A Study in the Meaning of* Ulysses (New Haven: Yale University Press, 1957), 108. See Kimball, "Joyce and Rank," 375–77, for Otto Rank's Freudian interpretation of the hostility toward the mother as it is found in *Ulysses*.

26. Thornton, *Allusions*, 181.

27. Budgen, *James Joyce*, 228.

28. See Thornton, *Allusions*, 16 and 428, on "Who Goes with Fergus?" and Joyce's attachment to it.

29. Richard Ellmann's comments on the restored passage in Frankfurt were substantially repeated in his review of the Gabler edition, "The Big Word in *Ulysses*," *New York Review of Books*, 25 October 1984: 30–31, and also apparently in his Julian B. Kaye Lecture in James Joyce Studies at Brooklyn College in September 1984, titled "*Ulysses* and the Word Known to All Men." See Brenda Maddox's characterization of Ellmann's Frankfurt address as an "attack" on "his rival Joycean interpreter, Mr. Hugh Kenner," in her "Love Makes the Joycean World Go Round," *Economist* (London), 23 June 1984: 85.

30. Hugh Kenner, *Dublin's Joyce* (Bloomington: Indiana University Press, 1956), 250, 262.

31. Jean Kimball, "Love and Death in *Ulysses*: 'Word known to all men,' " *James Joyce Quarterly* 24 (winter 1987): 143–60. See also Kimball, "Love in the Kidd Era: An Afterword," *James Joyce Quarterly* 29 (winter 1992): 369–77.

32. See Ernest Becker, *The Denial of Death* (New York: Free Press, 1973), 38–39, for an examination of the "fundamental threat" represented by the "sheer physicalness" of the mother. See also Suzette Henke, "Stephen Dedalus and Women: A Portrait of the Artist as a Young Misogynist," in *Women in Joyce*, ed. Suzette Henke and Elaine Unkeless (Urbana: University of Illinois Press, 1982), 82–84, on women as "emblems of the flesh—frightening reminders of sex, generation, and death" for Stephen Dedalus.

33. Scholes and Kain, *Workshop of Daedalus*, 44.

34. See Jung, *PU* 206–7, on the "phallic" significance of the mother's hand in his analysis of a patient's dream.

35. C. G. Jung, "The Psychology of the Unconscious Processes," trans. Dora Hecht, in *Collected Papers on Analytical Psychology*, ed. Constance E. Long (New York: Moffat, Yard, 1917), 352–444. The original, however, is *Die Psychologie der unbewussten Prozesse: Ein Überblick über die moderne Theorie und Methode der analytischen Psychologie* (Zurich: Rascher, 1917).

36. Jung, "Psychology," 418–19.

37. Jung, "Psychology," 423.

38. Jung, "Psychology," 425.

39. Jung, "Psychology," 436.

40. Note that Stephen's accompanying cry of "The intellectual imagination!" in "Circe"

echoes his identification in "Proteus" of Lucifer as "proud lightning of the intellect" (*U* 3:486) and that there is the same mix in both passages of Christ and Satan, with Stephen's Christ-derived "Come. I thirst" opposed to Lucifer in "Proteus" and The Mother's identification with Christ in "Circe" opposed to Stephen's identification with Satan.

41. Hugh Kenner considers this encounter "the only genuine hallucination in the chapter." See his "Circe," in *James Joyce's* Ulysses*: Critical Essays*, ed. Clive Hart and David Hayman (Berkeley: University of California Press, 1974), 351–52. Kenner also acknowledges the encounter as "one of the book's climaxes."

42. See Kenner, "Circe," 346–51, on these difficulties, as well as his listing of the "chain of bare happenings."

43. Kenner, "Circe," 351.

44. From a letter to William Haley. See Thornton, *Allusions*, 29, for the source, and note his suggestion that Stephen (and Joyce, for that matter) may have come across the phrase in Yeats's preface to Lady Gregory's *Cuichulain of Muirthemne* (1902). This quotation is first alluded to in "Nestor" as "I hear the ruin of all space, shattered glass and toppling masonry, and time one livid final flame" (*U* 2:8–10).

45. Thornton, *Allusions*, 62.

6. APPROACH TO THE ANIMA

1. Alicia Ostriker, "The Thieves of Language," in *Feminist Criticism: Essays on Women, Literature, Theory*, ed. Elaine Showalter (New York: Pantheon Books, 1985), 324.

2. David Hayman, "The Empirical Molly," in *Approaches to* Ulysses*: Ten Essays*, ed. Thomas F. Staley and Bernard Benstock (Pittsburgh: University of Pittsburgh Press, 1970), 105–8.

3. See Heather Cook Callow, " 'Marion of the Bountiful Bosoms': Molly Bloom and the Nightmare of History," *Twentieth Century Literature* 36 (winter 1990), 464–76, for the effect of Joyce's structuring of the novel, which gives male voices exclusive weight in the initial assessment of Molly, thus "foster[ing] initial sympathy for Bloom and distrust of Molly" (475).

4. See Kimberly J. Devlin, "Pretending in 'Penelope': Masquerade, Mimicry, and Molly Bloom," *Novel* 24 (fall 1991): 84–85, for her argument that "Penelope" might more accurately be called a "polylogue" or a "polyloquy."

5. See Derek Attridge, "Molly's Flow: The Writing of 'Penelope' and the Question of Women's Language," *Modern Fiction Studies* 35 (autumn 1989), "Feminist Readings of Joyce": 543–65, especially 544–46, on the effects of Joyce's omission of "graphic signs."

6. Fritz Senn, "Nausicaa," in *James Joyce's* Ulysses*: Critical Essays*, ed. Clive Hart and David Hayman (Berkeley: University of California Press, 1974), 262.

7. Devlin, "Pretending," 88.

8. Anne Robinson Taylor, *Male Novelists and Their Female Voices: Literary Masquerades* (Troy, N.Y.: Whitston, 1981), 210, 215.

9. Frances Restuccia, "Molly in Furs: Deleuzean/Masochian Masochism in the Writing of James Joyce," *Novel* 18 (winter 1985): 111, 114.

10. Colin MacCabe, *James Joyce and the Revolution of the Word* (New York: Barnes, 1979), 124.

11. Compare Bloom in "Circe": "Man and woman, love, what is it? A cork and a bottle" (*U* 15:1974).

12. Also an *unknown* woman, if we are to believe Stanislaus, who says that there was no

woman in his brother's life at this time—"many unindividualized women, but no woman" (*BK* 119).

13. Jung, *Letters*, 1:465.

14. Though the phrase is "pillar of cloud" in the Bible, Joyce consistently identifies it as "pillar of the cloud," a usage I adopt here.

15. Jung, *Letters*, 1:85.

16. Aristotle, *Generation of Animals*, trans. A. L. Peck (Cambridge, Mass.: Harvard University Press, 1963), 1:20.

17. This observation, from the third Tavistock Lecture in 1925, originated in Jung's 1912 *Transformations*, where the dragon was equated with "the resistance against incest" and the "cave dragon," Fafner, with the "terrible mother" (*PU* 275, note 67; and 292). In the 1952 revision of *Transformations* (*Symbols of Transformation*), Jung explained that "the dragon represents the negative mother-imago and thus expresses resistance to incest, or the fear of it" (*CW* 5:259). I should perhaps note that the Jungian reading I am exploring here is not in my view necessarily, or even primarily, a matter of direct influence, so that I have not limited my references to the 1912 work, whose style, as I have earlier pointed out, is notably convoluted.

18. See Ellmann, "Big Word," 30, for his observation that it "would hardly require a mother's ghost to divulge" that the word known to all men is *death*.

19. See S. B. Bushrui, "Yeats's Arabian Interests," in *In Excited Reverie: A Centenary Tribute to William Butler Yeats, 1865–1930*, ed. A. Norman Jeffares and K. G. W. Cross (New York: Macmillan, 1965), 293, for Yeats's comment on Harun al Rashid; 290, for the intense interest in Arabia in Yeats's circle (and Joyce's), especially in Richard Francis Burton's 1885 translation of the *Thousand and One Nights*, which Joyce must have known. W. B. Yeats, "The Gift of Harun Al Rashid" and notes, in *The Variorum Edition of the Poems of W. B. Yeats*, ed. Peter Allt and Russell K. Alspach (New York: Macmillan, 1957), 460–70, 828.

20. See Thornton, *Allusions*, 462.

21. See also Bloom: "Increase and multiply. Did you ever hear such an idea? Eat you out of house and home" (*U* 8:33–34).

22. On the "common impulse of all creative types to replace collective immortality . . . by individual immortality of deliberate self-perpetuation," see Otto Rank, *Art and Artist: Creative Urge and Personality Development*, trans. Charles Francis Atkinson (New York: Knopf, 1932), 45.

23. See Joyce on Christ as an all-around character: "He was a bachelor, and never lived with a woman. Surely living with a woman is one of the most difficult things a man has to do, and he never did it" (*JJ* 435).

24. See Thornton, *Allusions*, 62, on Stephen's probable debt to Douglas Hyde's *Love Songs of Connacht*.

25. Note Joyce's reminder to Martha Fleischmann that "Jesus Christ [the Word] put on his human body in the womb of a Jewish woman" (*Letters* 2:433). See also the Nicene Creed, where Christ "was incarnate by the Holy Ghost of the Virgin Mary: and was made man."

26. The constellation is in the shape of a *W*.

27. See Thornton, *Allusions*, 219.

28. Saint Augustine, *The Confessions of Saint Augustine*, trans. Edward B. Pusey (New York: Collier Books, 1961), book 7, section 12.

7. PROMISE AND PROPHECY IN "PENELOPE":
SHADOW AND ANIMA IN RELATION

1. Jung, *Letters*, 1:461.
2. Maddox, *Joyce's* Ulysses, 59, 11.
3. James Van Dyck Card, " 'Contradicting': The Word for Joyce's 'Penelope,' " *James Joyce Quarterly* 11 (fall 1973): 20. See also Marilyn French, *The Book as World: James Joyce's* Ulysses (Cambridge, Mass.: Harvard University Press, 1976), 257–59, on the "levels of contradiction" in Molly.
4. See Kimball, "Ambiguous Faithlessness," 457–58, for a summary of the critical history of Molly's fidelity, or lack thereof, from Edmund Wilson's charge in the thirties that she has been "continually and indiscriminately unfaithful to Bloom" to the itemized textual repudiation of Bloom's list by Don Gifford and Robert Seidman in the seventies. No one, of course, repudiates Boylan.
5. Adams, *Surface and Symbol*, 38.
6. French, *Book as World*, 257.
7. See Bertram Higgins, "The Natural Pander: Leopold Bloom and Others," *Calendar of Modern Letters* 1 (April 1925), 139, 140, on Bloom as one of a "unique confraternity," including "Gargantua, Sancho Panza, The Wife of Bath, Falstaff, Uncle Toby, Pickwick," all of whom embody "something constant in human nature," a designation that is echoed by Rebecca West's assertion that, in Bloom, "something true is said about man" (*Strange Necessity*, 36).
8. See Thornton, *Allusions*, 471, on this Psalm—113 in the Vulgate, 114 in the King James version of the Bible—and its connection to Dante's identification of the four levels of meaning in his letter to Can Grande Della Scala.
9. Compare this to the question and answer in "Circe" between Zoe and Bloom, when he is looking for Stephen: "You're not his father, are you?" to which Bloom answers, "Not I!" (*U* 15:1290–92).
10. Jung, *Letters*, 2:423.
11. John Henry Raleigh, *The Chronicle of Leopold and Molly Bloom:* Ulysses *as Narrative* (Berkeley: University of California Press, 1977), 210.
12. See Thornton, *Allusions*, 186.
13. Note that the Gabler edition restored to the text the "anterior" hemispheres, so that, although Bloom addresses only the "posterior" hemispheres, his satisfaction is in both breasts and buttocks.
14. See Wolfhard Steppe, with Hans Walter Gabler, *A Handlist to James Joyce's* Ulysses: *A Complete Alphabetical Index to the Critical Reading Text* (New York: Garland, 1986), 195, s.v. *Phenomenon*, *phenomenon*. See Higgins, "Natural Pander," 141–42, on Bloom and Stephen as "perhaps the most logically opposed pair that ever issued from [the] convention [of the opposition between man as "purely vegetative" and "man ideal"], and 145, for his observation that Bloom reacts "almost exclusively to the practical incidents of his environment," whereas for Stephen, "a thing perceived" suggests "a whole symphony of words and ideas."
15. See Levitt, "Radical Consistency," 82, on Bloom and Stephen as a "permanent union of sensibility," an "enduring community." Note Levitt's acknowledgment, 81–82, of Jungian echoes in his view of the relationship between Stephen and Bloom.
16. Jung, *Letters*, 1:405. Carol Gilligan, *In a Different Voice: Psychological Theory and*

Women's Development (Cambridge, Mass.: Harvard University Press, 1982), 1, 2, has similarly insisted that her hypothesis about the "different modes of thinking about relationships and the association of these modes with male and female voices" is the result of "empirical observation."

17. Note, however, Jung's reminder that there is a price to be paid for such a psychic gender interchange, concluding that "a man should live as a man and a woman as a woman" (*CW* 10:118) since "the masculinity of the woman and the femininity of the man *are* inferior, and it is regrettable that the full value of their personalities should be contaminated by something that is less valuable" (*CW* 10:127).

18. Stanley Sultan, *The Argument of* Ulysses (Columbus: Ohio State University Press, 1964), 317. See also Suzette Henke, "Joyce and Krafft-Ebing," *James Joyce Quarterly* 17 (fall 1979): 84–86; and Robert Byrnes, "Bloom's Sexual Tropes: Stigmata of the 'Degenerate' Jew," *James Joyce Quarterly* 27 (winter 1990): 303, for comment on Sultan's tracing of this pattern.

19. See French, *Book as World*, 47–48 and notes 30 and 32, for a useful summary of early attitudes toward Bloom's femininization. See also Joseph Allen Boone, "A New Approach to Bloom as 'Womanly Man': The Mixed Middling's Progress in *Ulysses*," *James Joyce Quarterly* 20 (fall 1982): 67–85, especially notes 1, 3, 4, for annotations of later critical approaches.

20. Bonnie Kime Scott, *Joyce and Feminism* (Bloomington: Indiana University Press, 1984), 7 and 206.

21. French, *Book as World*, 275. See Joyce's admiring comment in his 1900 essay, "Ibsen's New Drama," on the "curious admixture of the woman in [Ibsen's] nature," which contributed to his "marvellous [*sic*] accuracy" in portraying women (*The Critical Writings of James Joyce*, ed. Ellsworth Mason and Richard Ellmann [New York: Viking, 1959], 64).

22. French, *Book as World*, 48.

23. Diane E. Henderson, "Joyce's Modernist Woman: Whose Last Word?" *Modern Fiction Studies* 35 (autumn 1989), "Feminist Readings of Joyce," 517.

24. John Bormanis, " 'in the first bloom of her new motherhood' ": the Appropriation of the Maternal and the Representation of Mothering in *Ulysses*," *James Joyce Quarterly* 29 (spring 1992): 593, 599.

25. Suzette Henke, *James Joyce and the Politics of Desire* (New York: Routledge, 1990), 121.

26. Henke, *James Joyce*, 111.

27. Byrnes, "Bloom's Sexual Tropes," 305–6.

28. Budgen, *James Joyce*, 186–87.

29. Byrnes, "Bloom's Sexual Tropes," 322.

30. West, *Strange Necessity*, 31–32.

31. West, *Strange Necessity*, 36.

32. Horace Gregory in the New York *Herald Tribune* Book Section, 21 January 1934, quoted in Deming, *James Joyce*, 1:240.

33. Marshall McLuhan, *Understanding Media: The Extensions of Man* (New York: McGraw-Hill, 1964), 296.

34. Scott, *Joyce and Feminism*, 169.

35. Scott, *Joyce and Feminism*, 171–72.

36. Colum, "Confessions," 332–33.

37. Darcy O'Brien, "Some Determinants of Molly Bloom," in *Approaches to* Ulysses*:*

Ten Essays, ed. Thomas F. Staley and Bernard Benstock (Pittsburgh: University of Pittsburgh Press, 1970), 140, 139.

38. See John H. Lammers, "The Archetypal Molly Bloom, Joyce's Frail Wife of Bath," *James Joyce Quarterly* 25 (summer 1988), 487–88, for a summary review of archetypal approaches to Molly.

39. French, *Book as World*, 259.

40. Lammers, "Archetypal Molly Bloom," 489; see also Maria Tymoczko, "Sovereignty Structures in *Ulysses*," *James Joyce Quarterly* 25 (summer 1988): 445–64, on connections between Molly Bloom and the sovereignty figure from Irish myth.

41. Lammers, "Archetypal Molly Bloom," 488.

42. Note the echoes in Molly's "plan" of Ann Hathaway, the "boldfaced Stratford wench who tumbles in a cornfield a lover younger than herself" (*U* 9:259–60), as Molly vows to "make him feel all over him till he half faints under me" (*U* 18:1364).

43. Lammers, "Archetypal Molly Bloom," 498.

44. Lammers, "Archetypal Molly Bloom," 497.

45. Budgen, "Further Recollections," 534–35.

46. Jung's definitions in turn look ahead to Gilligan's contemporary distinction between masculine and feminine "voices" as characterized by the "logic of justice" *versus* the "ethic of care" (*Different Voice*, 30). The similarities between Gilligan's conclusions, based on long-term research with late twentieth-century girls and women, boys and men, and Jung's hypotheses of more than a half century before is a remarkable fact, especially since Gilligan, whose training has been Freudian, gives no indication of any awareness of Jung or his developmental theories: his name does not appear in her index.

47. See Alan Roughley's recent survey of the "major debate in Joyce studies about Joyce's attitude toward females, which, he says, became "a central issue in Joyce studies" in the eighties, *James Joyce and Critical Theory: An Introduction* (Ann Arbor: University of Michigan Press, 1991), 74.

48. Power, *Conversations*, 35.

49. Gea-Tellus is a markedly ambivalent figure. The Greek Gea, personification of the earth, source of all life, who produced Uranus without consort and with him produced the Titans, is also the mother who plotted with her children to overthrow her son-husband and fashioned the sickle with which Cronos castrated Uranus. Tellus, Gea's Roman counterpart, is the goddess of marriage, who was also "invoked in oaths as the grave of all things," according to Sir William Smith, *The Smaller Classical Dictionary*, rev. by E. H. Blakeney and John Warrington (New York: Dutton, 1958), s.v. Tellus. Joyce owned a 1917 edition of this dictionary.

8. BEYOND INTEGRATION: THE ARTIST AS PROPHET

1. See Henderson, "Joyce's Modernist Woman," 525, on the "matching voyages" of Molly and Leopold, which require "a double ending in two chapters," and her further note that "an epic with a double beginning for son and father calls for a double ending if the circles are to be unbroken."

2. Karen Lawrence, *The Odyssey of Style in* Ulysses (Princeton: Princeton University Press, 1981), 7, 10. Lawrence's study is, of course, indispensable in any serious consideration of styles in *Ulysses*. What I am concerned with in this discussion, however, is a struc-

tural tendency that seems to me to underlie or supplement all the stylistic experiments in the novel.

3. Lawrence, *Odyssey of Style*, 14.

4. See Thomas Jackson Rice, "The Complexity of *Finnegans Wake*," *Joyce Studies Annual 1995*, ed. Thomas F. Staley (Austin: The Harry Ransom Humanities Research Center and the University of Texas Press, 1995), 95, on Joyce's abandonment in *Finnegans Wake* of "stable characters, who possess histories and 'develop,' and replacing them with what may be one constantly mutating consciousness, supplanting temporal succession with an infinite '*noughttime*' (*FW* 349.06)."

5. See Jung, *CW* 7:271: "Whenever, through the assimilation of the unconscious, we admit the collective psyche into the sphere of the personal psychic functions, the opposing elements of which the former is composed separate themselves into various binary groups, each forming what one may call a 'pair of opposites.' "

6. See James Olney, *The Rhyzome and the Flower: The Perennial Philosophy—Yeats and Jung* (Berkeley: University of California Press, 1980), 327, on "Jung's recognition that the Collective Unconscious was a destroyer as well as a preserver."

7. Margot Norris, *The Decentered Universe of* Finnegans Wake (Baltimore: Johns Hopkins University Press, 1976), 4. See also Ole Vindig's report of Joyce's comment in the thirties that there were "no individual people in the book," "James Joyce in Copenhagen," in *Portraits of the Artist in Exile: Recollections of James Joyce by Europeans*, ed. Willard Potts (Seattle: University of Washington Press, 1979), 149.

8. John Bishop, *Joyce's Book of the Dark,* Finnegans Wake (Madison: University of Wisconsin Press, 1986), 214. Note the title of Robert M. Adams's review of Bishop's book, "While Mr. Whoever-He-Is Sleeps," *New York Times Book Review*, 18 January 1987, 14.

9. Margaret Schlauch, "The Language of James Joyce," *Science and Society* 3 (fall 1939), 489–90. See also the Polish novelist Jan Parandowski, "Meeting with Joyce," in *Portraits of the Artist in Exile: Recollections of James Joyce by Europeans*, ed. Willard Potts (Seattle: University of Washington Press, 1979), 161, for his opinion that, "with the death of its creator, *Finnegans Wake* . . . lost the only reader capable of enjoying it in the clear light of comprehension and not just in the fog of conjecture."

10. Schlauch, "Language," 489. Bishop, for example, according to David Kelly's note in Adams, "Mr. Whoever-He-Is," 15, "knows six languages and has 'dabbled in Hebrew and Aramaic.' " Note, however, that Bishop himself asserts that "any reader wishing genuinely to engage the *Wake* . . . must try to . . . attain to 'dummyship' and become as good an illiterate as HCE," Bishop, "*Joyce's Book*, 304.

11. Schlauch, *Language*, 490–91.

12. Bernard Benstock, *Joyce-Again's Wake: An Analysis of* Finnegans Wake (Seattle: University of Washington Press, 1965), 40. Note his reiteration of this negative opinion of the possibility of "a definitive comprehension of *Finnegans Wake*" in his survey of "The James Joyce Industry: An Assessment in the Sixties," *Southern Review* 2 (winter 1966), 228. See also James Atherton, *The Books at the Wake: A Study of Literary Allusions in James Joyce's* Finnegans Wake (New York: Viking, 1960), 11, for his tentative prediction that "a final literary evaluation of *Finnegans Wake* will never be made," since such an evaluation would depend on "complete understanding of the book," and "none seems to be in sight."

13. Rice, "Complexity," 80. See Rice's historical summary of approaches to "the *Finnegans Wake* problem," 80–81.

14. Rice, "Complexity," 81, 98.

15. Vindig, "James Joyce," 151. See Rice's questioning of the status of the *Wake* as a dream, "Complexity," 96.

16. Norris, *Decentered Universe*, 78. Note that Norris, in her *Joyce's Web*, 25, now asserts that the "waking referent" for interpreting *Finnegans Wake* as a dream "has emerged, and can now be found, in the early Joyce works themselves."

17. Margaret McBride, "A Portrait of the Artist as Schizophrenic: Issy as the Implied Narrator of *Finnegans Wake*." Paper presented at the Eighth Annual Miami J'yce Conference, Coral Gables, Florida, 4 February 1994.

18. N. J. C. Andreasen, "James Joyce: A Portrait of the Artist as a Schizoid," *Journal of the American Medical Association* 224 (2 April 1973): 71.

19. For Lyons's letter to the editor, headed "James Joyce and Medicine," see *Journal of the American Medical Association* 225 (16 July 1973): 313–14.

20. Dr. Andreasen's response follows Dr. Lyons's letter as a letter to the editor, *Journal of the American Medical Association* 225 (16 June 1973), 314. Note that in her response she identifies herself as "a former Joycean" and in the bibliographical note appended to her article mentions her conversations with Stuart Gilbert, Harriet Shaw Weaver, and Frank Budgen while she was studying Joyce as a Fulbright scholar in 1959.

21. Jung, *Letters*, 1:388.

22. For a more detailed discussion of the schizophrenic character of the art of these "two great initiators," see Jung, *Letters* 2:589–90, for his letter of 2 September 1960 to Sir Herbert Read. And see Read's response (2:591, note 8) on the fragmentation expressed in art as an attempt to tap "new sources of life . . . under the crust of tradition." Note also an echo of Joyce's "is there noone who understands me?" in Jung's wonderment that "there are no men in our epoch who see at least what I was wrestling with" (2:586).

23. Hans Prinzhorn, *Artistry of the Mentally Ill: A Contribution to the Psychology and Psychopathology of Configuration*, trans. Eric von Brockdorff (1922; Reprint, New York: Springer-Verlag, 1972), 271. See the introductory material in this English translation (v–xv) on the importance of this remarkable German psychiatrist with a background in music and the philosophy of art, who pioneered the study of schizophrenic art. Note also that, when Jung labeled *Ulysses* "cubistic," he pointed out that "Cubism is not a disease, but a tendency to represent reality in a certain way" (*CW* 15:117).

24. Power, *Conversations*, 19–20. Note Power's comment that "one musician, a friend of Joyce's, composed a piece to be played by a hundred mechanical pianos as well as numerous other mechanical noise-making devices" (20).

25. Jung, *Letters*, 2:81.

26. Stanislaus Joyce, "Early Memories of James Joyce," *The Listener* 41 (26 May 1949): 897.

27. Hoffmeister, "Portrait," 132. This kind of analysis brings to mind Mary Colum's observation in her review of *Ulysses* that, "when it comes to symbolizing, authors have from all time talked the greatest nonsense" ("Confessions," 333), but Joyce's descriptions are nevertheless consonant with the effect of *Finnegans Wake*.

28. David Hayman, "Some Writers in the Wake of the *Wake*," *Tri-Quarterly* 38 (winter 1977), 3.

29. Eric Neumann, *Art and the Creative Unconscious*, trans. Ralph Manheim, Bollingen Series no. 61 (New York: Pantheon Books; Princeton: Princeton University Press, 1959), 116–17.

30. See Ralph W. Rader's comment about Joyce's assigning his own "psychosexual bur-

dens" to Bloom, exempting Stephen from them: "we are not to suppose that the self-revelation is either unconscious or genuinely confessional," "Exodus and Return: Joyce's *Ulysses* and the Fiction of the Actual," *University of Toronto Quarterly* 48 (winter 1978–79): 162. At the same time, Rader's assertion in "Defoe, Richardson, Joyce, and the Concept of Form in the Novel," in *Autobiography, Biography, and the Novel*, by William Matthews and Ralph W. Rader (Los Angeles: William Andrews Clark Memorial Library, University of California, 1973), 51, that *A Portrait* and *Ulysses* "cannot be read without at least tacit awareness that they are versions of real life" is, I think, justified. Rader's discussion of the nature and significance of the relationship between Joyce's life and his fiction, in these essays and in "The Logic of *Ulysses*; or Why Molly Had to Live in Gibralter," *Critical Inquiry* 10 (June 1984): 567–78, is the most perceptive and fully developed analysis of this relation that I know about.

31. Hoffmeister, "Portrait," 131.

32. But note Bloom's apparent partial exemption from this kind of specificity, which I have noted in chapter 4.

33. See Hoffmeister, "Portrait," 131, where Joyce is also quoted as saying, "From *Dubliners* on, everything is 'work in progress,' though it does not bear that title."

34. West, *Strange Necessity*, 191–94.

35. See also Ellmann on Joyce's conviction of the "prophetic and magical nature" of *Ulysses* (*JJ* 525), and note Ellmann's assertion that Joyce regarded his books as "acts of prophecy" (*JJ* 551).

36. Joyce, of course, intermittently in letters considered his problems of composition or his developing vision of what he was working on, but after the works were published, they tended to drop from his correspondence. Thus, Power's reported conversations, especially as they relate to *Ulysses*, are as close as we come with Joyce to an extended discussion of a published work, the kind of review and evaluation that Henry James, for example, undertook—on a much grander scale, of course—in his critical prefaces.

37. Power, *Conversations*, 9.

38. Power, *Conversations*, 53.

39. Power, *Conversations*, 53.

40. Power, *Conversations*, 89.

41. For a discussion of the various ways World War I "break[s] into" the text of *Ulysses*, see Robert E. Spoo, " 'Nestor' and the Nightmare: The Presence of the Great War in *Ulysses*," *Twentieth Century Literature* 32 (summer 1986): 137–54.

42. Barbara W. Tuchman, *The Proud Tower: A Portrait of the World Before the War 1890–1914* (New York: Macmillan, 1966), 463.

43. Tuchman, *Proud Tower*, 463.

44. Tuchman, *Proud Tower*, xiv.

45. Tuchman, *Proud Tower*, xv. See also Spoo, " 'Nestor,' " 150, on the connection between "the eruption into history of [the war's] latent horror and treachery" and the dramatization in *Ulysses* of "this explosion of repressed forces."

46. Jung's essay "Wotan" was first published in 1936—in the context of German National Socialism and the Hitler movement and on the eve of an even more terrible war.

47. Robert Spoo, *James Joyce and the Language of History: Dedalus's Nightmare* (New York: Oxford University Press, 1994), 18.

48. Spoo, *James Joyce*, 5.

49. Coué, a French psychotherapist, founded a free clinic in Nancy in 1910 and, accord-

ing to the *Encyclopaedia Britannica*, was a popular lecturer in England and America in the early twentieth century.

50. Henry James, *Letters/Henry James*, ed. Leon Edel (Cambridge, Mass.: Harvard University Press, Belknap Press, 1974–84), 4:713, 715.

51. See Spoo, *James Joyce*, 98–105, for a discussion of Stephen's "nightmare" remark.

52. See Homans, *Jung in Context*, 140, on the "awareness and appreciation of the phenomenon of modernity" as "one of the outstanding features of Jung's system," and note Jung's claim that analytic psychology "does not stand in isolation but finds itself in a definite historical setting" (*CW* 10:16).

53. Morton P. Levitt, "A Hero for Our Time: Leopold Bloom and the Myth of *Ulysses*," *James Joyce Quarterly* 10 (fall 1972): 142–43.

54. Power, *Conversations*, 36. But see Joyce's claim to have written *Ulysses* "on an emotional basis as against an intellectual basis," so that "emotion has dictated the course and detail of my book" (95).

55. Power, *Conversations*, 54.

56. Homans, *Jung in Context*, 14.

57. Homans, *Jung in Context*, 109, 34.

58. See Lynne Layton and Barbara Ann Schapiro, *Narcissism and the Text: Studies in Literature and the Psychology of the Self* (New York: New York University Press, 1986), 30, on the increasingly inward turn of the novel even in the late nineteenth century, "a move that may be linked to the condition of pathological narcissism."

59. See Lynne Layton, "From Oedipus to Narcissus: Literature and the Psychology of Self," *Mosaic*, 18 (winter 1985): 97, on Kohut's theory, "whose *bedrock* is the development of a cohesive self" (Layton's emphasis). See also Young-Eisendrath and Hall, *Jung's Self-Psychology*, 19, on the agreement of contemporary psychoanalytic theorists with many of Jung's theories, "although they are largely ignorant of Jung's work." These authors quote Paul Roazen's observation in *Freud and His Followers* (1975) that "few responsible figures in psychoanalysis would be disturbed today if an analyst were to present views identical to Jung's in 1913" and cite Andrew Samuels's claim that "fifteen major contributions made originally by Jung have been rediscovered by psychoanalytic thinkers who give no credit to Jung."

60. That these inhibitions typically originate in childhood implies that they may be overcome through bringing them back into consciousness and seeing them with the eyes of maturity.

61. Homans, *Jung in Context*, 21.

62. See Thomas, *Dreams of Authority*, 257, for his observation that "Jung's rejection of some of Freud's basic claims in psychoanalysis parallels the course taken by many of the most prominent modernist writers."

63. Karen Newman, "Writing the 'Talking Cure': Psychoanalysis and Literature," *Poetics Today* 3 (spring 1982): 178, quoting Madelon Gohlke, " 'I wooed thee with my sword': Shakespeare's Tragic Paradigms," in *Representing Shakespeare: New Psychoanalytic Essays*, ed. Murray M. Schwartz and Coppelia Kahn (Baltimore: Johns Hopkins University Press, 1980): 181. Newman in her review essay cites Gohlke as one of the essayists in the collection who acknowledge the historicity of psychoanalysis.

64. Homans, *Jung in Context*, 97; Homans cites Jung's correspondence with Freud, his writings of the psychoanalytic years, and his autobiography as evidence of this shift in Jung's thinking.

65. See Layton, "Oedipus to Narcissus," 101, on Lasch's supposition that "the psychoanalytic concern with narcissism in the past thirty years is an index of a changing social structure and a changing character structure."

66. Homans, *Jung in Context*, 38. See his extended discussion of Heinz Kohut's psychology of narcissism and its application to the relationship between Freud and Jung (38–43).

67. Homans, *Jung in Context*, 39.

68. Jacoby, *Individuation and Narcissism* (unpaginated foreword note). Jacoby, a Jungian analyst, reports his recognition, on reading Kohut's first book, *The Analysis of the Self* (1971), of "an intimate kinship with my own psychological approach" and reports the reaction of his colleagues: "Why, that's pure Jung!" (ix). His book investigates the "overlap" in the systems of Jung and Kohut, which is obscured by "their diverse jargons" (x–xi), and notes that, though "Kohut forges into domains that . . . had previously been explored by C. G. Jung," he "seems to refuse to take notice of Jung's findings" (105). See also Young-Eisendrath and Hall, *Jung's Self-Psychology*, 158–61, for a comparison of Jung's self-psychology with Kohut's "more relational" understanding of the Self. And note that Gilles Deleuze and Felix Guattari have drawn attention to "the congruence of their own views and those of Jung," Peter Rudnytsky, "Oedipus and Anti-Oedipus," *World Literature Today* 56 (summer 1982): 464.

69. Homans, *Jung in Context*, 38.

70. Homans, *Jung in Context*, 39.

71. See Heinz Kohut, "Psychoanalysis and the Interpretation of Literature: A Correspondence with Erich Heller," *Critical Inquiry* 4 (spring 1978): 433–50, where he asserts the relevance of his self-psychology, which he identifies as the "latest development in scientific depth psychology," to "creativity itself," as well as to evaluation of "the products of [the artist's] creativity" (445). With no betrayal of any knowledge of Jung's psychology, Kohut writes to Heller: "With the advent of the psychology of the self, depth psychology can for the first time begin . . . to deal with the problems of the whole man" and therefore with the artwork as "an expression of [the artist's] self" (447–48).

72. Rader, "Exodus and Return," 153.

73. Power, *Conversations*, 74.

74. Power, *Conversations*, 75.

75. See Edmund Epstein, "James Joyce and the Body," in *A Starchamber Quiry: A James Joyce Centenniel Volume, 1882–1982*, ed. E. L. Epstein (London: Methuen, 1982), 73: "Joyce, almost alone among novelists, seems to consider it necessary to describe even the most embarrassing bodily functions as matter suitable for literature."

76. Power, *Conversations*, 53. See Mary Colum, "Confessions," 334, for her assertion that, with *Ulysses*, "written in the subconscious method," Joyce had introduced "a new literary form," entirely distinct from "the accepted form of the novel."

77. Power, *Conversations*, 54, 75.

78. Power, *Conversations*, 75.

79. Higgins, "Natural Pander," 141.

80. Budgen, *James Joyce*, 21.

81. Colum, "Confessions," 334.

82. West, *Strange Necessity*, 19.

83. Levitt, "A Hero," 136–37. See also Bakhtin, *Dialogic Imagination*, 163, for his discussion of "the rogue, the clown, and the fool" as "major protagonists" in the novel, especially the autobiographical novel, as "the bearer of the authorial point of view."

84. Theodore Holmes, "Bloom, the Father," *Sewanee Review* 79 (April 1971): 240–41.

85. S. L. Goldberg, *The Classical Temper: A Study of James Joyce's* Ulysses (New York: Barnes & Noble, 1961), 262, 314.

86. Byrnes, "Bloom's Sexual Tropes," 306.

87. Fiedler, "Bloom," 29.

88. William Troy, "Stephen Dedalus and James Joyce," in *William Troy: Selected Essays*, ed. Stanley Edgar Hyman (New Brunswick, N.J.: Rutgers University Press, 1967), 90.

89. Fiedler, "Bloom," 29.

90. Joseph Collins, "James Joyce's Amazing Chronicle," *New York Times Book Review*, 28 May 1922, 6. Collins also recognized, as many have not, that the "best training" for *Ulysses* is to read *A Portrait*.

91. West, *Strange Necessity*, 33.

92. West, *Strange Necessity*, 36.

93. Fiedler, "Bloom," 29. But see Rader, "Exodus and Return," 162, for his firm opinion that Bloom's "was emphatically not the mind that wrote *Ulysses*. That clear, keen mind was Stephen's matured—in his own phrase 'another now and yet the same.' "

94. French, *Book as World*, 42.

95. French, *Book as World*, 42.

96. French, *Book as World*, 38.

97. Holmes, "Bloom," 238–39.

98. French, *Book as World*, 166.

99. Vladimir Nabokov, *Lectures on Literature* (New York: Harcourt, 1980), 287.

100. Higgins, "Natural Pander," 141.

101. West, *Strange Necessity*, 36.

102. Norris, *Joyce's Web*, 22, 52.

103. Spoo, *James Joyce*, 8.

104. Spoo, *James Joyce*, 9.

105. Richard Kain, "Problems of Interpreting Joycean Symbolism," *Journal of General Education* 17 (October 1965): 235.

106. Hoffmeister, "Portrait," 130.

BIBLIOGRAPHY

Abel, Elizabeth, Marianne Hirsch, and Elizabeth Langland, eds. *The Voyage In: Fictions of Female Development*. Hanover: University Press of New England, 1983.

Abrams, A. M. *A Glossary of Literary Terms*. 5th ed. New York: Holt, Rinehart & Winston, 1988.

Adams, Robert Martin. *Surface and Symbol: The Consistency of James Joyce's* Ulysses. New York: Oxford University Press, 1962.

———. "While Mr. Whoever-He-Is Sleeps." *New York Times Book Review*, 18 January 1987, 14.

Anderson, Chester. "Leopold Bloom as Sigmund Freud." *Mosaic* 6 (fall 1972): 23–43.

Andreasen, N. J. C. "James Joyce: A Portrait of the Artist as a Schizoid." *Journal of the American Medical Association* 224 (2 April 1973): 67–71.

———. Letter to Editor. *Journal of the American Medical Association* 225 (16 July 1973): 314.

Anzieu, Didier. *Freud's Self-Analysis*. Trans. Peter Graham. Madison, Conn.: International Universities Press, 1986.

Appignanesi, Lisa, and John Forrester. *Freud's Women*. New York: Basic Books, 1992.

Aristotle. *Generation of Animals*. Trans. A. L. Peck. Cambridge, Mass.: Harvard University Press, 1963.

Arnold, Matthew. *Culture and Anarchy*. Ed. J. Dover Wilson. Cambridge: Cambridge University Press, 1950.

Atherton, James. *The Books at the Wake: A Study of Literary Allusions in James Joyce's* Finnegans Wake. New York: Viking, 1960.

Attridge, Derek. "Molly's Flow: The Writing of 'Penelope' and the Question of Women's Language." *Modern Fiction Studies* 35 (autumn 1989), "Feminist Readings of Joyce": 543–65.

Augustine, Saint. *The City of God*. Trans. Marcus Dods. New York: Modern Library, 1950.

———. *The Confessions of Saint Augustine*. Trans. Edward B. Pusey. New York: Collier Books, 1961.

———. *On Christian Doctrine*. Trans. D. W. Robertson, Jr. New York: Bobbs-Merrill, Library of the Liberal Arts, 1958.

———. *The Trinity*. Trans. Stephen McKenna. Washington, D.C.: Catholic University of America Press, 1963.

Bakhtin, M. M. *The Dialogic Imagination: Four Essays*. Ed. Michael Holquist, trans. Caryl Emerson and Michael Holquist. Austin: University of Texas Press, 1981.

Becker, Ernest. *The Denial of Death*. New York: Free Press, 1973.

Beebe, Maurice. *Ivory Towers and Sacred Founts: The Artist as Hero from Goethe to Joyce*. New York: New York University Press, 1964.

———. "Joyce and Stephen Dedalus: The Problem of Autobiography." *A James Joyce Miscellany*, 2d ser., ed. Marvin Magalaner, 67–77. Carbondale: Southern Illinois University Press, 1958.

Beja, Morris. *James Joyce: A Literary Life*. Columbus: Ohio State University Press, 1992.

Bell, Aubrey F. G. *Cervantes*. Norman: University of Oklahoma Press, 1947.

Benstock, Bernard. "The James Joyce Industry: An Assessment in the Sixties," *Southern Review* 2 (winter 1966): 210–28.

———. *Joyce-Again's Wake: An Analysis of* Finnegans Wake. Seattle: University of Washington Press, 1965.

———. "Text, Sub-Text, Non-Text: Literary and Narrational In/Validities." *James Joyce Quarterly* 22 (summer 1985): 355–65.

Berry, Patricia. *Echo's Subtle Body: Contributions to Archetypal Psychology*. Dallas: Spring Publications, 1982.

Bettelheim, Bruno. "Commentary by Bruno Bettelheim." In *A Secret Symmetry: Sabina Spielrein Between Jung and Freud*, by Aldo Carotenuto, xv–xxxix. Trans. Arno Pomerans, John Shepley, Krishna Winston. New York: Pantheon Books, 1984, augmented edition.

Bishop, John. *Joyce's Book of the Dark,* Finnegans Wake. Madison: University of Wisconsin Press, 1986.

Blackmur, R. P. "The Jew in Search of a Son." *Virginia Quarterly Review* 24 (1948): 96–116.

Bollettieri, Rosa M. B. "The Importance of Trieste in Joyce's Work, with Reference to His Knowledge of Psycho-Analysis." *James Joyce Quarterly* 7 (spring 1970): 177–85.

Boone, Joseph Allen. "A New Approach to Bloom as 'Womanly Man': The Mixed Middling's Progress in *Ulysses*." *James Joyce Quarterly* 20 (fall 1982): 67–85.

Bormanis, John. " 'in the first bloom of her new motherhood': The Appropriation of the Maternal and the Representation of Mothering in *Ulysses*." *James Joyce Quarterly* 29 (spring 1992): 593–606.

Brivic, Sheldon. *Joyce Between Freud and Jung*. Port Washington, N.Y.: Kennikat, 1980.

———. *Joyce the Creator*. Madison: The University of Wisconsin Press, 1985.

Buckley, Jerome Hamilton. *Season of Youth: The Bildungsroman from Dickens to Golding*. Cambridge, Mass.: Harvard University Press, 1974.

Budgen, Frank. "Further Recollections of James Joyce." *Partisan Review* 23 (fall 1956): 530–44.

———. *James Joyce and the Making of* Ulysses. New York: H. Smith and R. Haas, 1934.

———. "Joyce's Chapters of Going Forth by Day." In *James Joyce: Two Decades of Criticism*. 2d ed., ed. Seon Givens, 343–67. New York: Vanguard, 1963.

———. *Myselves When Young*. New York: Oxford University Press, 1970.

Bushrui, S. B. "Yeats's Arabian Interests." In *In Excited Reverie: A Centenary Tribute to William Butler Yeats, 1865–1930*, ed. A. Norman Jeffares and K. G. W. Cross, 280–314. New York: Macmillan, 1965.

Byrne, John Francis. *Silent Years: An Autobiography with Memoirs of James Joyce and Our Ireland*. New York: Farrar, Straus, & Young, 1953.

Byrnes, Robert. "Bloom's Sexual Tropes: Stigmata of the 'Degenerate' Jew." *James Joyce Quarterly* 27 (winter 1990): 303–23.

Callow, Heather Cook. " 'Marion of the Bountiful Bosoms': Molly Bloom and the Nightmare of History." *Twentieth Century Literature* 36 (winter 1990): 464–76.

Capra, Fritjof. *The Tao of Physics: An Exploration of the Parallels Between Modern Physics and Eastern Mysticism*. 2d ed. Boulder, Colo.: Shambala Publications, 1983.

Card, James Van Dyck. " 'Contradicting': The Word for Joyce's 'Penelope.' " *James Joyce Quarterly* 11 (fall 1973): 17–26.

Carotenuto, Aldo. *A Secret Symmetry: Sabina Spielrein Between Jung and Freud*. Trans. Arno Pomerans, John Shepley, and Krishna Winston. New York: Pantheon Books, 1982.

Castle, Gregory. "The Book of Youth: Reading Joyce's Bildungsroman." *Genre* 22 (1989): 21–40.

Coleridge, Samuel Taylor. *Biographia Literaria*. Vol. 1. Ed. J. Shawcross. 1907. Reprint, London: Oxford University Press, 1958.

Collins, Joseph. "James Joyce's Amazing Chronicle." *New York Times Book Review*, 28 May 1922, 6 and 17.

Colum, Mary. "The Confessions of James Joyce." *The Freeman Book, 1920–1924*. New York: B. W. Huebsch, 1924: 327–55.

———. *Life and the Dream*. Rev. ed. Chester Springs, Pa.: Dufour Editions, 1966.

Colum, Padraic, and Mary Colum. *Our Friend James Joyce*. Garden City: Doubleday, 1958.

Curran, Constantine. *James Joyce Remembered*. New York: Oxford University Press, 1968.

Curtayne, Alice. "Portrait of the Artist as a Brother: An Interview with James Joyce's Sister." *Critic* 21 (1963): 43–47.

Curtius, E. R. *European Literature and the Latin Middle Ages*. Trans. Willard R. Trask. Princeton: Princeton University Press, 1953.

Dante Alighieri. *The Inferno*. Trans. John Ciardi. New York: New American Library, Mentor Books, 1954.

———. *The Paradiso*. Trans John Ciardi. New York: New American Library, Mentor Books, 1970.

Deming, Robert, ed. *James Joyce: The Critical Heritage*. 2 vols. New York: Barnes & Noble, 1970.

Devlin, Kimberly J. "Pretending in 'Penelope': Masquerade, Mimicry, and Molly Bloom," *Novel* 24 (fall 1991): 71–89.

DiBernard, Barbara. *Alchemy and* Finnegans Wake. Albany: State University of New York Press, 1980.

Eliot, Thomas S. "*Ulysses*, Order and Myth." In *James Joyce: Two Decades of Criticism*. 2d ed., ed. Seon Givens, 424–26. New York: Vanguard, 1963.

Ellenberger, Henri. *The Discovery of the Unconscious: The History and Evolution of Dynamic Psychiatry*. New York: Basic Books, 1970.

Ellmann, Richard. "The Big Word in *Ulysses*." *New York Review of Books*, 25 October 1984, 30–31.

———. *The Consciousness of Joyce*. New York: Oxford University Press, 1977.

———. *James Joyce*. Rev. ed. New York: Oxford University Press, 1982.

———. *Ulysses on the Liffey*. New York: Oxford University Press, 1972.

———. *Wilde, Yeats, Joyce, and Beckett: Four Dubliners*. New York: Braziller, 1987.

Empson, William. "The Theme of *Ulysses*." *A James Joyce Miscellany*, 3d ser., ed. Marvin Magalaner, 127–54. Carbondale: Southern Illinois University Press, 1962.

Epstein, Edmund. "James Joyce and the Body." In *A Starchamber Quiry: A James Joyce Centenniel Volume, 1882–1982*, ed. E. L. Epstein, 173–83. London: Methuen, 1982.

———. *The Ordeal of Stephen Dedalus: The Conflict of the Generations in James Joyce's* A Portrait of the Artist as a Young Man. Carbondale: Southern Illinois University Press, 1971.

Escher, H. "*Die Errichtung der Zentralbibliothek in Zürich*." *Zentralblatt für Bibliothekswesen* 32 (1915): 86–104.

Fiedler, Leslie. "Bloom on Joyce; or Jokey for Jacob." *Journal of Modern Literature* 1 (1970): 19–29.

Fisher, David James. *Cultural Theory and Psychoanalytic Tradition*. New Brunswick, N.J.: Transaction Publishers, 1992.

Frank, Nino. "The Shadow That Had Lost Its Man." In *Portraits of the Artist in Exile: Recollections of James Joyce by Europeans*, ed. Willard Potts, 74–105. Seattle: University of Washington Press, 1979.

Franz, Marie-Louise von. *C. G. Jung: His Myth in Our Time*. Trans. William H. Kennedy. New York: C. G. Jung Foundation for Analytical Psychology, 1975.

———. "The Inferior Function." In *Lectures on Jung's Typology*, by Marie-Louise von Franz and James Hillman, 1–72. Dallas: Spring Publications, 1979.

———. "The Process of Individuation." In *Man and His Symbols*, ed. C. G. Jung, 158–229. Garden City: Doubleday, 1964.

French, Marilyn. *The Book as World: James Joyce's* Ulysses. Cambridge, Mass.: Harvard University Press, 1976.

Freud, Sigmund. *The Standard Edition of the Complete Psychological Works of Sigmund Freud*. 25 vols. Ed. and trans. James Strachey, in collaboration with Anna Freud. London: Hogarth and the Institute of Psycho-Analysis, 1953–74.

Gabler, Hans Walter. "The Seven Lost Years of *A Portrait of the Artist as a Young Man*." In *Approaches to Joyce's* Portrait*: Ten Essays*, ed. Thomas F. Staley and Bernard Benstock, 25–59. Pittsburgh: University of Pittsburgh Press, 1976.

Giedion-Welcker, Carola. "Meetings with Joyce." In *Portraits of the Artist in Exile: Recollections of James Joyce by Europeans*, ed. Willard Potts, 256–80. Seattle: University of Washington Press, 1979.

Gifford, Don. *Joyce Annotated: Notes for* Dubliners *and* A Portrait of the Artist as a Young Man. 2d ed. Berkeley: University of California Press, 1982.

Gilbert, Stuart. *James Joyce's* Ulysses: *A Study*. New York: Vintage Books, 1955.

Gillespie, Michael Patrick. *Inverted Volumes Improperly Arranged: James Joyce and His Trieste Library*. Ann Arbor: UMI Research Press, 1983.

Gillespie, Michael Patrick, with Erik Bradford Stocker. *James Joyce's Trieste Library: A Catalogue of Materials at the Harry Ransom Humanities Research Center, The University of Texas at Austin*. Austin: The Harry Ransom Humanities Research Center, 1986.

Gillet, Louis. "Farewell to Joyce." In *Portraits of the Artist in Exile: Recollections of James Joyce by Europeans*, ed. Willard Potts, 170–204. Seattle: University of Washington Press, 1979.

Gilligan, Carol. *In a Different Voice: Psychological Theory and Women's Development*. Cambridge, Mass.: Harvard University Press, 1982.

Gilson, Étienne. *The Spirit of Mediaeval Philosophy*. Trans. A. H. C. Downes. New York: Scribner, 1936.

Glover, Edmund. *Freud or Jung*. London: George Allen & Unwin, 1950.

Gogarty, Oliver St. John. *As I Was Going Down Sackville Street*. New York: Reynal & Hitchcock, 1937.

———. *It Isn't This Time of Year at All! An Unpremeditated Autobiography*. Garden City: Doubleday, 1954.

———. *Mourning Became Mrs. Spendlove and Other Portraits, Grave and Gay*. New York: Creative Age, 1948.

Gohlke, Madelon. " 'I wooed thee with my sword': Shakespeare's Tragic Paradigms." In *Representing Shakespeare: New Psychoanalytic Essays*, ed. Murray M. Schwartz and Coppelia Kahn, 170–87. Baltimore: Johns Hopkins University Press, 1980.

Goldberg, S. L. *The Classical Temper: A Study of James Joyce's* Ulysses. New York: Barnes & Noble, 1961.

Gordon, William A. "Submission and Autonomy: Identity Patterns in Joyce's *Portrait.*" *Psychoanalytic Review* 61 (1974–75): 535–55.

Grinstein, Alexander. *Sigmund Freud's Dreams.* 2d ed. New York: International Universities Press, 1980.

Hart, Clive. *James Joyce's* Ulysses. Sydney, Australia: Sydney University Press, 1968.

Hart, Clive, and Leo Knuth. *A Topographical Guide to James Joyce's* Ulysses. Colchester, U.K.: A Wake Newslitter, 1976.

Hayman, David. "The Empirical Molly." *Approaches to* Ulysses*: Ten Essays*, ed. Thomas F. Staley and Bernard Benstock, 103–35. Pittsburgh: University of Pittsburgh Press, 1970.

———. "Some Writers in the Wake of the *Wake*," *Tri-Quarterly* 38 (winter 1977): 3–38.

Haynal, Andre. *Psychoanalysis and the Sciences: Epistemology—History.* Trans. Elizabeth Holder. Berkeley: University of California Press, 1993.

Henderson, Diane E. "Joyce's Modernist Woman: Whose Last Word?" *Modern Fiction Studies* 35 (autumn 1989), "Feminist Readings of Joyce": 517–28.

Henke, Suzette. *James Joyce and the Politics of Desire.* New York: Routledge, 1990.

———. "Joyce and Krafft-Ebing." *James Joyce Quarterly* 17 (fall 1979): 84–86.

———. "Stephen Dedalus and Women: A Portrait of the Artist as a Young Misogynist." In *Women in Joyce*, ed. Suzette Henke and Elaine Unkeless, 82–107. Urbana: University of Illinois Press, 1982.

Herring, Phillip. *Joyce's Notes and Early Drafts for* Ulysses*: Selections from the Buffalo Collection.* Charlottesville: University Press of Virginia, 1976.

Higgins, Bertram. "The Natural Pander: Leopold Bloom and Others." *Calendar of Modern Letters* 1 (April 1925): 139–46.

Hillman, James. *Healing Fiction.* Barrytown, N.Y.: Station Hill, 1983.

Hodin, J. P. *Modern Art and the Modern Mind.* Cleveland: The Press of Case Western Reserve University, 1972.

Hoffman, Frederick J. *Freudianism and the Literary Mind.* 2d ed. New York: Vanguard, 1963.

Hoffmeister, Adolf. "Portrait of Joyce." In *Portraits of the Artist in Exile: Recollections of James Joyce by Europeans*, ed. Willard Potts, 127–36. Seattle: University of Washington Press, 1979.

Hogenson, George. *Jung's Struggle with Freud.* Notre Dame, Ind.: University of Notre Dame Press, 1983.

Holmes, Theodore. "Bloom, the Father." *Sewanee Review* 79 (April 1971): 236–55.

Homans, Peter. *Jung in Context: Modernity and the Making of a Psychology.* Chicago: University of Chicago Press, 1979.

———. Review of *A Secret Symmetry*, by Aldo Carotenuto. *Journal of the History of the Behavioral Sciences* 19 (1983), 240–44.

Jacobi, Jolande. *The Way of Individuation.* Trans. R. F. C. Hull. New York: Harcourt, 1967.

Jacoby, Mario. *Individuation and Narcissism: The Psychology of the Self in Jung and Kohut.* Trans. Myron Gubitz and Françoise O'Kane. London: Routledge, 1990.

James, Henry. *Letters/Henry James.* 4 vols. Ed. Leon Edel. Cambridge, Mass.: Harvard University Press, Belknap, 1974–84.

Jameson, Fredric. *Fables of Aggression: Wyndham Lewis, the Modern Fascist.* Berkeley: University of California Press, 1979.

———. *The Political Unconscious: Narrative as a Socially Symbolic Act.* Ithaca: Cornell University Press, 1981.

———. "'Ulysses' in History." In *James Joyce and Modern Literature*, ed. W. J. McCormack and Alistair Stead, 126–39. London: Routledge & Kegan Paul, 1982.

Joyce, James. *The Critical Writings of James Joyce*. Ed. Ellsworth Mason and Richard Ellmann. New York: Viking, 1959.

———. *Dubliners*. New York: Viking, Compass, 1968.

———. *Exiles: A Play in Three Acts*. New York: Viking, Compass, 1961.

———. *Finnegans Wake*. New York: Viking, 1958.

———. *The Letters of James Joyce*. 3 vols. Vol. 1, ed. Stuart Gilbert. Vols. 2 and 3, ed. Richard Ellmann. New York: Viking, 1966.

———. "A Portrait of the Artist" (1904). In *The Workshop of Daedalus: James Joyce and the Raw Materials for* A Portrait of the Artist as a Young Man, ed. Robert E. Scholes and Richard M. Kain, 56–74. Evanston, Ill.: Northwestern University Press, 1965.

———. *A Portrait of the Artist as a Young Man*. New York: Viking, Compass, 1964.

———. *Selected Letters of James Joyce*. Ed. Richard Ellmann. New York: Viking, 1975.

———. *Stephen Hero*. Ed. John J. Slocum and Herbert Cahoon. New York: New Directions, 1944.

———. *Ulysses: The Corrected Text*. 3 vols. Ed. Hans Walter Gabler, with Wolfhard Steppe and Claus Melchior. New York: Random, 1986.

Joyce, Stanislaus. *The Complete Dublin Diary of Stanislaus Joyce*. Ed. George Healy. Ithaca: Cornell University Press, 1971.

———. "Early Memories of James Joyce." *The Listener* 41 (26 May 1949): 896–97.

———. "James Joyce: A Memoir (1941)." Trans. Felix Giovanelli. *Hudson Review* 2 (winter 1950), 487–514.

———. *My Brother's Keeper: James Joyce's Early Years*. Ed. Richard Ellmann. New York: Viking, 1958.

Jung, C. G. *Analytical Psychology: Notes of a Seminar Given in 1925 by C. G. Jung*. Ed. William McGuire. Bollingen Series, no. 99. Princeton: Princeton University Press, 1989.

———. *The Collected Works of C. G. Jung*. 18 vols. Ed. H. Read, Michael Fordham, and Gerhard Adler, trans. R. F. C. Hull. New York: Bollingen Foundation and Princeton University Press, 1953–78.

———. *The Integration of the Personality*. Trans. Stanley M. Dell. New York: Farrar & Rinehart, 1939.

———. *Letters of C. G. Jung*. 2 vols. Ed. Gerhard Adler, with Aniela Jaffe, trans. R. F. C. Hull. Princeton: Princeton University Press, 1973–75.

———. *Memories, Dreams, Reflections*. Rev. ed. Recorded and ed. Aniela Jaffe, trans. Richard and Clara Winston. New York: Vintage Books, 1965.

———. *Psychology of the Unconscious: A Study of the Transformations and Symbolism of the Libido*. Trans. Beatrice M. Hinkle. New York: Moffat, Yard, 1916.

———. "The Psychology of the Unconscious Processes." Trans. Dora Hecht. In *Collected Papers on Analytical Psychology*, ed. Constance E. Long, 352–444. New York: Moffat, Yard, 1917.

Kain, Richard. "Problems of Interpreting Joycean Symbolism." *Journal of General Education* 17 (October 1965): 227–35.

———. "The Significance of Stephen's Meeting Bloom." *James Joyce Quarterly* 10 (fall 1972): 147–60.

———, ed. "An Interview with Carola Giedion-Welcker and Maria Jolas." *James Joyce Quarterly* 11 (winter 1974): 94–122.

Kenner, Hugh. "Bloom's Chest." *James Joyce Quarterly* 16 (summer 1979): 505–8.

———. "Circe." In *James Joyce's* Ulysses*: Critical Essays*, ed. Clive Hart and David Hayman, 341–62. Berkeley: University of California Press, 1974.

———. *Dublin's Joyce*. Bloomington: Indiana University Press, 1956.

———. *Joyce's Voices*. Berkeley: University of California Press, 1978.

———. "Molly's Masterstroke." *James Joyce Quarterly* 10 (fall 1972): 19–28.

———. "The *Portrait* in Perspective." In *James Joyce: Two Decades of Criticism*, ed. Seon Givens, 132–74. New York: Vanguard, 1948.

Kerr, John. "Beyond the Pleasure Principle and Back Again: Freud, Jung, and Sabina Spielrein." In *Freud: Appraisals and Reappraisals*, ed. Paul E. Stepansky, 3–79. Vol. 3 of *Contributions to Freud Studies*. Hillsdale, N.J.: Analytic, 1988.

———. *A Most Dangerous Method: The Story of Jung, Freud, and Sabina Spielrein*. New York: Knopf, 1993.

Kimball, Jean. "An Ambiguous Faithlessness: Molly Bloom and the Widow of Ephesus." *James Joyce Quarterly* 31 (summer 1994): 455–72.

———. "Autobiography as Epic: Freud's Three-Time Scheme in Joyce's *Ulysses*." *Texas Studies in Literature and Language* 31 (winter 1989): 475–96.

———. "Family Romance and Hero Myth: A Psychoanalytic Context for the Paternity Theme in *Ulysses*." *James Joyce Quarterly* 20 (winter 1983): 161–73.

———. "Freud, Leonardo, and Joyce: The Dimensions of a Childhood Memory." *James Joyce Quarterly* 17 (winter 1980): 165–82.

———. "The Hypostasis in *Ulysses*," *James Joyce Quarterly* 10 (summer 1973): 422–38.

———. "James Joyce and Otto Rank: The Incest Motif in *Ulysses*." *James Joyce Quarterly* 13 (spring 1976): 366–82.

———. "James and Stanislaus Joyce: A Jungian Speculation." In *Blood Brothers: Siblings as Writers*, ed. Norman Kiell, 73–113. New York: International Universities Press, 1983.

———. "Jung's 'Dual Mother' in Joyce's *Ulysses*: An Illustrated Psychoanalytic Intertext." *Journal of Modern Literature* 17 (spring 1991): 477–89.

———. "Love and Death in *Ulysses*: 'Word known to all men.' " *James Joyce Quarterly* 24 (winter 1987): 143–60.

———. "Love in the Kidd Era: An Afterword." *James Joyce Quarterly* 29 (winter 1992): 369–77.

———. " '*Lui c'est Moi*': The Brother Relationship in *Ulysses*." *James Joyce Quarterly* 25 (winter 1988): 227–35.

Kohut, Heinz. "Psychoanalysis and the Interpretation of Literature: A Correspondence with Erich Heller." *Critical Inquiry* 4 (spring 1978): 433–50.

Kristeva, Julia. *Desire in Language: A Semiotic Approach to Literature and Art*. Ed. Leon S. Roudiez, trans. Thomas Gora, Alice Jardine, and Leon S. Roudiez. New York: Columbia University Press, 1980.

Lammers, John H. "The Archetypal Molly Bloom, Joyce's Frail Wife of Bath." *James Joyce Quarterly* 25 (summer 1988): 487–502.

LaPlanche, Jean, and J.-B. Pontalis. *The Language of Psycho-Analysis*. Trans. Donald Nicholson-Smith. New York: Norton, 1973.

Larbaud, Valéry. "The 'Ulysses' of James Joyce." *Criterion* 1 (October 1922): 94–103.

Lawrence, Karen. *The Odyssey of Style in* Ulysses. Princeton: Princeton University Press, 1981.

Layton, Lynne. "From Oedipus to Narcissus: Literature and the Psychology of the Self." *Mosaic* 18 (winter 1985): 97–105.

Layton, Lynne, and Barbara Ann Schapiro. *Narcissism and the Text: Studies in Literature and the Psychology of the Self.* New York: New York University Press, 1986.

Levenson, Michael. "Stephen's Diary in Joyce's *Portrait*—The Shape of Life." *ELH* 52 (winter 1985): 1017–35.

Levitt, Morton P. "A Hero for Our Time: Leopold Bloom and the Myth of *Ulysses*." *James Joyce Quarterly* 10 (fall 1972): 132–46.

———. "The Radical Consistency of Point of View in 'Ulysses': A Traditional Reading." *James Joyce Quarterly* 26 (fall 1988): 67–88.

Lewis, Wyndham. "An Analysis of the Mind of James Joyce." In *Time and Western Man*, by Wyndham Lewis, 75–113. New York: Harcourt, 1928.

Litz, A. Walton. *The Art of James Joyce: Method and Design in* Ulysses *and* Finnegans Wake. London: Oxford University Press, 1961.

Lowes, John Livingston. *The Road to Xanadu: A Study in the Ways of the Imagination.* Boston: Houghton Mifflin, 1927.

Lyons, J. B. Letter to Editor. "James Joyce and Medicine." *Journal of the American Medical Association* 225 (16 July 1973): 313–14.

MacCabe, Colin. *James Joyce and the Revolution of the Word.* New York: Barnes, 1979.

Maddox, Brenda. "Love Makes the Joycean World Go Round." *Economist* (London), 23 June 1984, 85.

———. *Nora: The Real Life of Molly Bloom.* Boston: Houghton Mifflin, 1988.

Maddox, James H., Jr. *Joyce's* Ulysses *and the Assault upon Character.* New Brunswick, N.J.: Rutgers University Press, 1978.

Major, René. "Love for Transference and Passion for Signifiers: Between Sabina S. and Anna G." *Psychoanalytic Inquiry* 4 (1984), 174–88.

Martin, Timothy. *Joyce and Wagner: A Study of Influence.* New York: Cambridge University Press, 1991.

McBride, Margaret. "A Portrait of the Artist as Schizophrenic: Issy as the Implied Narrator of *Finnegans Wake*." Paper presented at the Eighth Annual Miami Joyce Conference, Coral Gables, Florida, 4 February 1994.

McGuire, William, ed. *The Freud-Jung Letters: The Correspondence Between Sigmund Freud and C. G. Jung.* Trans. Ralph Manheim and R. F. C. Hull. Bollingen Series, no. 94. Princeton: Princeton University Press, 1974.

McLuhan, Marshall. *Understanding Media: The Extensions of Man.* New York: McGraw-Hill, 1964.

Mercanton, Jacques. "The Hours of James Joyce." In *Portraits of the Artist in Exile: Recollections of James Joyce by Europeans*, ed. Willard Potts, 206–52. Seattle: University of Washington Press, 1979.

Nabokov, Vladimir. *Lectures on Literature.* New York: Harcourt, 1980.

Neumann, Eric. *Art and the Creative Unconscious.* Trans. Ralph Manheim. Bollingen Series, no. 61. New York: Pantheon Books; Princeton: Princeton University Press, 1959.

Newman, Karen. "Writing the 'Talking Cure': Psychoanalysis and Literature." *Poetics Today* 3 (spring 1982): 173–82.

Noon, William. "A Delayed Review." *James Joyce Quarterly* 2 (fall 1964): 7–12.

———. "James Joyce: Unfacts, Fiction, and Facts." *PMLA* 76 (June 1961): 254–76.

Norris, Margot. *The Decentered Universe of* Finnegans Wake. Baltimore: Johns Hopkins University Press, 1976.

———. *Joyce's Web: The Social Unraveling of Modernism.* Austin: University of Texas Press, 1992.

O'Brien, Darcy. "Some Determinents of Molly Bloom." In *Approaches to* Ulysses*: Ten Essays*, ed. Thomas F. Staley and Bernard Benstock, 137–55. Pittsburgh: University of Pittsburgh Press, 1970.

Olney, James. *The Rhyzome and the Flower: The Perennial Philosophy—Yeats and Jung*. Berkeley: University of California Press, 1980.

Ostriker, Alicia. "The Thieves of Language." In *Feminist Criticism: Essays on Women, Literature, Theory*, ed. Elaine Showalter, 314–38. New York: Pantheon Books, 1985.

Owen, Rodney Wilson. *James Joyce and the Beginnings of* Ulysses. Ann Arbor: UMI Research Press, 1983.

Parandowski, Jan. "Meeting with Joyce." In *Portraits of the Artist in Exile: Recollections of James Joyce by Europeans*, ed. Willard Potts, 154–62. Seattle: University of Washington Press, 1979.

Piaget, Jean, and Barbel Inhelder. "The Adolescent as a Total Personality." In *A Piaget Sampler: An Introduction to Jean Piaget Through His Own Words*, ed. Sarah F. Campbell, 59–70. New York: John Wiley & Sons, 1976.

Power, Arthur. *Conversations with James Joyce*. Ed. Clive Hart. New York: Barnes & Noble, 1974.

Prescott, Joseph. *Exploring James Joyce*. Carbondale: Southern Illinois University Press, 1964.

Prinzhorn, Hans. *Artistry of the Mentally Ill: A Contribution to the Psychology and Psychopathology of Configuration*. Trans. Eric von Brockdorff. 1922. Reprint, New York: Springer-Verlag, 1972.

Progoff, Ira. *Jung, Synchronicity, and Human Destiny*. New York: Julian, 1973.

Rader, Ralph W. "Defoe, Richardson, Joyce, and the Concept of Form in the Novel." In *Autobiography, Biography, and the Novel*, by William Matthews and Ralph W. Rader, 29–72. Los Angeles: William Andrews Clark Memorial Library, University of California, 1973.

———. "Exodus and Return: Joyce's *Ulysses* and the Fiction of the Actual." *University of Toronto Quarterly* 48 (winter 1978–79): 149–71.

———. "The Logic of *Ulysses*; or Why Molly Had to Live in Gibralter." *Critical Inquiry* 10 (June 1984): 567–78.

Radin, Paul. *The Trickster: A Study in American Indian Mythology*. London: Routledge & Kegan Paul, 1956.

Rahner, Hugo. *Greek Myths and Christian Mystery*. Trans. Brian Battershaw. New York: Harper & Row, 1963.

Rahner, Karl, ed. *The Teachings of the Catholic Church as Contained in Her Documents*. Comp. Josef Neuner and Heinrich Roos, trans. Geoffrey Stevens. Staten Island: Alba House, 1967.

Raleigh, John Henry. *The Chronicle of Leopold and Molly Bloom:* Ulysses *as Narrative*. Berkeley: University of California Press, 1977.

Rank, Otto. *Art and Artist: Creative Urge and Personality Development*. Trans. Charles Francis Atkinson. New York: Knopf, 1932.

———. *The Myth of the Birth of the Hero and Other Writings*. Ed. Philip Freund, trans. F. Robbins and Smith Ely Jelliffe. New York: Vintage Books, 1964.

Redfearn, J. W. T. "Ego and Self: Terminology." *Journal of Analytical Psychology* 28 (1983): 91–106.

Restuccia, Frances. "Molly in Furs: Deleuzean/Masochian Masochism in the Writing of James Joyce." *Novel* 18 (winter 1985): 101–16.

Reynolds, Mary. *Joyce and Dante: The Shaping Imagination.* Princeton: Princeton University Press, 1981.

Rice, Thomas Jackson. "The Complexity of *Finnegans Wake.*" *Joyce Studies Annual 1995*, ed. Thomas F. Staley, 79–98. Austin: The Harry Ransom Humanities Research Center and the University of Texas Press, 1995.

Riquelme, John Paul. *Teller and Tale in Joyce's Fiction: Oscillating Perspectives.* Baltimore: Johns Hopkins University Press, 1983.

Robertson, D. W., Jr. *A Preface to Chaucer: Studies in Medieval Perspectives.* Princeton: Princeton University Press, 1962.

Rodgers, W. R., ed. *Irish Literary Portraits.* New York: Toplinger Publishing, 1973.

Rogers, H. E. "Irish Myth and the Plot of *Ulysses.*" *ELH* 15 (1948): 306–27.

Rose, Danis. "The Source of Mr. Bloom's Wealth." *James Joyce Quarterly* 25 (fall 1987): 128–32.

Rosenzweig, Saul. *Freud, Jung, and Hall the King-Maker: The Historic Expedition to America (1909), with G. Stanley Hall as Host and William James as Guest.* St. Louis: Rana House, 1992.

Roughley, Alan. *James Joyce and Critical Theory: An Introduction.* Ann Arbor: University of Michigan Press, 1991.

Rudnytsky, Peter. "Oedipus and Anti-Oedipus." *World Literature Today* 56 (summer 1982): 462–70.

Samuels, Andrew. *Jung and the Post-Jungians.* London: Routledge & Kegan Paul, 1985.

Schepeler, Eva M. "Jean Piaget's Experiences on the Couch: Some Clues to a Mystery." *International Journal of Psycho-Analysis* 12 (1993): 255–73.

Schlauch, Margaret. "The Language of James Joyce." *Science and Society* 3 (fall 1939): 482–97.

Scholes, Robert E. "*Ulysses*: A Structuralist Perspective." *James Joyce Quarterly* 10 (fall 1972): 161–71.

Scholes, Robert E., and Richard M. Kain. *The Workshop of Daedalus: James Joyce and the Raw Materials for* A Portrait of the Artist as a Young Man. Evanston, Ill.: Northwestern University Press, 1965.

Schultz, Duane P. *Intimate Friends, Dangerous Rivals: The Turbulent Relationship Between Freud and Jung.* Los Angeles: Jeremy P. Tarcher, 1990.

Schutte, William. *Joyce and Shakespeare: A Study in the Meaning of* Ulysses. New Haven: Yale University Press, 1957.

Scott, Bonnie Kime. *Joyce and Feminism.* Bloomington: Indiana University Press, 1984.

Seidel, Michael. *Epic Geography: James Joyce's* Ulysses. Princeton: Princeton University Press, 1976.

Senn, Fritz. "Nausicaa." In *James Joyce's* Ulysses*: Critical Essays*, ed. Clive Hart and David Hayman, 277–311. Berkeley: University of California Press, 1974.

Shechner, Mark. *Joyce in Nighttown: A Psychoanalytic Inquiry into* Ulysses. Berkeley: University of California Press, 1974.

———. "The Song of Wandering Aengus: James Joyce and His Mother." *James Joyce Quarterly* 10 (fall 1972): 72–89.

Smalley, Beryl. *The Study of the Bible in the Middle Ages.* Oxford: Clarendon, 1941.

Smith, William. *The Smaller Classical Dictionary.* Rev. by E. H. Blakeney and John Warrington. New York: Dutton, 1958.

Spoo, Robert E. *James Joyce and the Language of History: Dedalus's Nightmare.* New York: Oxford University Press, 1994.

———. "'Nestor' and the Nightmare: The Presence of the Great War in *Ulysses.*" *Twentieth Century Literature* 32 (summer 1986): 137–54.

Stanford, W. B. *Ireland and the Classical Tradition.* Totowa, N.J.: Rowman & Littlefield, 1976.

———. "Joyce's First Meeting with Ulysses." *The Listener* 46 (19 July 1951): 99 and 105.

———. *The Ulysses Theme: A Study in the Adaptability of a Traditional Hero.* 2d ed. Ann Arbor: University of Michigan Press, 1968.

Steinberg, Erwin. "James Joyce and the Critics Notwithstanding, Leopold Bloom Is Not Jewish." *Journal of Modern Literature* 9 (winter 1981–82): 27–49.

———. "Reading Leopold Bloom/1904 in 1989." *James Joyce Quarterly* 26 (spring 1989): 397–416.

Steppe, Wolfhard, with Hans Walter Gabler. *A Handlist to James Joyce's* Ulysses*: A Complete Alphabetical Index to the Critical Reading Text.* New York: Garland, 1986.

Stern, Paul J. *C. G. Jung: The Haunted Prophet.* New York: Braziller, 1976.

Sting. "Synchronicity I." *Synchronicity.* The Police. A&M Records, Recording no. SP-3735. 1983.

Sultan, Stanley. *The Argument of* Ulysses. Columbus: Ohio State University Press, 1964.

Taft, Jessie. *Otto Rank: A Biographical Study Based on Notebooks, Letters, Collected Writings, Therapeutic Achievements and Personal Associations.* New York: Julian, 1958.

Taylor, Anne Robinson. *Male Novelists and Their Female Voices: Literary Masquerades.* Troy, N.Y.: Whitston, 1981.

Theoharis, Theoharis Constantine. *Joyce's* Ulysses*: An Anatomy of the Soul.* Chapel Hill: University of North Carolina Press, 1988.

Thomas, Aquinas, Saint. *Summa Theologiae.* 60 vols. New York: McGraw-Hill, 1964–72.

Thomas, Brook. *James Joyce's* Ulysses*: A Book of Many Happy Returns.* Baton Rouge: Louisiana State University Press, 1982.

Thomas, D. W. "A Fine Romance." *New York Review of Books*, 13 May 1982, 3 and 6.

Thomas, Ronald R. *Dreams of Authority: Freud and the Fictions of the Unconscious.* Ithaca: Cornell University Press, 1990.

Thornton, Weldon. *Allusions in* Ulysses*: A Line-by-Line Reference to Joyce's Complex Symbolism.* New York: Simon & Schuster, Touchstone, 1973.

Tindall, William York. *A Reader's Guide to James Joyce.* New York: Noonday, 1959.

Tolomeo, Diane. "The Final Octagon of *Ulysses.*" *James Joyce Quarterly* 10 (summer 1973): 439–54.

Toynbee, Philip. "A Study of James Joyce's *Ulysses.*" In *James Joyce: Two Decades of Criticism*, ed. Seon Givens, 243–84. New York: Vanguard, 1963.

Troy, William. "Stephen Dedalus and James Joyce." In *William Troy: Selected Essays*, ed. Stanley Edgar Hyman, 89–93. New Brunswick, N.J.: Rutgers University Press, 1967.

Tuchman, Barbara W. *The Proud Tower: A Portrait of the World Before the War, 1890–1914.* New York: Macmillan, 1966.

Tymoczko, Maria. "Sovereignty Structures in *Ulysses.*" *James Joyce Quarterly* 25 (summer 1988): 445–64.

Valente, Joseph. "Thrilled by His Touch: Homosexual Panic and the Will to Artistry in *A Portrait of the Artist as a Young Man.*" *James Joyce Quarterly* 31 (spring 1994): 167–88.

Van Waning, Adeline. "The Works of Pioneering Psychoanalyst Sabina Spielrein: 'Destruction as a Cause of Coming into Being.' " *International Review of Psycho-Analysis* 19 (1992): 399–414.

Vindig, Ole. "James Joyce in Copenhagen." In *Portraits of the Artist in Exile: Recollections of James Joyce by Europeans*, ed. Willard Potts, 137–52. Seattle: University of Washington Press, 1979.

Von Phul, Ruth. "Circling the Square: A Study of Structure." *A James Joyce Miscellany*, 3d ser. Ed. Marvin Magalaner, 239–77. Carbondale: Southern Illinois University Press, 1962.

Walcott, William O. "Notes by a Jungian Analyst on the Dreams in *Ulysses*." *James Joyce Quarterly* 9 (fall 1971): 37–48.

———. "The Paternity of James Joyce's Stephen Dedalus." *Journal of Analytical Psychology* 10 (1965): 77–95.

West, Rebecca. *The Strange Necessity*. Garden City: Doubleday, 1928.

Williams, William Carlos. "A Point for American Criticism." *transition* 15–17 (winter 1929): 157–66.

Wilson, Edmund. *Axel's Castle*. New York: Charles Scribner's Sons, 1931.

Winnicott, D. W. Review of *Memories, Dreams, Reflections*, by C. G. Jung. *International Journal of Psycho-Analysis* 45 (1964): 450–55.

Yeats, W. B. *The Variorum Edition of the Poems of W. B. Yeats*. Ed. Peter Allt and Russell K. Alspach. New York: Macmillan, 1957.

Young-Eisendrath, Polly, and James Hall. *Jung's Self-Psychology: A Constructivist Perspective*. New York: Guilford, 1991.

INDEX

Jean Kimball, University of Northern Iowa, has published articles on Joyce, focusing largely on psychoanalytic contexts for *Ulysses*, in the *James Joyce Quarterly*, *Texas Studies in Literature and Language*, *Journal of Modern Literature*, *Comparative Literature Studies*, and *Mosaic*, as well as in *Blood Brothers: Siblings as Writers*, edited by Norman Kiell. Her work on Henry James has appeared in *Nineteenth-Century Fiction*, *American Literature*, the *Henry James Review*, and in *Modern Judgements: Henry James*, edited by Tony Tanner, and *Henry James: The Best from American Literature*, edited by Edwin H. Cady and Louis J. Budd.